AUDIO
POST PRODUCTION
FOR FILM AND TELEVISION

Edited by Jonathan Feist

MARK CROSS

Berklee Press

Editor in Chief: Jonathan Feist
Vice President of Online Learning and Continuing Education: Debbie Cavalier
Assistant Vice President of Berklee Media: Robert F. Green
Dean of Continuing Education: Carin Nuernberg
Editorial Assistants: Dominick DiMaria, Sarah Walk
Cover Designer: Ranya Karafilly, Small Mammoth Design
Cover Photo Courtesy of Vancouver Film School

ISBN: 978-0-87639-134-1

1140 Boylston Street
Boston, MA 02215-3693 USA
(617) 747-2146

Visit Berklee Press Online at
www.berkleepress.com

DISTRIBUTED BY

HAL•LEONARD®
CORPORATION
7777 W. BLUEMOUND RD. P.O. BOX 13819
MILWAUKEE, WISCONSIN 53213

Visit Hal Leonard Online at
www.halleonard.com

Copyright © 2013 Berklee Press
All Rights Reserved

No part of this publication may be reproduced in any form or by
any means without the prior written permission of the Publisher.

This book is dedicated to my wife Megan and our two daughters Quinn and Keeley for their continued love and support.

CONTENTS

FOREWORD, by Kevin Becka (*Mix Magazine*) x

INTRODUCTION xi

CHAPTER 1. **Introduction to Post Production** 1
    Audio Post-Production Overview 1
        Dialogue 2
        Production Dialogue Editing 2
        Automated Dialogue Replacement (ADR) 3
        Sound Effects (SFX) 4
        Foley 4
        Music 5
        Basic DAW Setup for Audio Post Production 6

CHAPTER 2. **Evolution of Sound for Film and Television** 13
    The Timeline 13
    Fantasia and the Expansion of Theater Sound 15
    Multitrack Recording 15
    Multi-Channel Surround-Sound Playback 16
    Noise Reduction 17
    The Birth of the Pan Pot 17
    Developing Dolby Stereo 18
    The THX System 19
        The THX Playback System 20
    Digital Theater Sound 21

CHAPTER 3. **The Process of Making a Film** 23
    Development 24
    Pre-Production 24
    Production 25
    Post Production 26
    Distribution and Archiving 28
    Meet the Players 28
    Organization 29
        Film 29
        Television 30
        The Film Crew 30
        The Sound Crew 32

CONTENTS

CHAPTER 4. Post-Production Media 35
    Synchronization 35
        SMPTE Time Code 36
        Drop Frame/Non-Drop-Frame Rates 37
    Digital Audio File Formats. 38
    Film/Video Formats 39
        Video Quality Standards 40
    Digital Formats 41
    Telecine Machines and Process..................... 42

CHAPTER 5. Location Sound Recording...................... 45
    The Location Sound Crew 45
        The Production Sound Mixer..................... 45
        Boom Operator 48
        The Sound Assistant 50
        The Process.................................. 51
        Sound Logs 52
    In-Depth Look at Transfers 53
    More on Location Sound Recording 55
    A Closer Look at the Gear 57
        Microphones 57
        Shotgun/Hypercardioid, and Cardioid Microphones . . 57
        Lavaliere Microphones......................... 60
        Wireless Microphone Systems 61
        Zeppelins and Windsocks 62
        Boom Poles 63
        Mixing and Routing Devices 64
        DV Camcorder Audio.......................... 66
        Backup Systems 66
        Routing 67
        Hard Disk Multitrack Recorders 67
        Monitoring 69
        Headphones 69

CHAPTER 6. Working with Sound Effects 71
    Sound Design.................................... 72
    The Supervising Sound Editor 73
        Sound Design for *The Dark Knight* 74
    Backgrounds and Room Tones..................... 75
    Sound Effects Editor 76
    A Few Words about Conforming 79
    Delivering the SFX to the Dub Stage 80
    Sound Effects for Episodic Television................ 81

CONTENTS

CHAPTER 7. **Working with Dialogue** 83
Glossary of Production Dialogue and ADR Terminology . . . 84
The Dialogue Editor 87
The Assistant Dialogue Editor 88
Dialogue Editing in Television 90
Dealing with Production Dialogue in Reality TV 94
Real-Life Situations 95
Prepare Physical Studio Space for Voice Recording 96
Voice-Over and Narration in an ADR Session 98

CHAPTER 8. **Foley** 99
The Moves/Clothing Track 101
The Footsteps/Steps Track 101
The Props/Specifics Track 103
Recording Foley 104
Spotting Foley 104
Recording Foley 107
The Control Room 107
The Foley Stage 108
Foley at Home 110
    Monitors 111
    Headphones 111
    Microphones 111
    Props 111
    Surfaces 111
The Foley Mixer 112

CHAPTER 9. **Music Editing** 115
The Process 117
Temp and Source Music 120
Conforming Music 122
Techniques for Placing and Editing Music 124

CHAPTER 10. **Mixing Music for Film and Television** 127
Mixing Film Music 128
The Composer Studio 131
Mixing Music Demos 133
Mixing in Stems 134
Locked Picture 134
Pre-Records/Pre Lays 135
Clicks 136
Recording and Live Mixing (Orchestra) 137
    Recording the Orchestra, Demystified 137
The Decca Tree 139
The Mix/Deliverables 140

CHAPTER 11.	**The Pre-Dub/Temp Mix**	**143**
	The Pre-Dub/Temp Mix in Film	143
	The Pre-Dub/Temp Mix in Television	144
	The Pre-Dub Session	148
	Trimming	149
	Handles	149
	Fades and Crossfades	150
	Conforming	152
	Pre-Dubbing Trailers for Radio and Television	152
CHAPTER 12.	**The Final Dub**	**155**
	Dub Stages	155
	The Re-Recording Mixer	158
	Mixing Workflow on Pro Tools	160
	Goals	161
	Session Setup	161
	Creating the Mix Sessions	162
	Mixing the Reel	163
	Turning Back over to the Editor	163
CHAPTER 13.	**Templates**	**165**
	I/O Routing in a Final Dub Template	165
	Plug-ins and Processors for Mixing Dialogue, Sound Effects, Foley, and Music	173
	Dialogue Unit (DX)	173
	DX Compressor	174
	DX De-Esser	175
	DX EQ	176
	Reassigns	177
	Futz Track	181
	DX Reverb	182
	Sound Effects Unit (SFX)	184
	SFX Compressor	184
	SFX EQ	185
	SFX Reverb	186
	Foley Unit (FO)	187
	FO Compressor	188
	FO EQ	188
	FO Reverb	189
	Music Unit (MX)	190
	MX Trim	190
	MX EQ	191
	Mix Workflow	192
	Levels	193

CHAPTER 14. **The Music and Effects Mix** **197**
  The M&E. 197
  M&E Scenarios. 199
  M&E Mix Techniques 201
    Backgrounds 201
    Foley 201
    Mixing the M&E 202

CHAPTER 15. **Delivery and Archiving** **207**
  Deliverables, Formats, and Deadlines 207
  Quality Control and Quality Assurance. 210
  Session Management for Deliverables in DAWs 211
  Final Implementation and Delivery 212

AFTERWORD 213

ABOUT THE AUTHOR 215

INDEX 216

FOREWORD

So, you want a job in audio post production? Welcome to the roller-coaster world of a career in audio. Up you go: The gear used to make sound for picture is more affordable than ever. Independent filmmakers and producers of content for picture, broadcast, and live events can live and work outside the major production hubs of the past. Down you go: The gear is evolving at a breakneck pace. Hardware platforms, new software, and version changes happen with great urgency, so that gear providers can have a product to sell. It's harder than ever for users to keep up. In addition, budgets and shifts in production costs have resulted in the slow death of mentorship. Those wishing to create careers in audio post must rely on printed material, formal education, and the sometimes questionable wisdom of the Internet to avail themselves of the rich heritage, sum of knowledge, and solid professionalism needed to become a real pro.

As a professional recording engineer, journalist, and educator, I have an intimate relationship with the gear used for audio production and a unique view of the changes that have occurred in our industry in the last ten years. It's more important than ever to be sure you have a qualified and trusted source of knowledge to get the information right and assure yourself a place (and a job) in a career you'll love. That's where this book comes to the front line in your battle to stay abreast of what's happening now and in the future of audio post.

I've known Mark Cross for over fifteen years as a friend, brother in audio pain, and a professional with an enviable list of credits. Mark has mixed top-notch movies and television shows for the biggest names in the business and has been asked back time and time again—a sign that he's doing it right. Mark can also tell a great story, and that's what he's done here. He doesn't forget where it all started, laying out the history of film sound, woven with accurate and entertaining chapters on the modern technology used to practice the trade from the first push of the record button to final delivery. It's a good read, and I'm proud of Mark's accomplishments in this book. Enjoy.

—Kevin Becka, Technical Editor, *Mix Magazine*, Director of Education, Conservatory of Recording Arts and Science

INTRODUCTION

Audio post production plays a major role in any visual presentation, whether you're making a simple home movie, an industrial corporate presentation, a television or radio commercial, or working on a feature film. The audio is key in making the visual work. Making sure that the dialogue is clear and intelligible, that the sound effects and Foley complement the action of the video, and that the music works to move the overall mood can make or break any project.

The innovation of digital technology in media has had a tremendous impact on audio post production for film and television. This industry is now driven by the advent of digital audio, video, and effects within *digital audio workstations* (DAWs). The one thing that remains consistent is the need for motivated individuals who are educated and up-to-date in the processes and applications of this technology. If you are planning on working in this field, it is imperative that you master these techniques as well as developing creative problem solving skills.

This book offers a comprehensive overview of audio post production including the four basic elements: dialogue, music, sound effects, and Foley effects. By learning the tools and strategies used by working professionals, you'll be able to effectively participate in this fast-paced environment.

Post production is a team sport. It works best when everyone works together. Each member of the team makes a difference, and the whole is only as good as the sum of its parts. The final production, theatrical release, or episodic broadcast relies heavily on every step of the process, from inception to completion.

This book is very much in the same vein. It could not have been made possible without a cast of "behind the scene" professionals who selflessly offered their time and insight to help convey educational concepts specifically for this book. As you can see by the following credits, you are learning from the best of the best and for that we must give special thanks to:

Roll the credits, please....

    Megan Murphy, Co-Producer, *Curb Your Enthusiasm*

    Erin O'Malley, Producer, *Curb Your Enthusiasm*

    David Van Slyke, SFX, *Mixer, CSI, Mystery Alaska*

    Earl Martin, Mixer, *The Hills, Curb Your Enthusiasm*

    Frank Morrone, Mixer, *Lost, Cider House Rules*

    Phillip Rodrigues Singer, Foley Artist, *Rescue Me, Blown Away*

    Carli Barber, Music Editor, *Grey's Anatomy*

    Lisa Jaime, Music Editor, *Hairspray, Panic Room*

    Bill Macpherson, Location Sound, *U2: Rattle and Hum, Curb Your Enthusiasm*

    Vince Schelly, Boom Operator, *Curb Your Enthusiasm*

    Wendy Spence Rosato, Producer, *ER, Third Watch*

    Rich Weingart, Mixer, *Heroes, Lost*

    Kris Emery, Production Director, *Comedy Central*

    David Knauer, Mixer/Tech, *Audio Perception*

    Tristan Mathews, Coordinator/Director, *Curb Your Enthusiasm, Nothing for Something*

    Katie Rose, Foley Artist, *Beauty Shop, The Specialist*

    Dennis Sands, Scoring Mixer, *Dreamgirls, Finding Nemo*

    Maciek Malish, Dialogue Editor, *Lost, Starship Troopers*

    Josh Chase, SFX Editor, *The Middle, Scrubs*

    Eddie Rogers, Assistant Dialogue Editor, *Freeway, Lost*

    Martin Davich, Composer, *ER, Third Watch*

    Orlando Rashid, Editor, Mixer, *Jamie Foxx*

    Mehdi Hassine, Editor, Mixer, *Sigur Ros*

    Cecilia Perna, Foley Mixer, *The Middle, Scrubs*

    Steven Saltzman, Music Editor, *Straw Dogs, Priest*

    Larson Studios, Hollywood, CA

    RH Factor Post Production Sound, Burbank, CA

    Gray Martin Studios, Santa Monica, CA

CHAPTER 1

Introduction to Post Production

AUDIO POST-PRODUCTION OVERVIEW

Audio post production has been around for many years, and the process of working within it has morphed considerably. From using a razor blade and splicing tape to manipulating sound with a digital audio workstation (DAW), we have seen many of the tools and platforms progress while most the original concepts and techniques have stayed the same. One thing that remains consistent is that we continue dealing with dialogue, sound effects, Foley, and music.

These are the building blocks for every soundtrack. Although most of the projects we work on are dialogue driven, dialogue is dry and inanimate without the natural sounds that surround it. This plays a big role in helping to tell the story sonically. The sound effects and Foley will accentuate the actions of the characters and story, as the music moves and elevates the mood.

Sound design for film is the artistic creation, editing, and mixing of the audio elements in efforts to help tell the story of the film. When done correctly, it brings life to the otherwise lifeless moving pictures. Conversely, film brings meaning to the faceless soundscapes of a completed soundtrack. Sound and film should be seamless. There should be no defining point where one is separate from the other.

These are very specialized categories, and the people who work in these areas are superb craftsmen who can easily manipulate the most complex situations. The positions, titles, and teams can vary, because each project is unique and budget specific. It is nice to work on a team with your peers, all working towards the same goal, but it is not uncommon to get involved in a low-budget independent project where one person has to wear many different hats in order to deliver all of the audio post production elements single-handedly.

Here is a breakdown of the elements that are involved.

Dialogue

Dialogue is the communication that emanates from the actors. It authenticates the character on film as a person. It is through dialogue that the actor expresses feeling, motivation, and tells the story. Dialogue is also the tool that can be used to create the character.

The voice of Darth Vader in *Star Wars* is a great example of this. That deep voice behind the heavy breaths is the signature identity that defines the villain in that movie. It is difficult now to imagine Darth Vader with any other voice.

The accent and inflection of Tom Hank's performance of *Forrest Gump* is also legendary. However, capturing the dialogue in "Gump" was incredibly difficult—not because it was performed or recorded poorly; it was mainly because of the location.

The film was shot in the middle of summer in the Deep South. Anyone who has ever spent time in Alabama or Louisiana in the summer will understand that when the director yells, "Quiet on the set," thousands of crickets and cicadas probably will not respond. As you can imagine, the production sound on that picture was full of location interference. However, when you watch the movie, you never notice it. This is mainly because of the high level of craft in audio post production.

Production Dialogue Editing

In order for the *production audio* (recorded on the set or on location) to be included in the final mix for a film or television show, a *dialogue editor* needs to prepare it. This means locating the takes used by the picture editor from the recorded production audio and checking sync (so the audio matches the picture). This is done so that the *dialogue mixer* has the correct dialogue to use during the final mix.

Automated Dialogue Replacement (ADR)

Replacing or re-recording dialogue is very common in both film and television. Often, the dialogue is too noisy or otherwise deemed unusable because of poor line reading, airplane flyby, or set noise interference. This is also an opportunity to add voiceover narration or simply add dialogue that was never recorded. At this point, the line in question will be programmed/identified or "cued" for "looping."

This is also referred to as *ADR* (Automatic Dialogue Replacement). ADR is when the actor re-records the dialogue while watching the edited picture, matching the sync of the original line, or fitting the new lines with the actions. This process takes place on an ADR stage, a specialized recording studio set up specifically for dialogue replacement.

Fig. 1.1. ADR Stage at Larson Studios in Hollywood, CA

On the ADR stage, the actor and director are placed in a studio with a large screen (to project the film or television show) along with a microphone and headphones. They will both watch the segment that has been cued for ADR and determine how it should be redone. The engineer will be in the control room, setting up the "in" and "out" points of where the ADR will be recorded and will cue the actor with a sequence of beeps that they will hear in their headphones. Upon hearing the beeps, the actor will perform/speak the line to be replaced.

The post-production supervisor will try to schedule these sessions around the actors needed and the director's availability. They will try to get each actor to come in for one session and complete all the ADR needed for their character. This keeps session workflow smooth and costs down.

After the ADR has been recorded, the dialogue editor will check the sync carefully, modifying the take, if necessary, to precisely match it to the picture and prepare it for the final mix. This is done in a DAW. They often create *stems* (submixes) of the final/preferred lines to minimize the track count.

Sound Effects (SFX)

SFX (sound effects) are the additional sounds that will add color, texture, and (possibly) emotional feel to your soundtrack. This is handled by the *sound effects editors* and *sound designers*. They will add the computer beeps, gunshots, laser blasts, massive explosions, etc. and create subtler sounds to cover room tones and background ambiences such as wind, rivers, birds, and city traffic, to the existing production sound to create a sonic atmosphere that makes the audience feel as though they are right there in the movie.

Sound designers use a variety of techniques to make the sound effects complement the actions in any given scene. They will either create them or they will assemble them from various libraries, which can consist of hundreds of thousands of pre-recorded sounds. The designers will sync them with the picture and organize the sounds in a DAW. The final sound effects may consist of a layer of sounds, and they often create *stems* (submixes) of the SFX to reduce the track count.

Foley

The *Foley* (FX) process got its name from Jack Foley, the Hollywood sound editor regarded as the "father" of these effects. Foley effects are sounds that are created by everyday movement. This is also known as *sync effect acting*. Different from the environmental backgrounds ("BGs") and hard effects (SFX), Foley effects are sounds such as footsteps, object handling, the rustling of clothing, etc.

The people who create these effects are known as the *Foley walkers*. They are the artists who perform those sounds, doing this on a *Foley stage*—a studio that looks more like an old garage or storage space that consists of hundreds of shoes, props, and surfaces.

Foley walkers will watch the film and identify what sounds need to be recreated for each scene. One Foley walker may be wearing soft-soled shoes and walking on a hard surface to match one actor's steps, while the other wears work boots and walks on gravel to match another. They might switch to pick up a book, set down a coffee cup, scratch their heads, or kick a tire—whatever the scene requires.

This is all captured by the *Foley mixer*, who records the activity. The Foley mixer will be following and often directing the Foley walkers, based on a sheet that the sound supervisor created when he or she *spotted* (identified) the Foley effects that needed to be done. After the Foley effects are completed, the Foley mixer will edit the sounds to ensure that they are exactly in sync with the final picture and roughly balance the levels for the re-recording mixer. This is done in a DAW. Occasionally, they will create stems to reduce the track count in preparation for the final mix.

Music

Music for television and motion pictures falls into two general categories: score and source.

Score is the music created by the composer. Composers are usually hired by the director to write the dramatic underscore. This music is written specifically for the film or television show and often consist of musical "hits" that punctuate actions in the film. This can range from an intense action sequence to a tender romantic moment. The score can be big and extravagant and performed by a hundred-piece orchestra along with a fifty-voice choir, or it could be a simple arrangement for a small rhythm section or solo instrument.

The score is recorded and mixed by the *scoring mixer*, on a large scoring stage, or in a smaller studio, depending on how the music was composed and what the score needs. The music will be mixed (while referencing current dialogue and effects), in surround sound, and often delivered in stems, to give the re-recording mixers flexibility to make subtle level changes while maintaining the integrity of the final music mix.

Source music is what we hear coming from on-screen or off-screen devices, such as radios, televisions, or even ice-cream trucks. The source could also be a band performing at a concert, bar, or wedding. Source music may be original or licensed from a number of libraries that specialize in the creation of "generic" music. Songs (music with vocals) may occupy either function, depending on the dramatic intent of the director. If the music appears to be coming from a source in the film (like a car radio or telephone), it may be treated so that it will sound a bit lo-fi to achieve this effect of perception.

Basic DAW Setup for Audio Post Production

The process of creating, editing, and mixing the elements for audio post production is now done almost exclusively in digital audio workstations. Technology has come a long way, and we are very fortunate to have tools like this at our fingertips. DAWs now function as the multitrack recorder, the automated mixing console, the rack of outboard gear (compressors, EQs, reverbs, etc.), the patch-bay, the storage and backup medium, as well as the documentation too!

There are numerous DAW platforms, such as Avid's Pro Tools, Apple's Logic, and Steinberg's Nuendo, to name a few. It is very important to familiarize yourself with this technology, as they will become a big point of interest in your daily activities. Ultimately, which DAW you use comes down to what you are most comfortable with, as well as what program the project may already be using. You might use multiple platforms, because we are basically working with digital audio and video files. But I would recommend staying on a single platform, to eliminate any confusion along the way.

Setting up your DAW is a key point in starting your work. Because we are dealing with digital audio and video, we must make sure that we have a *resolved system*, where both the audio and video are totally in sync with the DAW and do not drift over time. This will include knowing the project's audio and video file format, time code type, sample rate, and bit resolution. Knowing this information about your project is key to setting up a resolved session on your DAW for audio post production.

Regardless of the DAW, you will either need to create a new session or open an existing one. If you open an existing session, the project's audio and video file format, time code type, sample rate, and bit resolution will already have been determined. You can check this in the DAW's preferences, settings, or session setup (depending on the DAW). This also means that these points have already been addressed, and that is what the project will resolve to.

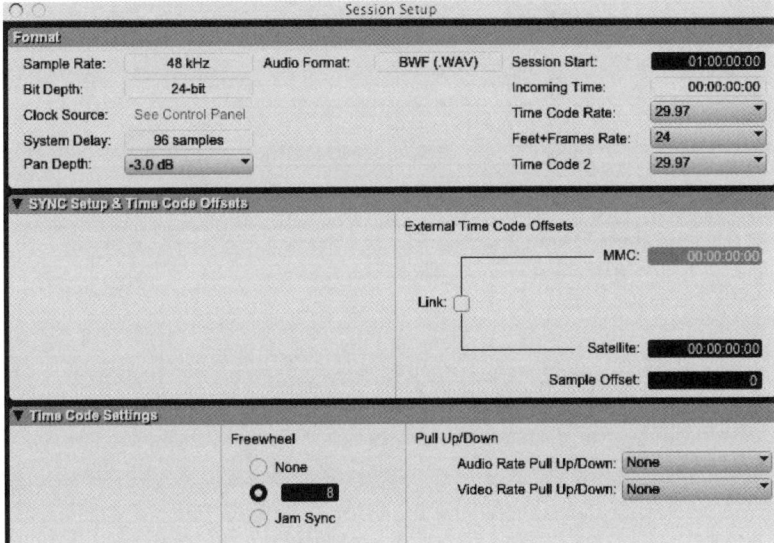

Fig. 1.2. Pro Tools Session Setup Page

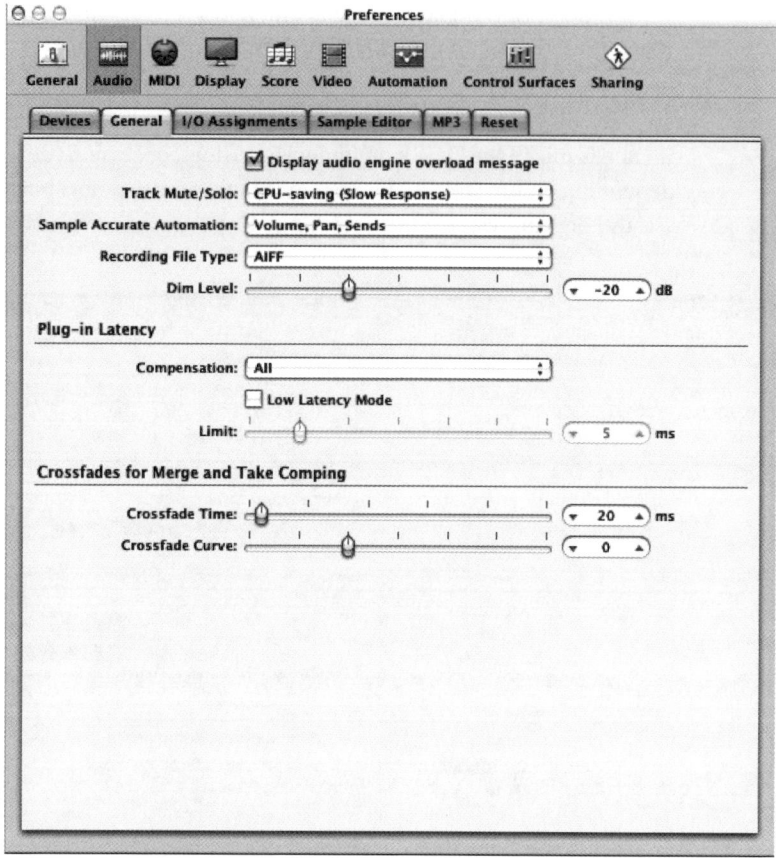

Fig. 1.3. Logic Session Preferences Page

Introduction to Post Production

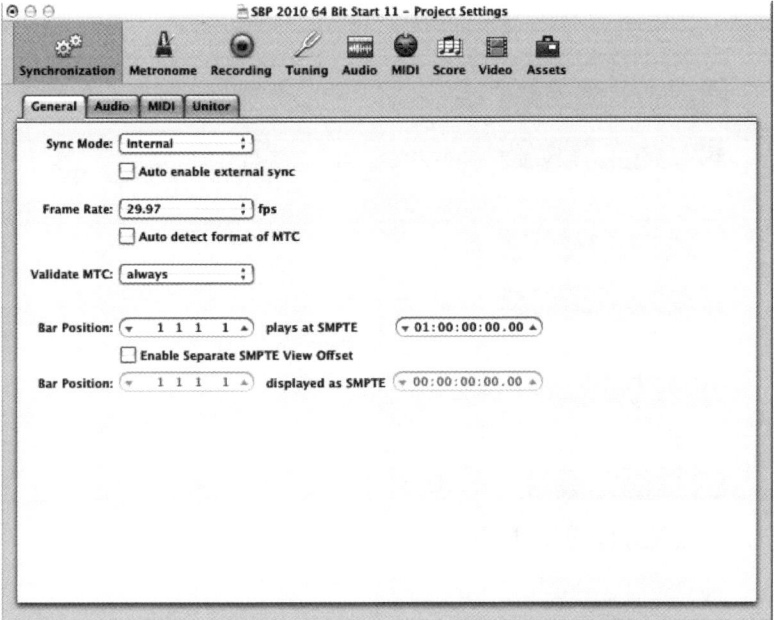

Fig. 1.4. Logic Session Settings Page

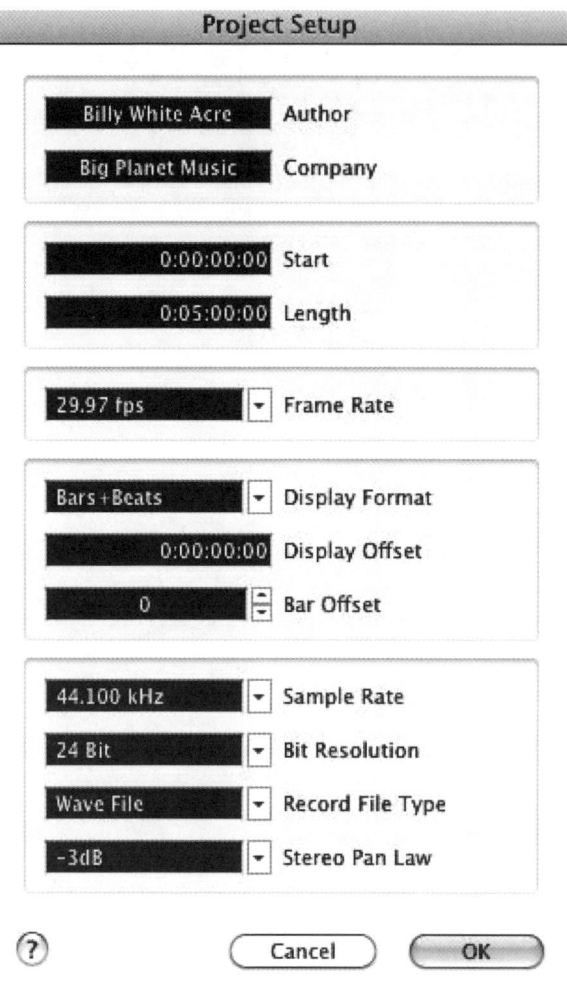

Fig. 1.5. Nuendo/Cubase Setup Page

If you are starting a new project/session, you will need to know all of this info up front. If you do not know this, you would ask someone in charge (the post supervisor, sound supervisor, the mixer, producer, etc.). If it is a small indie project and no one seems to have that information, it will be up to you to figure it out. A good place to start is by looking at the digital video properties. This should show the video format, frames per second (time code), sample rate, and bit resolution. This is exactly what you'll need to get started.

Once your session is up and running, with all resolution addressed, you can import the video into your DAW. Simply importing the video is just the first step. You will need to synchronize the video's time code (visual time code burned into the window of each frame of the video) with the time code resolution of the DAW session. Make sure that both the session audio and the video are in sync with the DAW, or they will drift in time and the audio will not match the actors or the action.

The video/movie will need to have its resolved time code burned into (printed on) the picture, in order for this to work effectively. If it is not, ask whoever is preparing video to make a new copy of the video with the time code visually burned into each frame. The file format, time code type, sample rate, and bit resolution must match precisely.

To synchronize the video with your DAW session, you will need to know the time code address of the movie start. In most cases, this is 1:00:00:00. (If it is a different time code address, use that number.) Position your movie file to start in your DAW at that time code address. Look at the first frame of picture. It should read 1:00:00:00. Now look at the SMPTE time code counter for the DAW. It should also read 1:00:00:00. This is a great start!

Now, use your cursor to select any random location in the movie file after the start of the video. For example, 1:01:24:19. That number should be burned into the frame of picture of the movie as well as the SMPTE time code reader of the DAW. If these numbers match, try this again at another random location (after the previous). If those numbers match again, then your system is resolved, meaning that both the time code of the movie and the time code of the session are matched and in sync.

If the numbers are off, nudge the movie file forwards or backwards (in increments of 1 frame or smaller) until the numbers match precisely. If they are still off, recheck your time code, sample rate, and bit resolution of the digital video. Just because someone told you what the time code rate is doesn't necessarily mean that they were correct. Information can get scrambled in translation, so it is important to get this figured out as ASAP.

This has happened to me many times. I am given a digital video file and told that it is drop frame time code. However, after going through this process, I was unable to resolve the video to my DAW session. At that point, I begin to experiment with different time code types until I find that the video is really at non-drop frame time code. When I contact the people who gave me the original video file and tell them what I have found, they usually respond with, "Oh yeah, sorry about that, it is non-drop frame."

When your project's audio and video file format, time code type, sample rate, and bit resolution are matched, the session is considered to be resolved and in sync. This means that both the audio and video will run together with no drift throughout the program. Synchronization is one of the biggest issues in audio post production and can be the source of numerous headaches along the way if it is not resolved. Be sure to address this first and foremost so that you do not have to deal with any sync issues as you work on your project.

We have introduced terminology and techniques that are possibly new to you. Not to worry, this brief introduction will unfold throughout each chapter. Read this at your own pace, and make sure that you understand the processes as you go. Sometimes, it helps to reread sections when they start to get technical; however, soon you will be comfortable with this and creatively addressing the audio post-production needs of any given project.

CHAPTER 2

Evolution of Sound for Film and Television

An awareness of the history and evolution of sound for film and television will help you understand most of the concepts and techniques that we use today. Knowing where we have come from also gives us a better appreciation for where we are. The post production industry has made great strides in the past few years, but a lot of our innovation is based on technology and techniques that were developed decades ago.

THE TIMELINE

In 1894, the Edison Company (owned by Thomas Edison) started experimenting with sound recordings printed to film under the supervision of W.K.L. Dickson. The very next year, they offered the *Kinetophone*, a device for viewing a sequence of pictures on an endless band of film that moved continuously over a light source and a rapidly rotating shutter, which created an illusion of motion. This led to the development of *Kinetoscopes* (Kinetophones with phonographs inside the cabinets to play audio simultaneously). Synchronization between sound and moving picture was achieved by connecting the two with a belt.

An updated version of the Kinetophone was developed in 1913. This had sound synchronized to the motion picture on a screen. This primitive synchronization was achieved by connecting the motion picture to a long pulley at one end of the theater and a phonograph at the other. Although this was considered to be cutting-edge technology at the time, the machines had some problems, and Dickson could foresee that they would need to transform them completely to keep up with his competitors.

Two of his main competitors were Josef Engel and Hans Vogt, who invented the Tri-Ergon Process in 1922. This was truly a groundbreaking advancement, as an optical audio recording was made directly onto the film itself, allowing sound and film to be played together (eliminating the synchronization issues for connecting the audio and video devices).

Synchronization was accomplished by using a photoelectric cell to turn sound vibrations into light waves that could be printed onto the edge of the film in a photographic process. When the film was replayed, another cell read the light patterns off the film and output an electrical waveform that could be amplified and fed into the speakers of the theater.

Hollywood took notice of these technological breakthroughs. At the time, they were still producing silent movies. Silent films had the story and dialogue printed as text onto the film, while live musicians in the theater played a music score written for the film.

But this all changed in 1927 when *The Jazz Singer* was released. Referred to as the first "talkie," *The Jazz Singer* was the first feature-length motion picture with synchronized dialogue sequences. Its release heralded the commercial ascendance of the "talkies" and the decline of the silent film era. No dialogue was actually written, so Al Jolson (the star of the film) improvised some lines, and it was a huge hit.

The next year, *Lights of New York* was released. This was the first all-dialogue feature film. Later that year, Walt Disney released *Steamboat Willie*, the first film to use post production for the entire soundtrack (dialogue, sound effects, and music). This was all considered to be cutting-edge technology, and the public bought right into it!

Theaters at that time utilized mono optical sound playback. The sound was printed on the film as photographic material by way of the Tri-Ergon process. While ideal for speech reproduction, music and sound effects did not fare as well.

The optical system had a limited audio bandwidth (40 Hz to 10 kHz maximum). It also had a limited dynamic range of about 40 dB. A good deal of noise was created by the system, as well. In addition, the optical storage and playback system was easier to employ and less expensive than the recording of magnetic audio tracks along the film. (Workable magnetic tape recording systems would not appear for another twenty-five to thirty years.)

Theater sound at that time was acoustically live, utilizing natural reverberation to amplify the voice of the on-screen talent. The original designs mimicked the designs of concert halls intended to accentuate acoustic music (opera, orchestral performances, and live theatrical performances).

Loudspeaker design was intended to compensate for low power (5 to 10 watt) tube amplifiers available at the time. An example of this would be the high efficiency horn-loaded designs by Altec called the "Voice of the Theater," introduced in 1947. However, it had a limited and uneven frequency response and a severe roll-off above 8 kHz. They also displayed very uneven dispersion characteristics.

This was theater sound in its embryonic stage. As the deficiencies of each system were identified, improvements were made by way of simple upgrades or large-scale technical innovations.

FANTASIA AND THE EXPANSION OF THEATER SOUND

In 1942, Disney released *Fantasia*, arguably one of the most important films, when it comes to sound engineering for motion pictures. *Fantasia* was the first film to use many of the technologies and techniques that we now use and take for granted. When looking back at some of these achievements, it is hard to comprehend how important they were. It is so simple to record, overdub, pan, and synchronize audio and video with current technology, that the thought of not having a multitrack recording device, or the reality that it took six engineers to operate the first pan pot, seems too far-fetched.

MULTITRACK RECORDING

John Volkmann, the recording engineer for *Fantasia*, did not have a multitrack tape machine to record the score for *Fantasia*. Multitrack was not invented until well over a decade later. In order to record separate sections of the orchestra, he had to use eight optical recording machines (all mono). Six machines were used to record the different sections of the orchestra (strings, brass, woodwinds, percussion, choir, and rhythm section), and two distant mics on the other two machines captured a balance mix of the entire orchestra.

This method gave Volkmann the ability to recombine the levels of each section in the orchestra or even re-record/overdub them, if need be. Later, a ninth machine (for the click track) was added as a guide for the animators to follow, in tempo with the score, to animate singing and dancing sequences.

MULTI-CHANNEL SURROUND-SOUND PLAYBACK

There were no surround theaters available in 1941 to play back the surround soundtrack for the film, so a special playback system called Fantasound was invented specifically for *Fantasia*. This system used two projectors. The first projector was for the visual images, as well as a mono mix of the entire soundtrack as backup. The second projector was printed with four mono optical tracks similar to the modern stereo optical track used today. This second machine technique was referred to as using a "follower."

Track 1 had control information in the form of various frequency tones and amplitudes that were used to modulate the volumes of certain speakers during the show. Tracks 2, 3, and 4 had the audio for the left, center, and right screen speakers, respectively. In addition, there were three other speakers called house left, house center, and house right, placed behind the audience. These speakers derived their signal from the screen left and right channels and were modulated by the control track as well. Thus, the first synchronized surround-sound system was born.

Because there were no surround theaters to play this back in 1941, Disney made *Fantasia* into a traveling road show. *Fantasia* would come to a large metropolitan area close to your town (like a circus or county fair coming to town). They would set up and calibrate the Fantasound playback system and check that everything was working correctly with the movie. After everyone in that location had come to see it, they would pack up and move to another town and repeat the setup and presentation.

According to *Fantasia* folklore, Disney planned to show this in Europe as well. Unfortunately, there was a tragic accident on the ship carrying the show over the Atlantic. The ship sank, and all of the elements of the first European presentation of *Fantasia* went with it to the bottom of the sea. I can see a discovery channel show created for this: "In Search of the Original Euro *Fantasia*...."

NOISE REDUCTION

At that time, optical tracks didn't offer much in the way of dynamic range, because each signal was recorded to tape, as hot as possible, to reduce the noise level (tape hiss) during playback. A control track could then be utilized during playback to later restore the dynamics to where orchestra conductor, Leopold Stokowski, felt they should be. This control track system was known as the "tone-operated gain-adjusting device" (TOGAD). This unique system controlled the levels of each of the main tracks. Disney engineers felt that if a future Fantasound format was ever developed, it should include level-dependent equalization as well, to achieve the dynamics needed for the film's orchestra. This was a very early form of noise reduction.

THE BIRTH OF THE PAN POT

Disney's chief engineer, William Garity, had the challenge of trying to simulate sound moving back and forth across the screen, following the characters actions. He determined that fading the sound volume between the speakers might be able to create the illusion of sound in motion. So, if the character was moving from left to center to right on the screen, the sound would start at full volume on the left and then slowly lower in level as the center volume of that sound would get louder; as the center volume began to lower, the right volume would start to get louder. This would simulate motion in the audio following the character.

A special 3-circuit differential junction network was created to accomplish the task. Thus, Disney could use it to mix down to a 3-track master. They called this device the "pan pot" (for "panoramic potentiometer"). Later, a 2-channel pan pot was created to vary the ratio between close and reverberant sound while maintaining constant level.

Mixdown required six engineers to control the various pan pots in real time, as each machine needed someone to operate the level control. (The mixing console had not been invented yet.) The mix was performed much like a modern film-scoring session, with Stokowski conducting engineers to engage the pan and level changes. Stokowski had marked all of these level and pan changes measure by measure in his musical score.

DEVELOPING DOLBY STEREO

In the late 1960s and early '70s, engineers at Eastman Kodak were developing Stereo Variable Area (SVA) soundtrack encoding. The concept of SVA was to use two optical channels to store multiple tracks of information on standard 35 mm film stock. The use of optical storage (still in use by theaters with mono sound, at the time) was greatly preferred due to its ease of implementation and lower cost (than magnetic storage). At the same time, Dolby Laboratories introduced Dolby A noise reduction for analog tape recording. Dolby A is a frequency-based compression system that delivers between 10 dB and 15 dB of tape hiss quieting.

In the mid 1970s, Dolby introduced the Dolby Motion Picture (MP) Matrix. The Dolby MP system utilized the SVA concept and added Dolby A noise reduction. This format was to find great acceptance, as it was compatible with mono, stereo, and stereo with surround-equipped theaters. It also eliminated the problems and expenses inherent to magnetic playback systems.

Dolby manufactured an encoding device, the SE-U4, which was a combing matrix used to condense the four channels (left, right, center, and surround) of audio into two. The two-matrixed tracks were then optically printed on film. This system was ideal, because it could be used in any theater.

- In a "stereo with surround" equipped theater, a decoding device read the two optical tracks from the film and decoded them into four discrete channels (left, center, right, surround). This system of encode/store/decode is referred to as a 424 matrix, creating what is commonly known today as an LTRT (which stands for Left Total, Right Total).
- A 2-channel stereo theater could read the two optical tracks from the film (no decoding required) and play them as left and right stereo.
- A mono theater could read both optical tracks as one mono signal fairly accurately.

The introduction of the Dolby Motion Picture (MP) Matrix and the LTRT were groundbreaking in the 1970s, because it started a standardization and universal master technique that could be implemented in a variety of theaters that were around at the time (both old and new). The LTRT has become a standard deliverable for mixers and is still in use today to accommodate older televisions and VCRs that utilize the 4-track surround format (like Dolby Pro Logic).

THE THX SYSTEM

In 1977, George Lucas saw the potential of the Dolby Stereo system. He was producing *Star Wars* at the time and went to great lengths to assemble a soundtrack that could take advantage of all the sonic capabilities of the Dolby Stereo system. A mutual effort between Lucas, Dolby, and the film's distributors (20th Century Fox) led to the setup of high quality sound in selected theaters around the United States. However, they did not originally take into consideration the playback systems and acoustics in the remaining 25,000 theaters that would be showing the film. Many of the intricacies within the soundtrack would be lost due to aging and poorly maintained sound systems found in many theaters at that time.

Then, with the sad state of theaters in mind, Lucas came up with the idea to create a set of standards for the quality of film soundtrack mixing and playback in theaters. He enlisted the talents of engineer Tomlinson Holman, formerly of Advent and APT, as chief engineer for post production. This project was to be dubbed the Tomlison Holman EXperiment, eventually shortened to THX.

The first step was to establish standard criteria for calibrating playback in the dubbing theater, also known as a "dub stage." The dub stage is a mixing stage in a theater-like environment. It looks very much like a movie theater, with a mixing console placed in the middle of it. This is where the soundtrack for the film is mixed.

A large wall of speakers was set up behind the screen to facilitate the front left, center, and right audio along with speakers strategically placed on the sides and rear for the left surround and right surround. Additionally, a subwoofer was placed under the screen in front, to accommodate the low end. This was the initial inception of the 5.1 surround-sound monitoring system. The walls, ceiling, and floors were treated with absorptive material to eliminate any standing waves or echo in the room. The concept was that the engineers would mix the film's soundtrack in a similar environment to where it was to be heard by audiences.

The first physical embodiment of the THX concept was in 1982, with the construction of the dubbing theater at the Sprocket Systems post-production facility in San Rafael, CA. The room was built with existing technology and equipment available in the audio marketplace. The only custom designed components were the THX crossover network and a modified Neve 8108 mixing console.

Once a high quality, high-resolution mixing environment had been constructed to allow the engineers and producers to hear and mix the soundtracks accurately, the real problem was addressed: the playback systems and acoustics in theaters.

The theaters were now designed to be acoustically "dead." According to the new spec, the audience should hear only the reverb, ambience, and effects as included in the soundtrack. The walls, ceilings, and floors should be treated acoustically to control the reflective surfaces in the room. The reverberation decay time (RT60) at 500 Hz should measure between .43 and .7 seconds, which is very short for a room large enough to hold 500 people. Additionally, the theater should have no parallel walls, to reduce the chance of flutter echoes and standing waves.

The *THX Baffle Wall* is a floor-to-near-ceiling wall located behind the screen. It has the front loudspeakers and a subwoofer mounted in it. The purpose of the wall is to launch a cohesive wave front through the screen, without any ill effects from the wall behind the screen. The wall is quite massive (three layers of drywall braced with metal ribs), and therefore helps increase the low frequency response as well.

The THX Playback System

There are no products actually manufactured by THX Lucas film. THX provides certification for the performance of the components that meet their criteria for quality and performance. Some one hundred manufacturers have placed THX certified components on the market for professional and consumer use. The only component specifically designed by THX is the *crossover*, which is the heart of the THX sound system.

THX was very successful and widely recognized as a standard for mixing and playback of a soundtrack for film upon its initial introduction. Shortly thereafter, the television industry embraced the technology on a smaller scale, as a basis for mixing television shows. Holman and Lucas had achieved their goal. A soundtrack mix that was created in a THX-approved dub stage translated accurately to a THX-approved theater.

DIGITAL THEATER SOUND

The Dolby Stereo Digital system is a 6-track digital surround system (Left, Center, Right, Left Surround, Right Surround, and Low Frequency Emitter, also known as L, C, R, LS, RS, LFE). This type of arrangement is often referred to as a "5.1 system" because there are five full-range speakers plus a subwoofer. The DTS system is often promoted through a logo with the text "The Digital Experience" at the front of a theater.

The Sony Dynamic Digital Sound (SDDS) system utilizes a discrete eight-channel 7.1 playback system, printed digitally on the film. There are five front channels (Left, Left Center, Center, Right Center, Right), as in a traditional 70 mm format, along with two surround channels (Left Surround and Right Surround) and a dedicated subwoofer track (LFE). The Sony system requires the use of a proprietary encode/decode technology.

The post-production industry is currently developing 7.1 technology for the mix and playback of the soundtrack. This includes left, center, right, and subwoofer up front, while having a surround left and surround right off to the sides, along with surround left and surround right behind you. There are a variety of established setup and placement specs available for a wide range of room dimensions. These are accessible via Dolby's website. Additionally, there are some futurists that are expanding that realm to even larger surround listening options. It will be interesting to see where this will lead us.

CHAPTER 3

The Process of Making a Film

The process of making a film or television show begins with an idea. This could be from a book, a play, a movie, a dream, or a manuscript. It goes through many stages as it develops, including scripting, casting, shooting, editing, mixing, and theatrical presentation, and it involves several steps that are each key to the project's progression.

Robert Altman's classic film *The Player* demonstrates part of this process in the opening scene. We observe one of the studio executives going through several movie pitches in just a few minutes. This sequence is very entertaining and quite an insight into the movie-making process. It is important to understand this process and the order in which they take place, as each step plays a major role in the next.

I can recall entering this world myself as an entry-level production assistant (PA) at a busy post-production studio in Los Angeles. My chores were to get coffee and lunch and go on runs for whatever was needed. I was young, energetic, and like most PAs, had no clue as to what was going on.

One day, I drove the boss home because his car was in the shop. As I drove, he decided to sum up the movie business as it related to the audio post-production process in about 45 minutes (the duration of our drive to his house—in Beverly Hills, of course). This conversation took me by surprise, as the boss was never a likeable or overly talkative person. His insights were so descriptive and accurate that I felt as if my clueless and inexperienced perception of the industry went from black and white to brilliant Technicolor!

By the time we arrived at his house, I thoroughly understood what we did at the studio and how everything worked together in a step-by-step process. Thanks, Andrew! The conversation went something like this; "Hey, you're new here, aren't you? Well, you're gonna need to know how this business works, if you wanna stick around. Oh, and turn left at the next light...."

So, here's how this business works....

DEVELOPMENT

The *development* stage in filmmaking is the writing and rewriting phase, where the story is "developed" (hence, the name). The project may have started out in a variety of different ways, so this is where it will be outlined and transformed into a *synopsis*—a two-page description of what the movie is about.

From there, the synopsis will develop into a *treatment*, which is a twenty- to thirty-page narrative defining the key points of interest (characters, mood, and story line). When the treatment is approved, a scriptwriter is hired to create the *screenplay*, which includes the complete dialogue and descriptions of the actions and sets. The screenplay process will further define and clarify the story, which may go through several revisions before it is approved.

The end of the development stage is punctuated with a finalized screenplay and the project receiving a "green light." This means that it has been approved and funded by the studio or production company, and it can move forward to the next step of production.

PRE-PRODUCTION

This is the point in which each step of the filmmaking process is carefully identified, planned, and defined, from the first day of shooting to the final post production and theatrical release, as well as archiving for a future rerelease on alternate media formats. A budget will be created at this stage, and that will define how intricate the production will be, along with the size and scope of the cast and crew.

The *pre-production* phase is where the story is visualized. This is done by way of *storyboarding*—a process where the project is story sketched in comic-book type format to define and conceptualize the story sequence.

As the cast and crew are hired, the production begins to take form. Many pre-production meetings will occur at this point, and this is where the key players (producers, director, writer, picture editor, director of photography, supervising sound editor, etc.) get together to plan the project.

The director will talk about his or her vision for the film, the picture editor and director of photography will talk about the look and feel of the film, the supervising sound editor will talk about sounds, the composer will talk about musical ideas, and the producer(s) will talk about the budget and schedule, etc. Pre-production is where they will do the major experimentation with the script, the sounds, the music, storyboarding, location scouting, set design, casting, etc.

PRODUCTION

The *production* phase is the actual filming of the project, and it is at this point that the sound department will be keeping a watchful eye on the location sound. They'll be making sure that the dialogue and ambiences are recorded properly, as well as determining whether any problematic set elements, power generators, and/or extraneous location noise could get in the way of capturing great production sound.

During this stage, it is good for the audio post-production crew to keep in touch with the film production team on set because last-minute set changes could directly affect the sound. Additionally, you will stay in touch with Transfer/Telecine (transfer from film to video for playback), to make sure that the dailies sound good.

Dailies are the assembled production takes (shoots) for the day, roughly put together. These get viewed at the end of each day of production, or sometimes at the beginning of the following day. Monitoring dailies serves as a barometer for how the production is progressing (or not progressing).

Dailies are extremely important, even though the picture is a very rough/grainy cut and the audio is often choppy and un-processed. The people viewing the dailies (the director, producers, department heads, and studio executives) look past all of that. They want to make sure that the actors are performing well and that the story and location are working. If it's a comedy, is it funny? If it's a drama, is it dramatic? Everyone will also be looking for any technical issues with sound and picture and address them ASAP!

POST PRODUCTION

Post production starts when the filming (principal photography) is completed or "wrapped." At this point, the editing begins and may continue all the way through, until the last possible minute. Editing could actually go on long after the initial release of the production. It is rumored that George Lucas continues to edit *Star Wars* with each new media format rerelease.

The picture editor will put together a *rough cut* of the film, and the sound supervisors will put together a rough mix (also referred to as the "temp dub") to accompany it as the soundtrack. The rough cut will be a bit more refined than the dailies, but not by much. It serves the same purpose, but it's now in a completed form. It will have more refined dialogue and may contain temp music and temp sound effects, while the actual music and sound design are still in the process of being composed or created.

The rough cut is screened for the key players to assess the film and make notes on improvements, and most importantly, how to proceed in post production. After this screening, the sound and video departments will address the notes, as well as fine-tuning their elements as the post-production process continues.

Depending on the budget, another temp dub might accompany each new cut of the picture. The main purpose of temp dubs is to check the project's progression and to make sure that everything is still on point. This process of creating new temporary versions of the film may repeat for as long as it takes to finalize the editorial process. Often, outside forces (such as focus groups) are brought in to give additional feedback, in case something was overlooked. Whether these steps happen depends on the project's budget. A lower-budget indie project may never have a temp dub because the filmmakers simply can't afford one.

Temp dubs can also serve as a "pre-dub" for the audio prep for the final film mix. The *pre-dub* is where all of the audio post-production elements are fine-tuned. The purpose of the temp dub is to introduce the elements to the mixers and to make a more manageable track count, so that the final mix (the final dub) doesn't get out of hand, in terms of how many audio tracks are used. With the advent of powerful DAWs, the track counts have increased in leaps and bounds. Pre-dubs are often essential to keep that in check.

An example of the track count getting out of hand comes from the Batman film, *The Dark Knight*. Hans Zimmer scored the opening bank robbery scene basing the "Joker's Theme" on a single sustained cello note. At that point, Zimmer developed a score that eventually became well over 800 Pro Tools tracks. The music mixer did his mix, which became close to 200 stems. (*Stems* are sub mixes of similar sounds/instruments that make up the final mix.) However, this was still far too many tracks to bring to a dub stage!

The music editor had to pre-dub his score mix in order to bring the track count down to just under a hundred stems—and that was just the music! Can you imagine adding hundreds of sound effects tracks along with Foley and dialogue? It becomes too complicated to manage. The pre-dubs are very important to the final mix and are often forming throughout the temp mixes.

All of this is in preparation for the *final dub*, where all of the audio soundtrack elements are mixed along with the final cut of the picture (see p. 19, "The THX System").

The final dub will be played back for the director, the producers, and department heads when it is completed. They each will document any audio flaws or fixes that they feel need to be considered before the final mix can be printed. Their notes will be assembled and addressed by the mixers until everyone feels that the mix is complete—or until the deadline has arrived, whichever comes first. This is usually the deadline.

DISTRIBUTION AND ARCHIVING

Distribution and *archiving* are the final stages of the process. At this point, the production might be prepared for theatrical release, screening, broadcast, or mechanical release on an alternate format, as well as direct Internet download. Feature films will have the big release campaigns, by way of advertisements, movie posters, press kits, star-studded premiers, and high-profile screenings at major film festivals (e.g., Cannes and Sundance). The studio will try to coordinate this stage of the project, with key times throughout the year where they feel the production will get the most attention and ultimately make the most money.

This is also when archiving occurs. *Archiving* is the process of backing up and storing the production and all of its elements in multiple mediums. Archiving is done for a variety of reasons. Backups are extremely important, as they assure that the project is protected against any problems beyond one's control (fire, extreme weather, etc.)—anything that could possibly destroy the production or its elements.

The studio can also use the archive to rerelease a production in the future, as well as in newer formats. A great example of this is the classic television show, *I Love Lucy*. It was on television in the 1950s, and I still see it broadcast on Sunday afternoons (over sixty years later). It was shot in mono, on film, so the studio had to go to the archives, transfer the elements to a digital format, and re-dub the episodes so that they could be broadcast according to today's broadcast specifications in digital and surround.

MEET THE PLAYERS

This is a good point to look at who is doing what in the filmmaking process. There are so many people involved these days, that in some cases, it takes 15 to 20 minutes to simply watch the end credits.

I remember, as a teenager, looking at the credits on the back covers of albums, while I'd listen to them. I started to notice the names of producers and engineers, as well as musicians, on the albums. Interestingly, as my record collection grew, a lot of the same names kept popping up. As my taste in music was developing, so was taste in people's work, besides just the artists.

This happened again with film, a few years later. I started noticing that I really enjoyed movies by certain directors, composers, and sound designers. I found that their involvement brought so much to the film that I would go to see it simply because they were involved. That piqued my interest in audio post production, and eventually led me west to investigate further.

ORGANIZATION

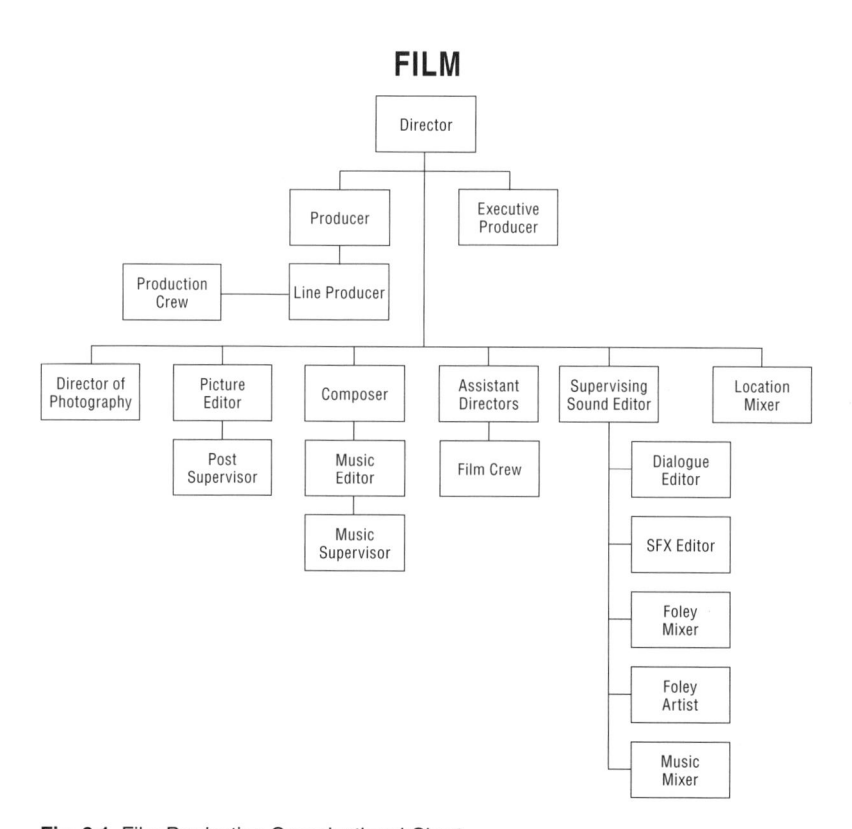

FILM

- Director
  - Producer
    - Line Producer
      - Production Crew
  - Executive Producer
- Director of Photography
- Picture Editor
  - Post Supervisor
- Composer
  - Music Editor
  - Music Supervisor
- Assistant Directors
  - Film Crew
- Supervising Sound Editor
  - Dialogue Editor
  - SFX Editor
  - Foley Mixer
  - Foley Artist
  - Music Mixer
- Location Mixer

Fig. 3.1. Film Production Organizational Chart

TELEVISION

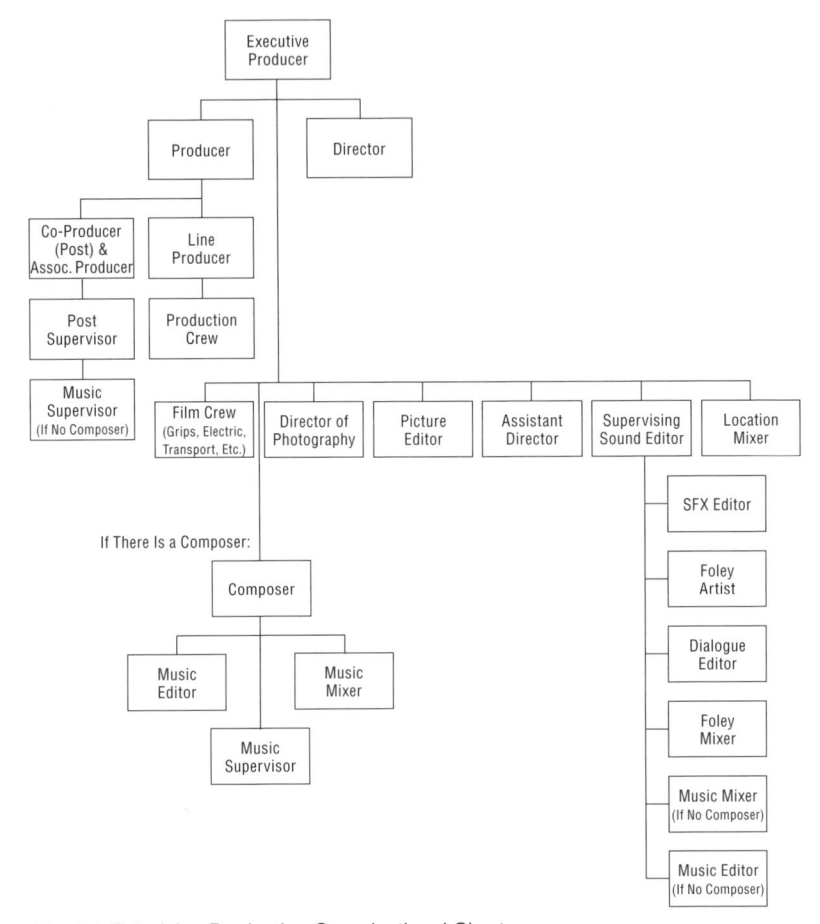

Fig. 3.2. Television Production Organizational Chart

Here is a list of a few people involved in the filmmaking process, along with a brief description of what they do.

The Film Crew

Producer(s): The producer is responsible for everything on the business side of the production. This includes money, budgeting, and hiring/firing, while they oversee the entire project.

Co-Producer: Working closely with the producers, the co-producer is considered a supervisor for the post-production department. Co-producers are responsible for the delivery requirements for the production including editing, color correction, and mixing. They also create and track the post-production department budget.

Executive Producer(s) (EP): The executive producer handles and/or finds the financing as well as the business and legal issues associated with the production. They can also be attached to the project creatively and will give notes on the project throughout the entire production.

Line Producer: The line producer creates and tracks the budget and also hires the crew. He or she oversees the day-to-day aspects of the production.

Production Assistant(s): Production assistants are also referred to as "runners" because they are usually running to get something (like coffee) or delivering something (like scripts or dailies). They are also involved in light office work. This is considered an entry-level position and is a great starting place for someone entering the industry, as it gives them direct contact with almost every aspect of the production in a very indirect way.

Director: The director is responsible for implementing the creative vision and scope of the project. The director guides how the talent will act out their roles, helps determine shooting locations and the look of the film, and has a hand in how the film's soundtrack is edited and mixed.

Assistant Director (AD): The AD runs the set and schedules the day. They are responsible for *making the day*—achieving every shot and activity scheduled for that day.

Director of Photography (DP): The DP is in charge of the look of the film. This includes the composition and resolution of the shots as well as the lighting and camera angles, etc. They work hand in hand with the director to make sure that everything looks like the way it was envisioned in pre-production. They have direct interaction with the camera and lighting people as well as the grip department.

Picture Editor: The picture editor takes the video/film along with production sound and edits it into a rough/final composite form known as the "rough cut." This is followed by a series of new cuts/versions. Their ultimate goal is to create the *final cut*.

Production Coordinator (POC): The POC runs the production office. They are responsible for numerous tasks, such as accounting, human resources, budget management, etc. Often, they are required to do all of these simultaneously, under extreme pressure and time-sensitive deadlines.

The Sound Crew

Supervising Sound Editor: The supervising sound editor is a creative role, working with the director, picture editor, and producer. This person is responsible for overseeing most aspects of post-production audio on a film or television show. Supervising sound editors coordinate sound editors, sound designers, Foley artists, recording engineers, and ADR (automatic dialogue replacement) recording for a project. They take all of the audible elements of the film (dialogue, music, sound effects) and guide them to form the soundtrack, which is an integral part of the storytelling.

Location Recordist/Mixer: The location recordist records the dialogue on set, as well as any wild takes and ambiance/room tones. He or she must capture these sounds on the set of the production (film or television show) cleanly, and without any outside interference, such as 60 cycle electrical hum, generator noise, or general interference. Any location dialogue that has extraneous noise in the background is deemed unusable and must be done over, often in costly ADR sessions.

Dialogue Editor(s): The dialogue editor edits and assembles the dialogue. He or she uses the location sound files to prepare the dialogue, along with any room tones, for the final dub. This is a specialized role and is mostly done using digital audio workstations.

SFX Editor/Mixer(s): Sound effects editors/mixers are charged with the creation, selection, and placement of sound effects for the project. They work closely with the supervising sound editor to create specialized sound effects specific to the project. Often, these are sound elements that have no real-life equivalent or cannot be achieved safely, (e.g., explosions, gunshots, etc.).

Foley Artist(s)/Walker(s): Foley artist(s)/walker(s) (also called the "sync effect actors") create the actual Foley sounds for the film. Foley is the art of recreating the sound that a body/object makes, in interaction with its environment, like the sound of a window closing in a certain room, the sound of a shirt tearing, or the sound of footsteps on a variety of surfaces.

Foley Mixer(s)/Editor(s): Foley mixer(s)/engineer(s) are in charge of capturing the Foley sound effects. They will record this on a Foley stage. The Foley stage contains numerous props and surfaces that are used by the Foley walkers/actors to recreate footsteps, clothes movement, and specific sound effects like doors slamming and glass breaking.

Music Mixer(s): Music mixer(s)/engineer(s) are in charge of recording and mixing the music score for the film or television show. The job might be as simple as mixing an electronic score in a DAW or as complex as recording a full orchestra on a scoring stage to multiple formats. Regardless, they are responsible for delivering the music stems to the dub stage for the final mix.

Music Editor(s): Music editors work closely with the composer and the music mixer. He or she is also in charge of creating a temporary score, or "temp score," while the picture is being edited together (usually put together from other film scores), as well as compiling songs for the production. The music editor will work with the composer by updating him or her with intricate notes on score ideas and picture edits.

Music Supervisor: The music supervisor handles the process of choosing, negotiating, and incorporating pieces of music into a film or television show. He or she often acts as a liaison between the creative and business ends of this process. The main responsibility of a music supervisor is to meet the needs of a project's director and producer, as well as catering to the creative goals of a project under a strict budget.

Re-Recording Mixers: Re-recording mixers are a team of engineers who mix the soundtrack (final dub) of the project. They will be given the final sound elements including dialogue, SFX, Foley, and music and will balance everything until the final soundtrack mix is achieved. This is done on a dub stage.

There are many other professionals involved in the process, beyond these key roles. To get a clearer idea of the vastness of people involved, watch the credits at the end of any feature film. The website www.imdb.com (Internet Movie Database) also lists all credited participants in a great number of films.

CHAPTER 4

Post-Production Media

This chapter is a bit more technical than the rest, mainly because post production is a technical field. We are constantly working with both new and old technology and often find ourselves on "the bleeding edge" of technical innovations. Take your time with this section, and refer back to it when you have the need to clarify or resolve a technical issue.

SYNCHRONIZATION

Synchronization is the basic process by which two playback systems (audio and video) communicate and keep time with each other. In order to create sound that works seamlessly with visuals, two playback systems may be necessary (one for audio, one for video). These two systems must be capable of playing back together in perfect time or "in sync" from the same point, without either one moving faster or slower than the other.

In synchronization, two things are necessary:

1. Positional Reference (where, in time)
2. Playback Rate (how fast)

Positional reference lets us know where we are in the film or audio track. Unique numbers are assigned to each segment of audio and frame of video (known as "time code"), in order to indicate exactly where you are at any given point.

Playback rate is how fast the frames are moving. In film and video, the playback rate is notated in the frame rate (frames per second, or fps). In digital audio, the playback rate is the sample rate (samples per second). The speed relationship between the audio and video must remain the same, in order to be in sync.

So the main questions are:

How do we get constant and reliable motion?

How do we get two devices to play together?

The answers to these questions can be realized with the use of SMPTE Time Code.

SMPTE Time Code

Just as bars and beat numbers are used to identify locations in a piece of music, time code allows us to identify where we are in audio and video. In visual systems, each frame of film is given a unique number. This is accomplished through the use of *SMPTE* (Society of Motion Picture and Television Engineers) *time code*, which is represented in hours, minutes, seconds, and frames, thus giving us positional reference by providing a unique address for any location on our film or in our audio. SMPTE time code is an industry standard for synchronization and was developed to broadcast video. SMPTE time code is expressed in an 8 digit number with colons separating each value of hours, minutes, seconds, and frames.

00h:00m:00s:00f

Fig. 4.1. Frame with Burned-in Time Code

Drop-Frame/Non-Drop-Frame Rates

When color video was developed, broadcasters wanted to keep the current black-and-white transmission intact at 30 fps. So, engineers came up with a system that allowed color television to be backward-compatible with the existing black-and-white televisions. Due to the frequencies involved, a slight adjustment had to be made to the frame rate in order for the new color system to work with both color and black-and-white televisions. The frame rate in color was slowed down by .1 percent, resulting in a rate of 29.97 fps. This small adjustment allowed the new color television broadcasts to be viewed on the older black-and-white television sets, and 29.97 fps is the current frame rate for all NTSC (National Television System Committee) video systems in use today.

Although the new frame rate solved the problem of compatibility, it created a new problem for video editors. The new 29.97 frame rate was a little slower than 30 fps; therefore, it would not display the correct time in relation to the clock on the wall. After a minute, a drift would occur, and this drift would increase as time went on. After an hour of real time, 29.97 SMPTE would read **"00:59:56:12"**—a difference of over 3 seconds. For relatively short programs, such as commercials, this was not a problem. However, for anything longer than one minute, the time-code drift became significant.

This is where *Drop Frame Time Code* steps in.

Drop Frame SMPTE time code skips (or "drops") some frame numbers in order to achieve an accurate real-time display. The video frames themselves are not lost. The time code merely skips certain frame numbers along the way, so that it can display the current real time more precisely. The frame count of Drop Frame SMPTE is determined by how the frame numbers are skipped.

In order to lose those extra 18 frames in each 10-minute increment, drop frame must skip 2 frames (frame :00 and :01) every minute for the first 9 minutes and none in the 10th minute. This gives us a total of 18 frames in 10 minutes. This cycle repeats every 10 minutes. As there are 1,800 frames of video in 10 minutes at 30 fps, the 18 frame numbers that are skipped (*remember, no video frames are skipped, just their numbers*) correlate to the .1 percent speed change to color video at 29.97 frames per second.

You can always visually identify Drop Frame Time Code (DFTC), as the colon (:) is changed to a semi-colon(;) between the seconds and frames.

For example:

    Drop Frame Time Code (DF):   **01:14:06;08**

    Non Drop Frame Time Code (NDF):   **01:14:06:08**

STANDARD FRAME RATES:

24 frames per second (film)

25 frames per second (European or PAL video)

29.97 frames per second (NTSC Color video)

30 frames per second (audio only or black-and-white television)

23.976 frames per second (HD video that converts to NTSC video)

STANDARD SAMPLE RATES:

44.1 kHz: the current standard music sample rates for CDs and music

48 kHz: the film and video standard

88.2 kHz: hi-res music sample rate for audio CDs. Easily converts to 44.1 kHz.

96 kHz: newer hi-res sample rate for better frequency response. Can be used for video, since it is a multiple of 48 kHz and is easy to convert.

DIGITAL AUDIO FILE FORMATS

Post-production media (both audio and video) comes in a variety of ever-changing formats. It can be difficult to stay on top of this, because manufacturers always seem to be introducing something better and often smaller. We have come a long way since the days of wax, lacquer, vinyl, tape, and film. However, in some instances, we are still supporting a few of those formats. For the purpose of this book, we will examine the digital formats in use today.

In audio, we are working with audio files in a few different formats: AIFF, WAV, SDII, MP3, and CAF, to name a few. Both AIFF and WAV (also known as "broadcast wave") are the most common. The broadcast wave format has become the preferred format throughout the industry. This is mainly because of its ability to include a time stamp within the meta-data of the file. The time stamp is very important, as it refers to the location origin of the file. This is useful, especially when editors start to move things around.

CAF (Apple's Core Audio Files), SDII (Sound Designer II/older Pro Tools format), and other file formats are definitely out there, and we need to be aware of them. Fortunately, most DAWs can convert audio files to the file format used in your session, either automatically or as a manual option when you're importing. Today, file format conversion is of good quality, and not as big of an issue as it was in the past. Some DAWs even support multiple file formats within the same session. This is a good thing, as it helps our workflow move steadily forward.

FILM/VIDEO FORMATS

Film: Physically, film is a strip of plastic that is 35 mm wide (less commonly, 16 mm or 8 mm), with sprocket holes on the sides so that it can be driven by a projector. This plastic is coated with an emulsion containing light-sensitive silver ion with variable crystal sizes that determine the sensitivity, contrast, and resolution of the film. When the emulsion is sufficiently exposed to light, it forms a latent (invisible) image. Chemical processes can then be applied to the film to create a visible image. This process is called "film developing."

Film is costly and fragile, because it uses chemicals to create the images. However, it is still preferred by cinematographers for depth of field and detailing, as they can easily alter the look by the way they process it. Film also has a much higher resolution than video—beyond High Definition (HD). It does not always look real, which adds to its mystique and artistic features. Film has a "look" to it. Compared to video, in film, people seem to glow a bit more, and edges are softer. It is a universal medium, as it can be played almost anywhere on the planet, and it has a proven shelf life.

Video: *Videotape* is a means of recording images and sound onto magnetic media (originally tape), as opposed to movie film. It was developed in WWII for broadcast television. The original format was black and white (B&W). The only upgrade that was made to video was to transform it from black and white to color. The main problem with this was that the industry had to find a way to make both B&W and color compatible. The industry couldn't force the consumer to buy new television sets so that they could experience color TV.

After considerable research, the NTSC (National Television System Committee) introduced a system that encoded the color information separately from the brightness, and greatly reduced the resolution of the color information in order to conserve bandwidth. The brightness level remained compatible with existing B&W television sets, at a slightly reduced resolution, while color televisions could decode the extra information in the signal and produce a limited-color display. (See page 37).

Video Quality Standards

Video quality is described in terms of resolution and aspect ratio.

Resolution is the number of pixels per inch. Pixels are dots used to display an image on a screen or printed matter. The word "pixel" is a blend of the words "picture" and "element." The higher the pixel count, the better the image.

Aspect ratio refers to the shape of the frame, width to height.

Standard Definition (SD): Standard Definition resolution is 720 x 486 pixels—considered a standard amount to create a good image. Standard definition has an aspect ratio of 4:3. This (4:3) ratio goes back to the original movie theater screens.

High Definition (HD): The pixel count for HD is greater than SD. HD resolution can be 1920 x 1080 or 1280 x 720. HD has an aspect ratio of 16:9, so the framing is proportionally wider than SD.

1080i/1080p: With the introduction of the HD DVD and Blu-ray high definition disc formats, as well as HD televisions that are capable of HDTV's highest resolution of 1920x1080, the terms 1080i and 1080p are being used more than ever before. The big difference in the terms, of course, is the *i* (for interlaced) and *p* (for progressive), which indicate how the image is stored and how it is displayed.

In the analog world of televisions, interlaced vs. progressively scanned video is an important distinction. Interlacing involves showing every other line of video in one frame and then supplying the remaining lines on the next pass. Standard analog television signals are interlaced by necessity, because standard analog televisions were never designed to handle anything but an interlaced signal.

New HDTVs are inherently progressively scanned devices. Their circuitry displays video all at once, so if they receive interlaced signals, those signals are de-interlaced to progressive signals before they are displayed. Until recently, few HDTVs could accept a 1080p signal due to cost savings or other technical limitations. HDTVs capable of only the lower 1280x720 HDTV resolution will usually only accept interlaced video at the higher 1920x1080 resolution.

DIGITAL FORMATS

QuickTime: QuickTime is a cross-platform software technology developed by Apple for video playback and multimedia. It is also the media player format supported by many DAWs.

MPEG: MPEG stands for "Motion Picture Experts Group." MPEG is used to denote a whole family of audio and video compression algorithms developed by MPEG. The formats are MPEG-1 (MP3 audio format), MPEG-2 (DVD and HDTV encoding), and MPEG-4 (next generation codecs). All MPEG codecs are supported by QuickTime.

AVI Codecs: AVI stands for "Audio Video Interleave." This is the standard multimedia format used for PCs in Windows. As Mac-based DAWs support both Avid and QuickTime files for movies, Windows users must install QuickTime on their systems

DV Codecs: DV, or "Digital Video," is an international standard for consumers, semi-pro, and professional digital-equipment, such as DV camcorders.

TELECINE MACHINES AND PROCESS

The Telecine process is used when film is transferred to video. This is done for a variety of reasons. One is to facilitate the creation of dailies (see chapter 3). Additionally, as television became more popular, producers were interested in showing their movies on television. They had to figure out a way to get their movies into a format that television could easily work with, because film and television resolution are different. The Telecine process was developed to facilitate this.

To understand the Telecine process, it is best to break things down on a technical level. A single film frame is the smallest visual entity that can't be subdivided. Frames are displayed at a rate of 24 per second (fps) in theatrical projection, while the standard in NTSC video (US TV) is 29.97 fps.

If we simply sped up the movie reel to 29.97 fps, and kept one film frame as one video frame, the action would speed up about 20 percent. This increase in speed would be noticeable, even to the most untrained eye. Therefore, it is not considered a realistic option.

The more effective solution is to take advantage of the fact that video frames are built in two passes—two consecutive "fields" of lines. In the Telecine process, the odd-numbered lines (1, 3, 5…) are "scanned" or drawn on the display. Then, the even lines are similarly scanned.

If the film reel is slowed down by an unnoticeable 0.01 percent to 23.976 fps, the ratio between the film and television frames is exactly 4 film frames for 5 television frames. The 5 television frames are a total of 10 consecutive fields of lines.

A sequence of 4 film frames is usually given the letters A, B, C, and D.

One solution for transferring the 4 film frames into the 5 television frames is the following (also known as the *2-3 pull-down process*):

- frame A into the entire first frame of video.
- frame B into the entire second video frame and into the first field of the third video frame.
- frame C into the second field of the third video frame and into the first field of the fourth video frame.
- frame D into the second field of the fourth video frame and into the entire fifth video frame.

If we slow this down and look at it frame by frame, it will appear disjointed and odd. However, when it is played at normal speed, it creates the illusion of fluid motion.

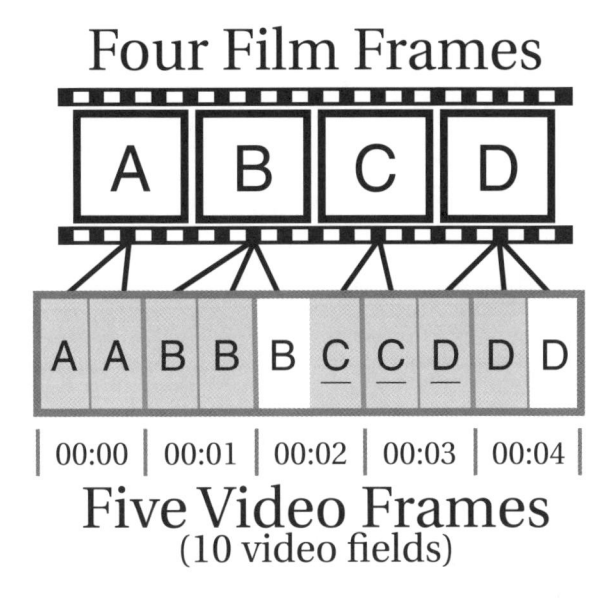

Four Film Frames

| A | B | C | D |

| A | A | B | B | B | C | C | D | D | D |

| 00:00 | 00:01 | 00:02 | 00:03 | 00:04 |

Five Video Frames
(10 video fields)

Fig. 4.2. 2–3 Pulldown Process

CHAPTER 5

Location Sound Recording

Recording high-quality sound while shooting on location is essential to a great-sounding film. Careful attention to capturing sound during the filming process will also save time and money in post production. All of this is in the hands of the location sound crew. They are in charge of recording the sound on set in sync with the camera, as well as interior and exterior scene ambience (room tones). This is achieved by utilizing a variety of gear and techniques.

THE LOCATION SOUND CREW

The location sound is recorded by a crew of two to three people. The team consists of the production sound mixer (team leader) along with the boom operator and assistant. When the budget is tight, the boom operator will double as the assistant. They will be on set/location setting up before the shoot begins and often remain afterwards to capture room tones and live ambience.

The Production Sound Mixer

The production (or location) sound mixer is responsible for capturing all sound on the set. This is usually a union position and includes putting together the location sound budget and equipment as well as hiring their support crew. The duties include recording the live production dialogue and the production FX in sync with the camera, as well as interior and exterior scene ambience (room tones). These recordings will be included in the final mix and in the reference mix to be used by the dialogue editor, sound effects editor, music editor, and picture editor.

The production sound mixer will arrive on location with his or her equipment, which includes microphones, wireless systems, booms, mixer, audio storage, headphones, cables, tools, and cue/log sheets for making notes and logs. They must be prepared to capture a wide variety of sound on location while considering the format of the finished product. They will also be dealing with outside interference such as weather, air traffic, and loud generators on set.

The production sound mixer is considered a department head, and is thus responsible for capturing all aspects of production sound. This includes the hiring of a boom operator and utility sound technician, planning the technical setup (including both sound equipment and ancillary devices involved in syncing and time offsets), anticipating sound-related problems on location, and ordering and preparing the sound equipment to be used on the set.

The production sound mixer typically records to a portable multitrack hard-disk recorder (usually with a small mixer) that facilitates splitting out each actor's wireless lavaliere mic to a separate track and then combining the comp mix to another. Often, when filming on video, they will also record their comp mix directly into the camera, for sync and safety reasons. Most of their gear (hard disk recorder, mixer, monitor, wireless receivers, sound logs, etc.) is arranged on a mobile sound cart. This allows them to move around quickly and efficiently to capture the sound for each scene.

LOCATION SOUND MIXER BILL MACPHERSON

Bill Macpherson was the location sound mixer for *The Sarah Silverman Program*, *Curb Your Enthusiasm*, and U2's *Rattle and Hum*, a documentary on the rock band U2 on tour. On *Rattle and Hum*, he and his crew had to go on tour with the band. Because the film was about the band on tour, the audio crew had to be close by and available at a moment's notice. This meant that the sound crew *had* to stay at all of the luxury "rock star" hotels and share all of the first class travel amenities. It was work nonetheless. Bill did an extraordinary job and the film sounds fantastic! Of course, location sound is never this glamorous!

Here is Bill in action, on set in Hollywood.

Fig. 5.1. Bill McPherson, Location Sound Engineer

Here is Bill's sound cart.

Fig. 5.2. Sound Cart

Boom Operator

The boom operator is the first assistant to the production sound mixer. The principal responsibility of the boom operator is microphone placement. This includes using a boom (fishing pole-like mic stand) with a microphone attached to the end. Sometimes, when the situation permits, they will use a *fisher boom*, which is a more intricate and specialized piece of equipment that the operator stands on; a fisher boom allows precise control of the microphone at a much greater distance away from the actors than what is possible with a normal boom. The boom operator also attaches wireless microphones to actors or anyone whose voice requires recording.

Here is boom operator Vincent Schelly setting up the wireless receivers for the Sanken Lavaliere mics.

Fig. 5.3. Adjusting Transmitters for the Wireless Mic Setup

Boom operators are the people who hold and operate the microphone attached to the long pole, which in film lingo is called the "boom." The boom operator must decide where to place the boom mic based on a combination of factors, including the location and projection of any dialogue, the frame position of the camera, the source of lighting (and shadows), and any unwanted noise sources.

They also handle and set up various sound equipment and report directly to the production sound mixer. The boom operator must try and get as close to an actor as possible, without getting the microphone into the shot. The microphone must be optimally placed for recording dialogue, effects, or music.

Here is Vincent Schelly operating a boom on set in Hollywood.

Fig. 5.4. Boom Operator Vincent Schelly

Being a boom operator is not an easy job. It requires a steady hand, good arm muscles, and technical skill. The boom operator should be one of the most knowledgeable technical people on the set. They must have a fundamental understanding of a number of aspects of a film, including wardrobe, the script, and cameras. Knowledge of the wardrobe helps them plant lavaliere microphones inconspicuously. Knowing the script keeps them on par with the actors' lines, as they must follow it closely with the microphones. Also, they must be able to follow the camera and its lenses to keep the boom out of the shot.

Because more and more filming is done on location and the equipment has become more compact, lighter, and simpler to operate, one person often performs many of the above audio engineering functions. Also, since the boom operator is standing around all day, holding the microphone in the air, it is important that the boom pole be light, to help avoid injuries. The work can be very tiring and straining on the arms, back, and shoulders. Some days may be as long as twelve hours, with a majority of the time spent standing. Boom operators work on stage and on location, which might require a bit of traveling.

Typical tasks for a boom operator:

- Place the microphone so there is no shadow on the set or actors.
- Plant a microphone on every actor in the take.
- Set up the boom, operate it, and break it down for storage at the end of the day.
- Assist the production mixer in all microphone placements.
- Ensure that mics are placed in the optimum positions to record the sound.
- Voice-slate wild and ambient sound.
- Keep audio cables away from electrical cables so that they will not pick up AC hum.
- Pick up and deliver sound equipment and supplies.
- Consult with production personnel to set up stage properties to achieve desired effects.
- Generally assist the production mixer in any required duties.
- Hold the fish pole microphone over the actors.

The Sound Assistant

If there is a budget for a third person on the location sound team, they will be hired as the sound assistant. The sound assistant is in charge of the *sound kit/sound cart*. This will contain a variety of mics, cables, connectors, etc., as well as any other required audio gear for a remote set location. The assistant is an entry-level position and a good way to start out in this area of the business. If there is no budget for an assistant, these responsibilities are covered by the boom operator.

The sound assistant (also called the 2nd boom op/cable/etc.) is basically available to assist the location sound mixer and the boom operator. Most of his or her time will be spent in keeping the sound cart organized and performing quality control on the log sheets, as well as making sure that the digital audio files and meta-data are thorough and accurate. Sound assistants are most commonly present on big budget projects. They are union engineers, but work at the capacity of entry-level sound people.

> **THE UNION**
> Most post-production jobs are union jobs, and the union that most audio post-production engineers belong to is the International Alliance of Theatrical and Stage Employees (IATSE). Union jobs have certain advantages, in that the union makes sure that you are not being taken advantage of—that you are compensated fairly for a days work, that you get extra pay when you work overtime and on holidays, that you get fed on set at reasonable times, as well as offering you health insurance options. You can get more information on IATSE at www.iatse-intl.org/home.html.

The Process

Production sound is captured throughout the film shoot. Audio engineers are part of the crew and work on location (wherever that may be) to record the production sound. They have to be ready for any and all situations, including extreme weather (along with its effect on both themselves and the gear). Their gear must constantly be in working condition, with backups available on a moment's notice. If they are on location away from home, they need to be familiar with the local area in case they need to do a quick fix or repair. They also must be prepared to be away from home for a long period of time.

Sound Logs

Sound logs and accurate file-encoded meta-data, documentation, and organization are a big part of the location sound engineer's job. The sound log is very important because it includes the precise identification data for each file. Each log entry includes three key points of information:

- **Roll:** the hard drive, Compact Flash, or film reel number
- **Scene:** the scene number in the script that is being filmed
- **Take:** the number for each take recorded for that scene

PRODUCTION SOUND REPORT

TITLE:		PRODUCTION CO.:	DISC/ROLL #:
SOUND MIXER:			DATE:
PHONE:	MEDIA:	❏ MASTER ❏ COPY	PAGE____OF____
RECORDER:	SAMPLE FREQ:	BITS:	BWF FILE TYPE ❏ MONO ❏ POLY
TIME CODE:	TONE:	MONO MIX ON CH#____	FORMAT: ❏ UDF ❏ FAT16 ❏ FAT32
DAILY INSTRUCTIONS:			

	SCENE	TAKE	SEGMENT/FILE#	#OF PRINTS	NOTES	1	2	3	4	5	6	7	8	9	10
1															
2															
3															
4															
5															
6															
7															
8															
9															
10															
11															
12															
13															
14															
15															
16															

Fig. 5.5. Sound Report

The sound log will also include SMPTE time code, the circled (or preferred) take, and comments. No comments usually indicate a circled take. Comments usually refer to interference or problems with that particular take (airplane flyover, car drive-by, rain, or extreme wind gust, etc.). The location recordist will get a line script before the shoot and enter in as much critical data regarding roll and scenes as possible so that they can focus on takes and comments during shooting.

Most current digital-multitrack field recorders and mixers have the ability to enter this info directly into the WAV file meta-data. This can be done on the machine itself or by interfacing a keyboard to type in the data. Embedding this information directly into the files' meta-data makes all the difference in organization. Both the dialogue editor and the assistant dialogue editor rely heavily on the sound log and meta-data to put their sessions together. Upon completion of the project, they may also print out a hard copy document of this information to deliver with all of the media.

IN-DEPTH LOOK AT TRANSFERS

Film-to-video transfers or *telecine* is the process in which the film and location sound is transferred to video to create dailies that the director and producers can review as a barometer for how the production is developing. In television, the process is simplified, as the sound is taken directly from the camera (which originated from the location sound mixer). There is a backup system, which includes a safety copy of the comp mix on set as well as the individual radio mics (lav mics) for each actor.

In film, the process can be a little tricky, as many variables come into play. First of all, the sound and film are usually separate entities that need to be synchronized and combined so that they can be telecined. The post-production facility that is responsible for the telecine process can do this. However, the location sound mixer must provide accurately time-stamped audio files, as well as detailed sound logs for reference.

If there is a call for a direct sound transfer from one medium to another, special care must be taken, with an acute awareness of system alignment and synchronization. If the sync is off ever so slightly, the production sound will have to be manually re-sync'd against picture. Even a small amount of drift will snowball over time, so synchronization plays a major role in this process.

The logs must be complete so that each bit of production sound can be referenced to the film footage that it was recorded with. This is key in creating and/or referencing an EDL (Edit Decision List). The EDL is created and updated as the film cut evolves, reflecting cuts that have been made and referencing where the media originated.

EDLs are a standard in the post-production process. They are the map that directs offline to online—in other words, used as a guide when bringing a sequence up to a better resolution.

```
001  NO_REEL   A       C         00:01:00:00 00:01:30:00 00:59:00:00 00:59:30:00
* NOTE:   NO CINEMA TOOLS DB RECORD WITH SOUND FOR THIS CLIP WAS FOUND.
* FROM CLIP NAME:  Bars and Tone (HD 1080i60)

002  NO_REEL   A2      C         00:01:00:00 00:01:30:00 00:59:00:00 00:59:30:00
* NOTE:   NO CINEMA TOOLS DB RECORD WITH SOUND FOR THIS CLIP WAS FOUND.
* FROM CLIP NAME:  Bars and Tone (HD 1080i60)

003  NO_REEL   A       C         00:01:00:00 00:01:00:01 00:59:58:00 00:59:58:01
* NOTE:   NO CINEMA TOOLS DB RECORD WITH SOUND FOR THIS CLIP WAS FOUND.
* FROM CLIP NAME:  Bars and Tone (HD 1080i60)

004  NO_REEL   A2      C         00:01:00:00 00:01:00:01 00:59:58:00 00:59:58:01
* NOTE:   NO CINEMA TOOLS DB RECORD WITH SOUND FOR THIS CLIP WAS FOUND.
* FROM CLIP NAME:  Bars and Tone (HD 1080i60)

005  NS11      A       C         10:26:15:17 10:26:17:01 01:00:15:12 01:00:16:20
* FROM CLIP NAME:  HN_1_4(a)

006  NS11      A2      C         10:26:15:17 10:26:17:01 01:00:15:12 01:00:16:20
* FROM CLIP NAME:  HN_1_4(a)

007  NS11      A       C         10:26:17:01 10:26:24:11 01:00:16:20 01:00:24:06
* FROM CLIP NAME:  HN_1_4(a)

008  NS11      A2      C         10:26:17:01 10:26:24:11 01:00:16:20 01:00:24:06
* FROM CLIP NAME:  HN_1_4(a)

009  NO_REEL   NONE    C         00:00:00:00 00:00:05:01 01:00:20:12 01:00:25:13
AUD    3
* NOTE:   NO CINEMA TOOLS DB RECORD WITH SOUND FOR THIS CLIP WAS FOUND.
* FROM CLIP NAME:  63 Air Horn; Professional Hockey Gam.mp3

010  NO_REEL   NONE    C         00:00:00:00 00:00:05:01 01:00:20:12 01:00:25:13
AUD    4
* NOTE:   NO CINEMA TOOLS DB RECORD WITH SOUND FOR THIS CLIP WAS FOUND.
* FROM CLIP NAME:  63 Air Horn; Professional Hockey Gam.mp3

011  NS11      A       C         15:38:56:05 15:38:56:11 01:00:24:06 01:00:24:12
* FROM CLIP NAME:  HN_1H_4(b)

012  NS11      A2      C         15:38:56:05 15:38:56:11 01:00:24:06 01:00:24:12
* FROM CLIP NAME:  HN_1H_4(b)
```

Fig. 5.6. EDL

The numbers in figure 5.6 (001, 002, 003...) are the edits in the sequence. These edits are called "events." Every time the picture editor makes an edit on the video or audio tracks, the edit shows up as an event on the EDL. After the event number is a sound reel number (NS11). Note that there are no reel numbers for events 001 to 004 (001 NO_REEL). However, event 005 calls for the sound reel NS11. That means if the re-recording sound mixer needs to capture that event again, they would pull reel NS11 to find the media.

Directly below that information is the (* From Clip Name) area. This will tell you either the sound effect file (as it appears in events 009 and 010), or the scene and take (from the sound log or file meta-data).

Finally, we have the SMPTE time code numbers in the columns on the right hand side of the page. The first TC number is source in. The second TC number is source out. Source refers to where (on the dailies tape or backup sound file) the re-recording mixer can find that particular clip. The third TC number is the record in and the fourth TC number is the record out. Record refers to where the re-recording mixer needs to place that source clip in the sequence.

In some cases, the final location sound delivery process is extremely simple. Bill Macpherson records directly to a Fostex PD 606 hard disk recorder (as well as two other backups). The Fostex allows him to save directly to DVD-RAM discs that can easily be dropped and dragged into AVID or Final Cut Pro Sessions. (Picture editors commonly use the AVID and FCP to cut picture and assemble the show.) There really is no transfer or telecine process, at this stage. At the end of the day, he just burns a DVD and sends it off to editorial.

MORE ON LOCATION SOUND RECORDING

There are a few things to be aware of when recording sound for picture. The principles of location sound are the same for most situations. A good rule of thumb to remember is that sound conveys emotion while picture conveys information. No matter who the audience is, at the very least, they expect natural "transparent" sound. So, the better your soundtrack, the less it is consciously noticed.

As you work to capture location sound, it is best to visualize the audio path as a chain of a gear. Like an actual chain, the audio path is only as strong as it's weakest link. This means that a high-quality, accurate recording device paired with a low-quality microphone will not result in anything better than what the microphone is capable of recording. While it is not practical for location sound mixers to always use the best quality location sound equipment made, it is recommended to use components that match each other in features and quality.

While "poor quality" sound can be manipulated and adjusted all along the audio path in different ways, it is best to adjust and compensate for this before it ever enters the audio path. Despite all of the best post-production tools and technology available, what you hear is what you get. If you record poor quality sound, it will always be poor quality sound.

Scout the location for sound as well as for picture. Go to the location you will shoot at, close your eyes, and listen to the room or environmental characteristics. If it's an exterior, listen to the ambient noises you will have to work with. You'll be asking questions like; which sounds can you eliminate? Which sounds can you minimize and how?

When you arrive at the shoot location and have set up thoroughly, do a sound check. If the actors are there, set up your audio equipment and have them rehearse the scene. If it's an interview, set up your microphones, have the talent speak, and listen how their voices project and what levels you should set. If you are setting up before talent is on the set, have a crew member speak and get some levels on that.

The best way to learn how to enhance your location sound is to work with professionals. When you are starting out, look for opportunities on a small project or a friend's independent film. Try to get out there and become an active participant in the process. Production is a collaborative process and learning from the ideas and skills that your colleagues possess are what will help you grow.

One of the most enjoyable aspects of location sound recording is that it is never perfected. Once you reach a certain level of competence with sound, the nuances of fine-tuning the sound come into play. It is better to think in terms of enhancing the sound on your projects than trying to repair major audio disasters. There are always new challenges to face and new problems to resolve. Moving forward into high-definition, digital filmmaking, DVD, multimedia, and surround sound, the requirements and appetite for high quality sound will increase.

Fig. 5.7. Location Sound Setup (Courtesy of Rode Microphones)

A CLOSER LOOK AT THE GEAR

Microphones

Shotgun/hypercardioid, cardioid, and lavaliere microphones are used in most shooting situations. Besides physical construction and size, the main factors that categorize microphones are their pickup patterns and characteristics. Certain pickup patterns are better than others for picking up different subjects and specific portions of the audio frequency spectrum.

Shotgun/Hypercardioid, and Cardioid Microphones

The term "shotgun" describes a type of microphone that is a long narrow tube, not unlike the barrel of a shotgun. They fall into two categories: long shotgun and short shotgun. A longer shotgun usually has a narrower angle of acceptance of sound and rejects more sound from the sides, also referred to as "off-axis." Shorter shotguns usually pick up more sound from the sides and will not isolate a single element as much as a longer shotgun will.

Shotgun microphones are more directional than other types of microphones. Hypercardioid and cardioid microphones have a slightly wider angle of acceptance than shotguns, but they are narrower than most other microphone types. The official terms are variants of the term "cardioid": hypercardioid and supercardioid.

58 CHAPTER 5

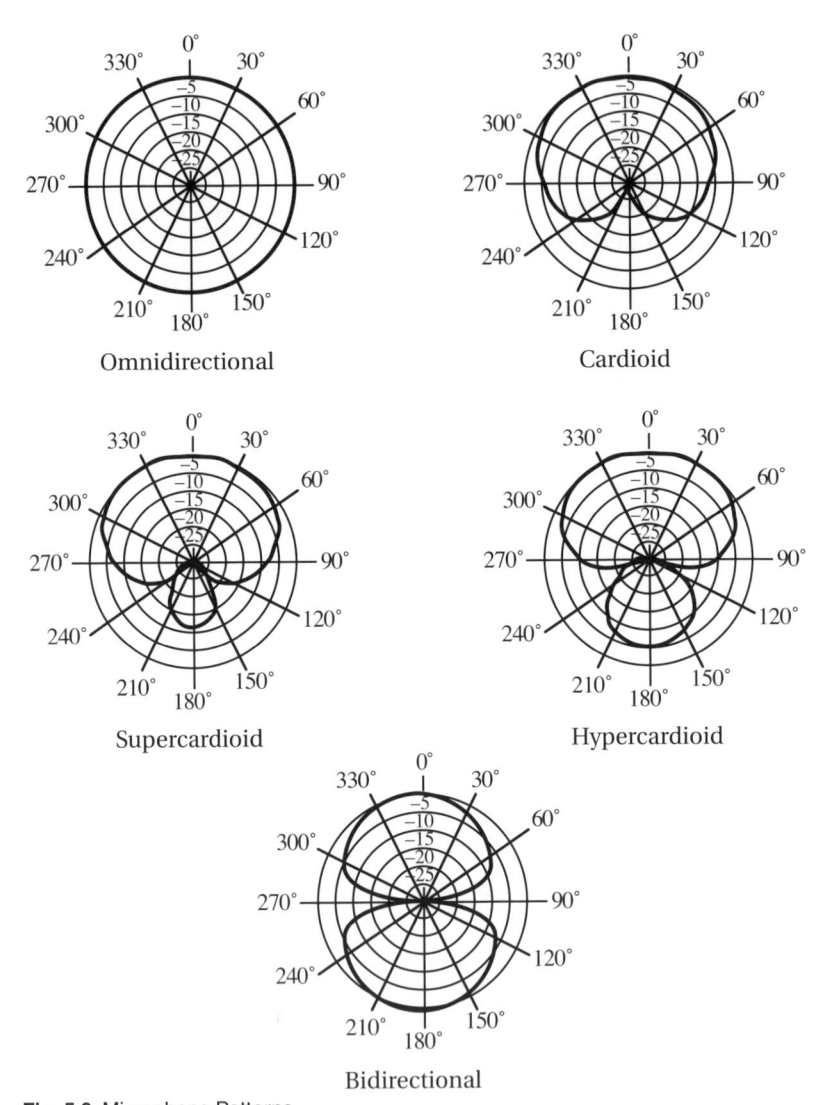

Fig. 5.8. Microphone Patterns

Omnidirectional

Cardioid

Supercardioid

Hypercardioid

Bidirectional

In location sound recording, these kinds of microphones are aimed at talent as they record dialogue, and they help to isolate the spoken sound from most of the extraneous background sound. A shotgun or cardioid mic is almost always mounted to a microphone boom so that it can be suspended about two to three feet above the talent, depending on framing. To understand why, consider what lies behind the talent. If the mic is pointed at the talent's mouth and positioned level with the camera, the microphone will also pick up whatever sound comes from behind the talent, as well as their voice. By pointing the microphone element down from above, the floor or ground will be behind the talent, rather than other activity, which helps to isolate the voices.

Above all other factors, the distance between the mic and the sound source will have the largest influence on the overall sound in your recordings. Regardless of pickup pattern, cost, or quality of your mic, if it is placed too far away or aimed improperly, then your sound quality will be diminished.

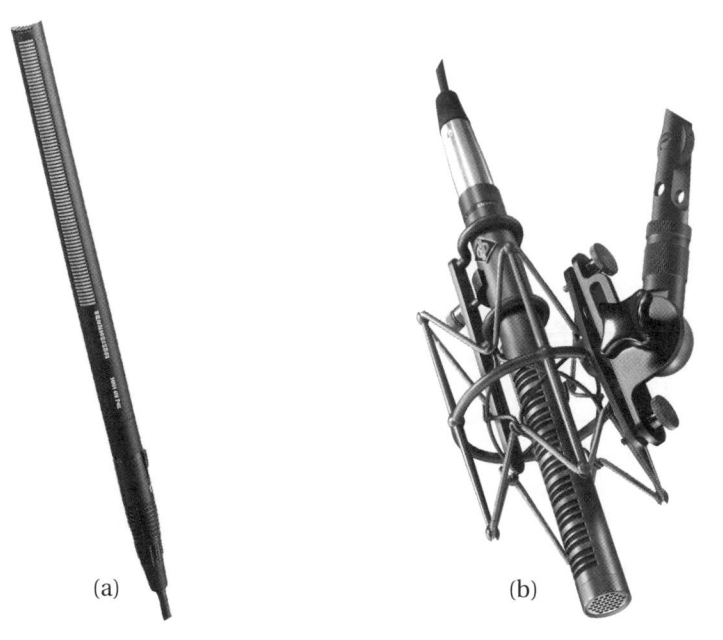

Fig. 5.9. Shotgun Mics (a) Sennheiser 416 (b) Neumann KMR 81 (with a Shock Mount, on a Boom). Courtesy of Sennheiser.

Lavaliere Microphones

A *lavaliere* is defined as "a pendant worn on a chain around the neck," which should give you a good idea about what a lavaliere microphone (or "lav") is. The most popular lavaliere microphones today are incredibly small—smaller than a match head. So small, that they can easily be hidden in the talent's hair of even behind a tiny button on a shirt.

Lavaliere microphones come in usually one of two options: omnidirectional or unidirectional. An *omnidirectional lav* picks up sound fairly well from all sides. A *unidirectional lav* has a pickup pattern much more like that of a shotgun or hypercardioid microphone. Because a unidirectional microphone must be aimed at the talent's mouth, the opportunities for hiding the microphone are mostly eliminated, limiting the use to mostly planting the microphone in the center of the talent's chest.

Besides being used on talent, certain lavaliere microphones are also handy for using as a *plant* microphone. A *plant* microphone is typically placed in a hidden spot on the set to pick up talent as a supplement to or instead of a boom microphone. Plant microphones can also come into play when scenes are shot with a Steadicam or with large dolly moves, where it may be impractical to have the boom operator try to follow the camera. Another instance could be that wardrobe restrictions make using body mounted lavalieres tough or impractical.

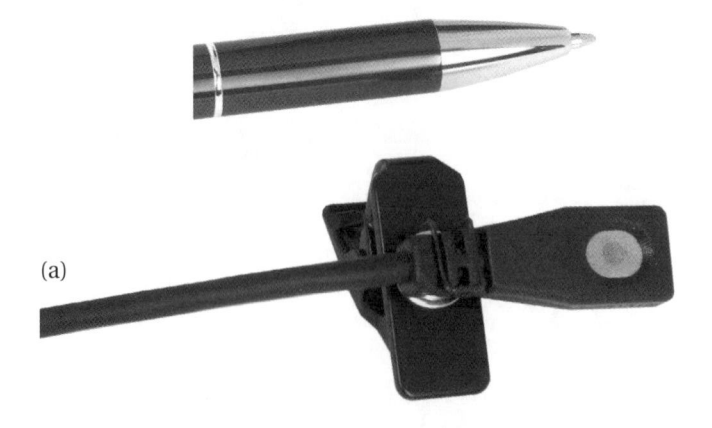

(a)

(b)

Fig. 5.10. (a) Lavalier mic, next to a pen, for scale. (Courtesy of Lectrosonic)
(b) Lavalier mic (Courtesy of Rode Microphones)

Wireless Microphone Systems

There are two types of lavalieres that are typically used in production: wired or wireless. While wireless transmitters can be used with handheld microphones, they are most commonly teamed with lavaliere microphones. Some sound mixers also use wireless systems on their boom mics. This is very typical in reality type "run and gun" shows. Also, some location sound mixers use wireless systems to "cut the tether" from the sound mixer to the camera. A wireless system consists of a single transmitter and a single receiver.

Wireless systems are improving, but the bandwidth that wireless systems operate on is becoming more and more crowded. *Diversity* (dual) *antenna systems* are considered far superior to *single antenna systems,* because in a diversity system, if the reception between transmitter and receiver is weak or encounters interference on one antenna, the system can switch over to the other antenna. The UHF (ultra high frequency) band is generally considered more effective and less crowded than the VHF (very high frequency band).

When using wireless systems, consider renting rather than purchasing. You may not need wireless systems all of the time, so it makes more sense to rent the best rather than buy something middle of the road. When using wireless systems, it is essential that you feed the system brand new batteries often. Wireless systems eat a lot of batteries and begin to perform poorly as the batteries get weaker. If using wireless all day during a typical 10-hour day, plan on replacing the batteries after every four to five hours of use.

Zeppelins and Windsocks

A *zeppelin* is a protective enclosure that encapsulates a microphone. The name evolved from the resemblance to the German gas dirigibles of the 1920s and '30s. The function of the zeppelin is not only to protect the somewhat delicate microphone element but also to filter out extraneous wind and HVAC air movement. Ideally, you should have separate sizes of zeppelins for both long shotguns and shorter shotguns and cardioids.

Fig. 5.11. Zeppelin (Courtesy of Rode Microphones)

Windsocks are synthetic fur-covered sleeves that slip over a zeppelin. Most offer Velcro tabs and/or zippers to snugly fit a zeppelin. Windsocks offer a much higher degree of wind resistance than using a zeppelin alone. Some manufacturers even offer two different lengths of fur on their windsocks: shorter hair for moderate wind and longer hair for strong wind.

Besides diminishing wind noise and buffeting, using a furry windsock will cut out some high frequency response, so you should not use one all of the time. You need to listen to what the microphone is picking up, and choose to use or not use a windsock in addition to the zeppelin accordingly. There are also socks that are "velvety" instead of furry, which work very well in winds up to 15 mph and give minimal high-frequency attenuation.

Fig. 5.12. Wind Socks (Courtesy of Rode Microphones)

Boom Poles

Once you have at least one good shotgun, hypercardioid, or cardioid microphone, and a microphone mount, zeppelin, windsock, or a slip-on windscreen, how do you use them? The first step is to obtain a boom pole. Boom poles are available in a variety of lengths, styles, and materials, with the most popular poles being made of aluminum and carbon fiber. Generally, it is better to have two lengths of boom pole: a short one for travel and small setups and a longer one for larger wide shots. Aluminum boom poles are generally heavier than carbon fiber, but they are cheaper and easier to repair. If you shoot more narrative style projects, it may be worth spending the extra money for a lighter carbon fiber model.

Fig. 5.13. Using a Boom Pole (Courtesy of Rode Microphones)

Mixing and Routing Devices

Most professional productions use a portable audio-mixing console. The exceptions are single-camera shoots where the audio is just being used for reference or background ambience. But if you are shooting dialogue, you should be using an audio mixer. It's really that simple. If you are shooting with a stationary camera and AC power is accessible, you can get a great result with small desktop mixers. With a location audio mixer, you get:

- **Tone generator.** Tone generators record reference tones at the head of each reel to give the editor a constant point of reference for the levels that the audio was recorded at.
- **Roll-offs and cuts.** Location audio mixers often have high and low roll-offs and cuts. These are useful for eliminating rumble, hiss, and other undesirable sounds before the sound is sent to camera.
- **Pre-amps.** Almost all location audio mixers have considerably higher quality microphone pre-amps than almost any camcorder.

- **Slate microphone.** A slate microphone is located on the mixer to let the operator insert their voice onto the mixer's output. It is very useful for audio slates—for example, you can say, "Room tone:30" when you go to record room tone.
- **Monitoring.** Location audio mixers usually have a tape return circuit that lets the operator compare the output of the mixer to the output of the recording device by flipping a switch.
- **Panning and mixing.** A mixer lets you determine the panning of as many channels of microphones as it has capacity for. With a 4-channel mixer, you could route three lavaliere microphones to the right channel on the camcorder and the boom to the left channel. Some of the more professional mixers have multiple outputs.
- **Microphone power.** Some mixers can power certain wireless receivers.
- **Phantom power.** Almost all location audio mixers can supply phantom power to at least one of their outputs, and some can provide it to more than one. This saves camcorder battery power, if the camcorder has phantom power. If the camcorder doesn't have phantom power, the mixer is able to provide the phantom power instead of requiring a separate microphone power supply.
- **Better metering.** Most camcorders do not have very accurate, high quality audio meters. Most location audio mixers have very high quality audio meters.
- **The ability to "ride" gain.** Generally, most location sound mixers "ride" gain, smoothly setting the gain levels being sent to the recording device as the talent's levels rise and fall. This does not mean raising and lowering the volume levels as the talent speaks; it means making sure that the signal being recorded does not clip.

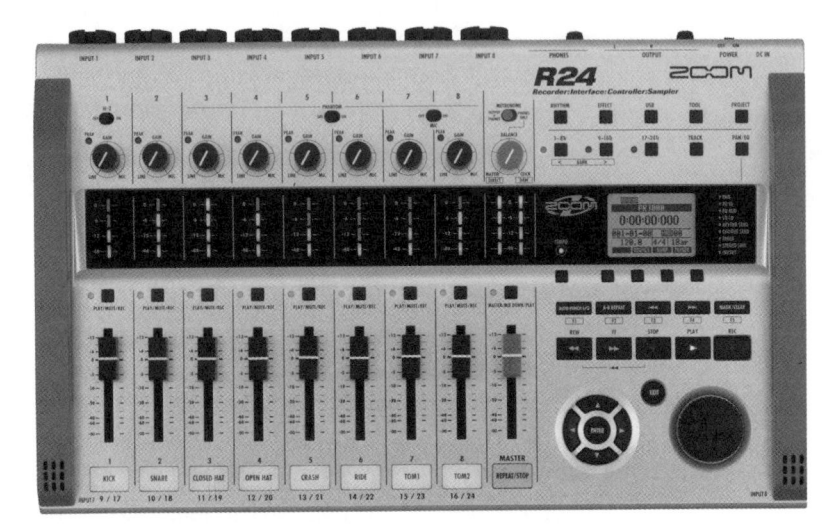

Here is a location sound mixer:

Fig. 5.14. Zoom Mixer R24 (Courtesy of Samson Technologies)

DV Camcorder Audio

The most commonly used recording device for most would be a camcorder. A few common consumer camcorders have decent sound quality, but the most popular consumer camcorders generally have major sound issues, straight out of the box. These limitations are exclusive to each model and have nothing to do with the quality of the audio that is fed into each unit from your mixer.

Backup Systems

Location sound mix engineers often utilize separate audio recording devices as a safety or backup. It can be in the form of additional multitrack recorder hard drives, CompactFlash, or DVD-RAM. Regardless, backup is extremely important. If you have ever experienced a computer/hard drive crash or meltdown, you know what I mean. I can't say enough about having a few good backups available. It is well worth the investment.

Routing

Realistically, you need the mixing console's output to go to the camera as well as your digital audio recording device. The audio from the camcorder will serve as a guide for aligning the audio from your digital audio recording device. In this way, both devices will receive an identical signal.

One thing to consider when doing this is synchronization. It is best when one machine is the *master* (generating SMPTE time code), which then *jam syncs* (regenerates) the time code to the slave machine. In most professional instances, the location mixer's multitrack recorder is the master, jam syncing time code to the camera, which acts as the slave machine.

If you keep comprehensive sound reports and are organized, it is more efficient to edit your show, approve the cut, and then add the "quality" audio at the end—*post conform* the audio, as the process is called. If your mixer has dual audio outputs, route one to the camcorder and one to the digital audio recording device.

Hard Disk Multitrack Recorders

There are a lot of digital multitrack hard-disk field recorders available today. The quality and technology has evolved to where most are quite good. The industry standard for decades was an analog 2-track stereo Nagra tape deck. This was and still is extremely durable and trustworthy. However, the current digital machines have the same durability along with numerous new features that make them very attractive. Considering that the Nagra was only a stereo machine, the fact that the newer machines can record six to eight tracks allows for much more flexibility in capturing the individual radio mics, as well as the comp mix.

Zaxcom makes the Deva, the Fusion, and the Nomad; Aaton makes the Cantar X2; and Sound Devices makes the 788P. They are all digital multitracks and are very portable and durable. All are good and are available at different price points. Some are better than others, but it all depends on the application and the project. They vary regarding input and output, interface, reliability, verification, and whether material can be transferred to another format to archive.

Here is the Sound Devices 788 Hard Disk Recorder.

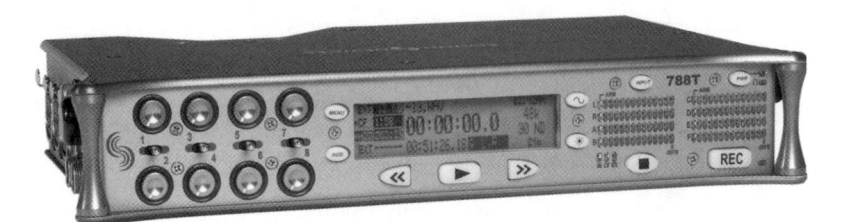

Fig. 5.15. Hard Disk Recorder (Used with Permission, Copyright Sound Devices, LLC)

These machines can easily interface with mixers and feature large internal hard drives. In most cases, they can record to additional/alternate media simultaneously. This is great for backups, protecting you if one of your drives fails. Most have (qwerty) keyboards that allow you to quickly input data for the sound log.

Besides price, the difference between these machines is mainly what application you may need it for. If you are on an *ENG* (electronic news gathering) project, you would look to the more portable recorder. ENG is a "run and shoot" style of work that is often on location (instead of a sound stage) and tends to be quite unpredictable in nature.

If you are on a sound stage or elaborate film set, you may look to a recorder with more bells and whistles. This is all budget and project specific. I would recommend renting a few of these recorders for different situations to help you decide which one would work best for you.

One of the key features that set the field recorders apart from other recording devices is its *pre-buffer*. The pre-buffer is a user-defined length of time that the recorder will record before you engage it with the Record command. This means that once you turn the machine on (with the pre-buffer enabled), the recorder is constantly recording. This helps in case you don't hear the director say "Action!" or miss the Record command, and you can still capture the sound.

Monitoring

The monitoring system on your recording device is the last part of the equation. It can be difficult to judge your audio efforts if you cannot hear what is being recorded properly. If you have invested in a decent audio mixer with a tape-return monitor circuit, monitoring lets you compare the audio signal you are sending the recording device with what the monitoring circuit in the recording device is reporting back to you. By comparing these and by listening on accurate audio monitors in your edit system, you can begin to accurately assess the quality of what you are recording.

Headphones

The last component in the audio chain is your headphones. The headphones used to monitor recording serve several very specific purposes:

- You must be able to judge the characteristics of the room, your talent's voice, sound effects, and ambient levels.
- You will need to be able to determine if your microphones are picking up the traffic outside, the helicopter in the distance, etc.
- They must be portable enough that you will always bring them and use them on everything that you shoot that has audio.
- They must be efficient enough to output high enough sound levels from weak or inefficient headphone circuits.
- They must cover your entire ear. You cannot judge what your recording device is recording with headphones that only partially cover your ears. You will be hearing too much of the live sound and not enough of what the recording device is recording to make informed judgments about what you are recording.

One of the best headphones and the industry standard are the Sony MDRV-7506s. While the Sonys are not the most accurate headphones available, they are extremely efficient, they are small for a full ear design, they fold up to about half of their own size, and they come with a screw-on mini-to-quarter-inch adapter. There is a consumer version called the Sony MDRV-600s that sounds close to the same. They cost about the same, but they are bigger. They still fold up but not as small as 7506s do. They are more comfortable than the 7506s for wearing for long periods of time.

As you can see, the task of a location sound crew and the gear they use is vast and often unpredictable. They are constantly dealing with a variety of factors such as weather, set design, and script changes (to name a few) while existing in remote locations far from any support. Having great location sound is the foundation for a transparent and realistic soundtrack, so being flexible and carefully maintaining gear will make all the difference. Everything captured on location will directly affect the post-production process with regards to dialogue, sound effects, Foley, and in some situations music. That said, preparation and planning is key to having a great experience.

CHAPTER 6

Working with Sound Effects

Sound effects (SFX) play a key role in audio post production. Their presence can make all the difference in selling a scene, punctuating a presentation, or simply defining the action or visual on the screen. The use of SFX is an art form that has been around for decades, and the process of choosing and adding them has become much more streamlined and organized with the aid of DAWs, databases, and search engines. These technological advances allow you to store, recall, sort, and organize an extremely large amount of SFX in fairly short order. Today, SFX are organized by utilizing meta-data embedded in the audio files to categorize and define them.

In the past, each individual sound effect was stored on a filmstrip or reel of analog tape. One by one, the effects were categorized, logged, filed, and backed up. So, you had thousands of sound effects stored in numerous vaults, and it took a long time to access each one. When you did find the effect or effects that you were looking for, you had to load that reel on a tape machine and fast-forward/rewind to locate the audio, in order to audition each one. If you didn't like what was on that reel, you had to repeat the process, again and again, until you found the effects that worked in your project. When you found what you needed, the effects had to be transferred to another tape machine or medium, so that you could preserve the original source. Although the sound of an effect from a library stored on analog tape is sonically superior to those stored in most digital mediums, this process is daunting and quite time-consuming.

Today, sound effects are available to anyone, in the form of mega libraries on multiple CDs, DVDs, or hard drives. You can simply type "door slam" into a search engine of a database and find several hundred door slams, which you can easily audition at the click of a mouse. That is a much more streamlined process than the analog method from the not-so-distant past.

Sound effects in film and television can fall into four categories:

- Hard SFX: tangible sounds (gunshots, door slams, etc.), typically from a CD/hard drive SFX library
- Background/Ambient: wind, rain, room tones, atmosphere
- Movement: servo motors, car drive-bys, truck brakes
- Natural/Foley: acted out sound effects, such as footsteps

SOUND DESIGN

What is sound design? If you ask ten different people, you will most likely get ten different answers. The term *sound design* was first introduced in 1972, as the credit was given to Walter Murch for his awesome work in the classic *Apocalypse Now*. It referred to the person responsible for every aspect of sound for the film. The term went on to designate the supervising sound editor in audio post production. Presently, it has morphed again and is loosely used to describe a creative/technical person who creates both sonic and musical textures for film, television, radio, Web design, etc. Despite the varied opinions, most will agree that SFX are absolutely integral to the audio post-production process in completing a film or television show. They enhance, and, at times, overcompensate for the action in the film.

The post-production industry has embraced digital technology because of the efficiency and quality it can bring to the sound effects. However, sound designers and SFX editors may use both digital and analogue technology to capture and create sound effects that have never been heard before, or to artistically construct specific "new" sounds to complement the director's vision, as well as to sonically augment a scene.

Sound is very subjective and dependent upon the visual context and the mood set up in the image. The soundtrack of real life is too dense for film. In the real world, our minds select certain noises and filter out others. For instance, we mentally foreground the person speaking to us, even if the background is louder. In film, the sound effects editors and re-recording mixers have to focus on the competing sounds for us.

Focusing on selected sounds can create tension, atmosphere, and emotion, and it can also impart personality to film characters. Sound is a means to lend depth and expand space to the two-dimensional image on screen, while locating us within the scene. A crucial difference between visual and aural manipulation of the audience is that even sophisticated audiences rarely notice the soundtrack. Therefore, sound effects can speak to us emotionally, and they can almost subconsciously put us in touch with a screen character.

THE SUPERVISING SOUND EDITOR

The *supervising sound editor* is involved in any given project early enough to observe the dailies, or at least the rough cut, following the wrap of principal photography. It is their job to assess the project's production sound to see what sound effects are needed to enhance the soundtrack. That will give them a barometer of exactly what the sound effect needs will be.

The supervising sound editor maintains a comprehensive list, including library and custom sound effects, of what the SFX team needs to gather or create. If there is a budget for creating custom sound effects, the supervising sound editor will scout locations that seem appropriate for both internal and external sound effect recording. This may include renting a sound stage on a studio lot or an afternoon at the local police's firing range to capture custom sound effects for a project. Each project is different, and the locations and sound needs vary considerably between them.

When the supervising sound editor has completed this list, they will put together a crew to acquire the sounds. The team may include some creative sound editors that work primarily in edit bays, with DAWs and several massive sound effect libraries, as well as an experienced sound recordist to capture custom sound effects for the project.

It's wise to have an experienced, professional, custom sound-effects recordist. Most engineers are not familiar with the task of capturing these sounds. They can be quite dynamic in nature and can easily go from a whisper to a scream in an instant. Often, there are not opportunities to get a second chance at recording a key moment, so experience is key to getting this done effectively. Additionally, a good field sound-effects recordist will know of additional aspects of the sound that may be needed, along with knowing how to deal with extraneous sounds like generators and traffic.

Sound Design for *The Dark Knight*

Supervising sound editor/sound designer Richard King had some interesting experiences creating the sound design for the Batman feature film, *The Dark Knight*. This was a big-budget project, and he had the opportunity to create some unique and authentic sounds. The Batpod (a large, very impressive-looking motorcycle) definitely needed its own sound. King incorporated the concept of the *Shepard tone*—a continually ascending tone, which creates the illusion of continually ascending (or descending) pitch. This concept was used with the Batpod, so it sounds like it's always accelerating. The Shepard tone works best with fairly pure sounds. This led them to electric motors, which also matched the sleek look of the Batpod. They recorded a lot of big electric motors and a couple of electric race cars, like the Tesla and a Wrightspeed X1 prototype, even putting them on a dynamometer, which allowed King to record extreme acceleration and engine torque in a very controlled fashion without the car actually moving.

The Batpod has huge wide tires, and he knew they would be an important component. The team spent a lot of time recording different kinds of tires, like off-road tires on trucks and knobby tires on all-terrain vehicles, just experimenting, trying to find a good tire sound. One day, King was running on a treadmill, and he accidentally dragged his running shoe over the back of the tread, as it was moving. He thought, "That's a cool sound!" So, he recorded it, and integrated it with the other tires into the Batpod tire sound.

Along with collecting sounds for the Batpod, the studio invested in a car that they drove onto a stage in Burbank and never drove off. By the time they were finished with it, it was undrivable. King placed microphones all over the car (inside and out) and proceeded to demolish it any way he could—breaking windows, hitting it with sledgehammers, and eventually, tearing it apart with the assistance of the Jaws of Life provided by the Burbank Fire Department. This gave them an expansive library of new and unique sounds that they could use in the film.

King also wanted to get a new take on gunfire sounds, so his crew spent a day at the Burbank Police outdoor firing range. They assembled as many weapons as possible and set up microphones all over the range. The weapons were fired, and the sounds were recorded. However, during a playback in the middle of the session, they noticed that they were getting an extreme amount of bass response from one of their microphones. This low end was adding an incredible impact to the sounds he was capturing. When they went to see what was happening, they noticed that particular mic had accidentally fallen off of its mic stand and was lying on the ground. Therefore, it was picking up an incredible amount of low end from the ground rumble. King quickly used this to his advantage. This mistake opened his eyes to new possibilities in mic techniques, and to this day he lays mics on the ground when recording gunfire.

BACKGROUNDS AND ROOM TONES

Background sound effects (BGs) is a term for sound effects that don't always need to sync to anything in particular, instead providing general background ambience of the scene. This will include room tones, matching ambient sounds, wild sounds, and buzz tracks. Exceptions are random birds, ambient police car sirens, distant voice mumbles, etc. that are slipped in to enhance the background effect.

BGs come in handy for a variety of situations. They are great ways to set up a location for a scene. Indoors and outdoors, every space has a sound when it is at rest. These sounds (when mixed correctly) can make you feel as if you are right there in the location of the scene. They can also help ADR sound natural, even though it was recorded in a pristine studio, without the ambience present in the original production dialogue.

BGs can also help to match bad or uneven location dialogue. You *may* record in a room where sounds from a loud AC vent or power generator are picked up by one (but not all) of your location mics. You can add noise to your production dialogue to mask or match the noisy dialogue tracks. This is called adding a *buzz-tone*.

These are all techniques that dialogue editors have been using for years to prepare for the final mix. Here are a few definitions of the common terminology:

- Room Tone: The sound of a room at rest, without any movement or dialogue. Usually used behind ADR to help match it to the production sound.
- Matching Ambient Sound: Creating or recording ambience to match presence from another scene/take.
- Ambient Sound: air, wind, room tone, city noise.
- Wild Sounds: Sound that doesn't need to be synced but adds realism to the environment on screen (e.g., recording a playground).
- Buzz Track: Sound that alleviates any unnatural silences in film (air conditioner noise, or extra room tone).

SOUND EFFECTS EDITOR

The sound effects editor's primary function is to add SFX to the production sound in a DAW session to be delivered to the dub stage for the final mix. The sounds need to correspond to what is on the screen, and also create realistic room tones and backgrounds, in order to make the visuals feel and sound dramatic and realistic. When done correctly, it will ultimately authenticate the scene sonically.

The process of adding and assembling these effects begins in a DAW. The picture editor provides the SFX editor with the *OMF* (Open Media Framework) files—a portable format for digital audio and picture files, used by picture editors. As the picture editor is assembling the film or television show, the SFX editor will be working with and referencing the production sound from the location sound crew. They may even experiment with temp music and temp SFX along the way. As the cut of the picture comes together, so does the production sound. The picture editor works closely with the director to assemble the final cut. Therefore, it is important that the sound effects editor has that OMF, as a reference, to start their session.

The sound effects editor usually starts with the BGs, as they go through the show. This is called the *backgrounds pass*. They assemble and add the BGs as well as adding markers to the session for each cut and scene change. These markers help them to map out the show in the DAW for any shifts and specific areas of interest. They work using the notes from the spotting session, along with any temp effects that have been added. The temp SFXs are there as a guide for what to put in and where to put it, but they are never discarded, because the director may ask for them in the final mix. Occasionally, SFX editors cut up the backgrounds so that certain sounds, such as bird chirps or car horns, don't fall directly on dialogue.

The backgrounds pass is primarily used as an overview. The second backgrounds pass is done to fine-tune the sounds and fill in any gaps or moments of interest. Backgrounds can really help the pacing of a scene. For example, if the action is in a busy office, the SFX editor might add printer sounds, phones ringing, or drawers opening when no dialogue is spoken. This will help to keep the scene moving along and sounding more alive and real.

The next pass is to add *hard effects* (doors, cars, etc.). This is to cover whatever you see (cat, dog, door shut, window open). A good search engine will come in handy for this section. The search engines and database applications can work in conjunction with most libraries and DAWs, so that you could simply type in a few key words describing what you need and instantly multiple sounds will become available. Once the specific sound is chosen, it is cut in so that the sounds match and are in sync.

A final run-through is then done to check the sound effects, as well as making volume adjustments or sonic treatments along the way. In addition to covering the basic sound effect needs from the spotting session, the sound effects editor will address other areas of the sound that seem to be having problems. A bad dissolve or a dialogue issue can be covered by using a random yet unnoticeable sound, such as a car drive-by. This can make all the difference, just by fixing an audio issue that would otherwise call attention to itself.

Here is Josh Chase, cutting sound effects for an episodic television show:

Fig. 6.1. Josh Chase, Sound Effects Editor

Here is his workspace:

Fig. 6.2. Sound-Effects Editing Workspace

A FEW WORDS ABOUT CONFORMING

Conforming is the process of adding a newer (and often shorter) picture cut to the most recent audio mix of dialogue, music, and effects (and sometimes all of them). Picture changes occur all of the time, and conforming the existing soundtrack to the current picture version is necessary as editors prepare the final dub, often up to the very last minute.

Sound editors do not always have the luxury to wait for the final locked picture to begin their work. To make sure that they have enough time to complete their work, they begin work with early versions of the picture and expect that conforming will be necessary. When a new picture cut becomes available, the assistant editors (dialogue, sound effects, and music) conform the current audio session to this new cut. They refer to the EDL (edit decision list) to see where picture edits were made. As discussed in chapter 5, the EDL is a comprehensive list of every picture edit: when and where it occurred and how much material was added or removed.

The conforming process is almost always a shortening of the soundtrack's duration, so numerous audio edits are involved. Unfortunately, this is not easily done with a universal cut and time shift of all tracks at any given edit. Some tracks will need fades or crossfades to make the cuts seamless. The assistant editor will pay close attention to the conforming process to avoid any audible hits that could happen when cutting in the middle of a long background region, music sequence, or dialogue phrase.

There are applications available for DAWs that do this automatically. However, even the best applications require a bit of finessing to make the audio edits transparent. Most editors start with one of these applications and then take a second pass to smooth out any edits that need fades. The advent of new technology and DAWs makes this automated process more accurate and streamlined, but the conforming process is still precise and tedious work.

DELIVERING THE SFX TO THE DUB STAGE

When the SFX editor is finished, the session is delivered to the dub stage. The mixers must be able to navigate through the sound effects tracks quickly and efficiently, and the track layout of the final SFX session is key to making this work. Film and television situations require different layouts. Films are much more involved and could have hundreds of tracks. Episodic television shows are more planned and regimented.

The typical layout for an episodic television show will include:

- 26 mono SFX tracks
- 10 stereo SFX tracks
- 16 Stereo BGs
- 6 mono BGs

Hard SFX tracks are set on top of the session, BGs are in the middle, and the temp SFX and OMF are located at the bottom. The session is cleaned up as well. Most DAWs let you save a copy of the session for delivery. This "Save Copy" option allows the editor to strip out any audio or regions/clips that are not part of the final session delivery. This helps to minimize the deliverable file size, as well as keeping the session organized and easy to navigate through.

The sound effects editor will be available during the final dub, in case of any last minute changes or any notes that the mixers have regarding the sound effects. In some instances, a sound effects editor will wait in a nearby edit bay so that they can easily address any last-minute issues. Sound editors can also be available virtually. This gives them more freedom to do other things, as well as having their own dedicated workspace.

SOUND EFFECTS FOR EPISODIC TELEVISION

Veteran sound designer and former Berklee professor David Van Slyke has been creating unique effects and sound design for numerous films and television shows for many years (most notably *CSI*, for which he has won several Emmy Awards). He began his career in the 1980s and '90s working on Synclaviers and Audio Frame DAWs. This naturally morphed into using Pro Tools for all of his projects. When asked about SFX libraries, David quickly responds that he has them all, and adds that, along with the libraries, he is constantly creating new and unique sounds, creating a palette of SFX that exceeds well over 2 terabytes. For that purpose, he carries a portable Olympus digital stereo-field recorder so that he can capture any sound that presents itself at any possible moment. David is always open to opportunities to record unique sounds. Along with his ever-growing library, he has customized his searchable Soundminer database so that each and every sound is available at any given time.

Working on an episode of *CSI* begins with a spotting session. During this 60 to 90 minute session, the director, picture editor, composer, and sound designer go through the episode from start to finish and identify key moments for music and sound effects. After years of doing *CSI*, David has an idea of what sounds will work and what will not work. The director and producers rely on David to use his craft and expertise to make it a great sonic moment.

The biggest challenges that he encounters is the time frame of working in episodic television. He has one week to spot, create, and deliver his sound effects track, and he is expected to hit a home run every time! This can require an 80-plus hour workweek. He often looks to his assistant to help with backgrounds and room tones. They use Digidelivery to deliver their elements (which usually exceeds 2 gigabytes) over the Internet. The recordist at the dub stage (final mixing room) will retrieve the deliverables and set them up on a dedicated Pro Tools system on the dub stage.

David views sound design as an artistic craft that he has honed for the past two decades. He sees the future of sound design morphing more toward simplicity. Technology has certainly helped in this regard. The onset of Pro Tools has allowed the sound designer to focus more on the craft and less on the overall delivery. One big change came a few years ago, when the re-recording mixers no longer asked for cues sheets from the sound designers. Cue sheets are hard copy track sheets that reflect when and where sound effects were located on a Pro Tools, DA-88, or 24-track reel-to-reel tape machine. Creating cue sheets usually took several additional hours. Now, that time is spent creating and fine-tuning unique sound moments that elevate the show's sonic landscape. Technology has also simplified the process so that everything that he needs is right at his fingertips.

Working in sound effects as an editor or as an assistant editor can be artistically rewarding, as well as professionally challenging. It is a lot of fun to participate in creating the sonic soundscape of a project, but the extreme deadlines can certainly take their toll. I have done this on occasion and have walked away with a renewed appreciation for the pros that do this every day. It is a lot of hard work, but the people that I know who do this full-time truly love their jobs and are thankful to have that opportunity.

CHAPTER 7

Working with Dialogue

Dialogue is the most interesting and often the most important element in audio post production. It is through voice that the actor expresses feeling and motivation, and it authenticates the speaker in a film as a person. Most projects are dialogue driven, so intelligibility of any character is paramount. Therefore, dialogue is at its best when captured properly on set. It will have the honest emotion and feel from the actor's performance. This is a big deal because that is very difficult to replicate. That is why *production dialogue*—dialogue recorded live, as the scene is being filmed—is often considered the first choice for the re-recording mixers.

Production dialogue also includes subtle external sounds such as live sound effects, background ambience, and room tones. Some of those effects can be replicated by Foley artists or sound effect editors, but having the production effects available can help the final mix as well as the M&E (music and effects) mix. Although production dialogue is always preferred, dialogue replacement (ADR) is a common process available to fix any dialogue that has been deemed unusable. When dialogue replacement is done properly, it appears seamless and unnoticeable.

GLOSSARY OF PRODUCTION DIALOGUE AND ADR TERMINOLOGY

Let's define some relatively new terms associated with dialogue and ADR.

Production Dialogue and Editing: Production dialogue is the audio recorded on the set or on location. This can be from mini lavaliere mics on the actors or from a boom mic held overhead (or a mix of both). It often includes important leakage of the natural ambiences, as well as any production SFX.

ADR (Automated Dialogue Replacement): The process of replacing dialogue in a studio after production has completed or wrapped. This is suggested in cases where the production audio is too noisy, or otherwise deemed unusable.

Spotting the ADR (ADR Cues): To prepare for the ADR session, the supervising sound editor or dialogue editor will "cue" the line for ADR. This means creating a sheet or script of the dialogue performances in question for the actor so that they know which lines to replace. This sheet will include location of the lines expressed in SMPTE time code "ins and outs," as well as any alternate lines (if needed).

ADR Cue Sheet: List of selected lines from a script that need to be redone or replaced in an ADR session. This is a standardized document that includes any reference information including project title, date, actor, line to be replaced, list of how many takes were done, etc.

Reel: DAT:	LINE	
ROLE		
CUE#		REASON
T/C IN: T/C OUT:	TAKE 1 2 3 4 5 6 7 8 9 10 11 12 13 14 15 16 LOCATION	

Reel: DAT:	LINE	
ROLE		
CUE#		REASON
T/C IN: T/C OUT:	TAKE 1 2 3 4 5 6 7 8 9 10 11 12 13 14 15 16 LOCATION	

Reel: DAT:	LINE	
ROLE		
CUE#		REASON
T/C IN: T/C OUT:	TAKE 1 2 3 4 5 6 7 8 9 10 11 12 13 14 15 16 LOCATION	

Reel: DAT:	LINE	
ROLE		
CUE#		REASON
T/C IN: T/C OUT:	TAKE 1 2 3 4 5 6 7 8 9 10 11 12 13 14 15 16 LOCATION	

Reel: DAT:	LINE	
ROLE		
CUE#		REASON
T/C IN: T/C OUT:	TAKE 1 2 3 4 5 6 7 8 9 10 11 12 13 14 15 16 LOCATION	

Fig. 7.1. ADR Cue Sheet

Walla: A sound effect for the murmur of a crowd in the background. Walla is often used as subliminal aural communication and sets a mood or a tone. The word "walla" was created in the old radio days when they needed the sound of a crowd in the background. They found that if several people simply repeated "walla, walla, walla, walla," it sounded like a crowd talking. The audience did not really hear the words, just the buzz of voices.

Loop Group: A group of actors brought together to create this murmur is known as a "loop group" or a "walla group." Nowadays, walla actors make use of real words and conversations, often improvised, tailored to the languages, speech patterns, and accents that might be expected of the crowd to be mimicked.

ADR Stage: A specialized studio where actors can record dialogue lines in sync with the picture. It consists of a large recording room equipped with a large monitor or screen to display/project the film. The stage will also be set up to comfortably accommodate the actor, director, and occasionally, the sound supervisor. There are usually two microphones (one up close and one distant, to capture both perspectives), along with a stand for a large script.

Fig. 7.2. ADR Stage at Gray Martin Studios, Santa Monica CA

Fig. 7.3. ADR Stage at Larson Studio, Hollywood CA. Photo by Molly Quaid.

THE DIALOGUE EDITOR

The *dialogue editor* is in charge of preparing production dialogue for the pre-dub or dub stage. Their efforts are vast and often overlooked. If a dialogue editor does a great job, their work is not noticed at all. Of course, the reverse of that statement applies as well. What most people do not take into consideration is that when a scene is shot from several different angles, the production audio will vary from shot to shot. When the picture is cut together, the visual becomes interesting and engaging, but the respective production sound from those shots are often choppy, noisy, and may have level discrepancies. It is the dialogue editor's job to ensure that the scene is sonically transparent.

The dialogue editor's work is best described as both *cleaning* and preserving the production dialogue, while preparing it to be mix-ready for the final dub. The cleaning process is mostly used in dealing with extraneous noises that interfere with the dialogue. This could be from lip smacks, or when an actor knocks something over, or bumps into a prop. The dialogue editor tries to make the dialogue appear seamless and transparent. This is done through precise editing, crossfades, and good use of filler (room tone). There are many issues that any given dialogue editor will be faced with on a television show or movie, like ADR, missing lines, or missing shots that aren't available until the last minute.

THE ASSISTANT DIALOGUE EDITOR

Behind every great dialogue editor is an incredible *assistant dialogue editor*. The assistant is another unsung hero in this part of the editorial process. An assistant acts as the interface between the picture department and the dialogue editor. Once the location sound is captured, the location sound crew passes their work over to the picture department, and then, in turn, the picture department will send it over to editorial. This has been the standard operating procedure for decades. The assistant understands how to navigate through this protocol to make sure that all of the dialogue is available for the dialogue editor.

The assistant gathers the following items, in preparation for dialogue editing:

- locked picture (in the form of a QuickTime movie)
- guide track (audio from the QuickTime movie)
- sound reels and sound logs from production (the location sound)
- OMF from the picture edit session
- EDLs, hopefully both picture (picture cuts) and audio (alternate takes from location sound)

The assistant editor's job is to assemble all of this in a DAW session for the dialogue editor, making sure everything is complete and ready for editing. Efficiency and accuracy are key to being a great assistant. The QuickTime movie, OMFs, and the guide track act as the foundation of the session. They need to be resolved with regards to QuickTime movie, time code, file format, sample rate, and bit resolution, to all work together.

Next, the assistant must address the sound reels from production. The location sound is usually captured digitally on the set. This is done with a 4-, 6-, or 8-track digital multitrack recorder to facilitate multiple actors in any given scene. The first track will be a live mixed comp of all dialogue and production. The next track will be the same, but 6 dB lower, in case of any extreme levels that could blow the input and distort the track. The next four to six tracks are pre-fader/pre-mixed individual lavaliere mics from the actors, often referred to as the "radio mics." These radio mic tracks can come in very handy if the first mixed comp track isn't working, for whatever reason.

The audio sound files from the location sound team will be encoded with meta-data that identifies the scene, actor, take, etc. This is equivalent to the sound log used to document all of this information. *Demuxing* (mux is an acronym for "multiplexed") is the process in which multitrack files are split out and identified individually. In most cases, the assistant dialogue editor does this with an auto-assembly program, along with the EDL. Some tools for demuxing are Titan, Virtual Katy, and Post Conform.

The auto-assembly application is looking for the following data/file names:

- sound roll
- source
- destination
- scene
- take

In an ideal world, most dialogue would be taken from the comp track, but in reality, the dialogue comes from wherever it fits best. If a line is missing, the assistant needs to dig into these files to find it or to provide alternate choices.

As soon as all of this is complete (along with adding the room tones and any wild takes) and the dialogue session is assembled, the assistant can send it to the dialogue editor, along with a line script and a current version of the picture to begin work, as well as the EDL from the picture department. The EDL will have critical data regarding any picture edits and alternate takes. The dialogue editor relies heavily on the assistant dialogue editor to prepare everything accurately, efficiently, and on time. It is crucial for this to be done correctly in order for everyone to meet their respective deadlines. It is often said that audio post production is a team sport, because each person passes their work to the next person in the chain, and so on, and so on.

DIALOGUE EDITING IN TELEVISION

A dialogue editor's preparation for a television series can be difficult. Everything is happening very quickly, and there is rarely time to talk with the location sound people beforehand. A fair amount of trust between the dialogue editor and the location sound editor must exist in order for this process to go smoothly. There is always feedback on what is or what is not working, but the biggest issue is that the sound location crew can be as many as four or five episodes ahead of what editorial is dealing with.

Room tones/filler are paramount, and the location sound crew understands that. The dialogue editor is looking for more than just good takes and documentation. They need a good bed of room tone from each location, which they can use for filler. These room tones can make or break the ADR, and the directors are really counting on them to make the production sound, as well as the ADR, to appear as real as possible.

The *DX* (short for "dialogue") *editor* will work very closely with the sound supervisor. Together, they go to the spotting session with the director. The spotting session for each episode is for both dialogue and sound effects. The director and sound supervisor, along with the DX and SFX editors, will identify any problems or special treatments required in that episode. The spotting session is also where the ADR is cued. Even though the dialogue editor may have nothing to do with recording the ADR, it is good for them to know where it will be located, so that they can plan for it.

TRACK ABBREVIATIONS

Because there is so little room available to label tracks in most DAWs, a system of short abbreviations has developed that is standard in the industry.

DX	Dialogue
SFX or FX	Sound Effects
MX	Music
FO	Foley

ADR is often done to make the story more understandable—to add to established shots or added thoughts to help clarify the plot. It is usually done because of an actor's performance or delivery, but it can also be because of a technical problem, such as dealing with extraneous noises, for example, rain, a moving vehicle, or an actor accidentally knocking over a prop.

When ADR is identified (cued), the dialogue editor will put the line in question on a separate track called the "X track." The X track is where all original production dialogue that is deemed unusable will reside. Often, a line of dialogue is redone in an ADR session, but when the project gets to the dub stage, the mixer may want to use all or part of the original track instead, because of how well it works with picture. An experienced mixer can often smooth or fix the most problematic dialogue tracks. This is a great benefit, as the original dialogue is almost always preferred in a final mix because of its authentic delivery and raw emotion.

If the ADR is available while the dialogue editor is putting together the dialogue session, he will add some filler/room tone (on a separate track) to make it feel more like the original. This can make all the difference. ADR is often done in a dry/lifeless studio, and the room tone helps it to sound more like the production dialogue that was captured live on set.

There are two types of ADR that they will spot for: *principal ADR* for the main actors and *group ADR* for crowd scenes. Most shows will have cues for both on each episode. ADR for the principal actors is tricky because of availability and location. Most post production is done in Los Angeles, even if the show is being shot in New York, London, Hawaii, or wherever.

Oftentimes, the principal ADR is captured at a post-production studio near the set. When it is completed, the audio files are sent over to the dialogue editor or directly to the final dub. The group ADR is almost always done in Los Angeles. This is because there are so many great loop groups available, as well as numerous full-service post-production studios equipped with great ADR stages.

There are a few things that the dialogue editor will do to prepare a session for a mix. They need to prepare a methodical track layout in a DAW that is consistent from reel to reel (in film) or act to act (in television). The layout is based on a structure and what would logically work for the mix. But there is no set rule.

Some editors choose to *checkerboard* the dialogue—create multiple tracks in the DAW session, and then separate the dialogue into unique tracks for each character. It is called "checkerboarding" because of the way the session looks when you are finished. Although this seems logical, it takes up a lot of tracks on the mixing console, as well as screen clutter in the DAW.

Fig. 7.4. Checkerboarding Dialogue in a DAW

As an alternative to checkerboarding, some dialogue editors will prepare the session layout based on sound and timbre. The editor envisions the easiest way for it to be mixed, and prepares the track splits to accommodate any special treatment and backgrounds for the main characters in that scene. They will go to the comp track first, but if it is too boomy or noisy, they will go for the radio mics and add some filler. It's about making quick and efficient choices, as well as preparing the session so that the final dub mixer can easily navigate through it.

A fair amount of patchwork needs to be done, when dealing with ADR and technical problems. A lot of this can be dealt with using creative take choices, crossfades, volume graphs, and light processing. Dialogue editors will often go to an alternate take if they have to really doctor something up. This is a great place to continue using production dialogue even if you simply need to grab a word or a syllable. S, T, or B are great letters/syllables to cut on, but the main goal is to be transparent. The EDL will provide a roadmap for where to grab any alternate takes.

> **PLUG-INS FOR EDITING DIALOGUE**
>
> Here are some go-to plug-ins that dialogue editors favor for treating dialogue.
>
> - Bias SoundSoap, for reducing digital harshness of iso mics or reducing rain on a tarp over the camera
> - iZotope Declick, for dealing with digital *snats* (crackles and pops in the audio)
> - iZotope Decrackle, for frying pan or clothing issues
>
> These are great tools for cleaning up poorly recorded dialogue, as are occasionally applying EQ and compression. This can be done on a new track in order to preserve the original audio file, but most experienced dialogue editors will just deliver the cleaned up file.

Dialogue editors will also include the option to extend dialogue regions. The professional term for these extensions is *handles*, and they are used to augment the audio regions/clips at the beginning or the end. This enables the re-recording mixer to extend and crossfade smoothly between shots with differing background tones. These are great for the mixer to have available in case they feel that extending the audio region will help the sequence play better. Handles are standard when dealing with post-production elements, especially dialogue and sound effects.

In addition to the X track, the PFX track(s) is created. *PFX* are the production effects that are captured on set with the dialogue. They can be door slams, cup downs, footsteps, vehicle sounds, etc. These effects are put on a separate track(s) labeled PFX. This is mainly to keep the level separate from the dialogue, and to let you backfill them with room tone. Although the supervising sound editor may decide that certain PFX are to be redone as sound effects and/or Foley, the original source is always good to have available to use or possibly layer along with any new sounds. The PFX are often routed to a separate PFX stem for the M&E (the music and effects mix used to dub the film in a foreign language for international distribution).

Each show has its own deliverable requirements. Currently, the standard delivery platform is a Pro Tools session. The dialogue editor will do all prep and patchwork in Pro Tools. This makes it easy to integrate with all of the other elements. The dialogue editor will clean up the session by eliminating unused tracks and regions and do a "Save copy in…" command, which includes only the project's audio files for final delivery, creating a new session. This session might be further compacted to make it quicker and more efficient for uploading and downloading via Internet.

DEALING WITH PRODUCTION DIALOGUE IN REALITY TV

My friend Earl Martin (Gray Martin Studios) handles the audio post production for several popular television shows, most of which are unscripted and few rarely follow an outline. This can make for some interesting dialogue situations. More often than not, the producers are putting together the script/story line as it happens. Because of this, they rely heavily on post-production editorial (both video and audio) to construct and complete each episode. In these situations, the dialogue editors are not just prepping dialogue for the mix; they are also writing (rewriting?) the script (what script?), along with shaping the story.

This is carefully done by creating what Earl calls, "Franken-bits." This process is where the actor says (or mumbles) something in the take, and the director (in post production) instructs the dialogue editor to grab syllables, words, and phrases from alternate takes to make them say something completely different to either create a story or make the story more interesting. This can be successfully achieved through creative dialogue editing, alternate takes, and ADR, to slip new dialogue (Franken-bits) into the actor's mouth when he or she is not featured, or hopefully, off-camera. This makes the post production a big part of the show's budget (both time and money).

One show in particular was based around good-looking/fashion savvy adolescents running around Hollywood, living their lives, and trying to be entertaining in the process. It was hard to use a boom (an overhead mic that is suspended over the actors on a long pole) because of the wide camera shots. It was also difficult dealing with lavaliere mics because often the girls (and sometimes the boys too) were wearing close to nothing at all. In those situations, the location recordist chose to use a *cavity mic*, which is a wireless lavaliere mic that is attached to a cavity on the body of the actor/actress. Although this may seem like a clever workaround, it also exhibits a new host of dialogue issues.

During the first ADR session for this show, Earl couldn't figure out why there was so much low end (low frequencies) in the production dialogue track from the set. He realized by observing the wide angle shots that they must have used a cavity mic. This is common practice and usually hidden in clothing, or hair, or taped to a body cavity.

To simulate what he was experiencing with the dialogue track, place your hand against your chest and start speaking. You will instantly notice the low end rumble that your hand is feeling when you talk. This is what was getting picked up by the cavity mic and translating to the track!

So when Earl was doing ADR for the show, he realized that in addition to having a close and distant shotgun mic on the ADR stage, he also had to use a lavalier/cavity mic to make sure that there was some sonic consistency in the dialogue track. These decisions are what can make or break a good dialogue track. The additional low end can be filtered out in the mix, but having it there initially adds continuity to the track.

REAL-LIFE SITUATIONS

When I began my career in Hollywood, I was working at a post-production studio that specialized in sound effects, Foley, ADR, and music score mixing. It was a wonderful opportunity at an exciting era in film. One of my first jobs was to assist in a series of ADR sessions for a film that was having some problems with its post-production elements.

This feature film was shot in Canada and scheduled to do the post production in Hollywood. Unfortunately, someone made a catastrophic error that created a situation where the location sound could not leave Canada. Therefore, every word of dialogue had to be redone in ADR. This was a feature length film, and ultimately, it became three weeks of daily twelve-hour ADR sessions that included every cast member, along with loop groups, as well as voice casting for characters when the actors were not available to do the ADR session.

Although this was considered a colossal blunder, it created an opportunity for me to learn a new skill and make some extra cash, as we put in many hours of overtime. Despite my inexperience, I was happy to take advantage of this situation that ultimately taught me almost every aspect of ADR. I had become quite the pro when the project was completed, and when the next project came through the door, I was chosen for the session.

There were some valuable Hollywood lessons learned on this project, as well. One was to always say "yes" when someone asks you to do something at the beginning of your career. Even though I had little or no experience, I had the interest and the motivation. And that was enough to get me started. I also had the natural instinct to keep my eyes and ears open and my mouth shut—especially when it came to dealing with a totally foreign process of fixing messy or missing dialogue. Additionally, I learned that accidents happen all the time, and that getting on the solution side of any problem made you an asset to the project. These lessons were essential to developing my career.

PREPARE PHYSICAL STUDIO SPACE FOR VOICE RECORDING

As you have seen, ADR is done most effectively on an ADR stage. This specialized recording room, along with its companion control room for the engineer and gear, is ideal for dialogue recording. You would need some additional gear and space to do this in your personal studio, but there are a few things that you can do as a workaround, in the meantime.

If only one room is available in your home studio, you will need to set it up to perform a dual function of both control room and ADR stage. A few adjustments are necessary, to achieve this. Your computer screen(s) need to be quiet and to display both your DAW and the QuickTime movie simultaneously. This works best if you have two monitors.

Any gear that makes substantial noise (computer tower, air conditioner, etc.) will need to be located in a separate room. If your studio is located in a spare bedroom, you may utilize the closet as a machine room, for the noisy gear. Most electronic gear needs to be cool to run effectively. One workaround for this is to route a separate send and return from your central air conditioner into the machine closet. You could also purchase an additional air conditioning unit dedicated for that space.

You will need to record and play back with headphones (both for you and the voice talent). So, make sure that you have several working sets of headphones that fully cover your ears. A *headphone distributor* is great as well, if you have more than more person there for the ADR session.

You will want to set up at least one microphone on a mic stand in your studio to record the voice talent. A proper ADR stage will have two mics: one close (about a foot and a half away from the talent) and one distant (about three feet from the talent). A music stand is very handy to hold the script or ADR cue sheet. It will need to be strategically placed so that the voice talent can see both the script and the QuickTime movie (for visual cues).

You will need to spot the ADR and cue it in the ADR sheet for the voice talent to use as a guide, so having a word processing program and a printer are extremely useful.

ADR is cued through both audio (beeps) and visual cues (SMPTE time code). The beeps are an industry standard, and are used as an audio cue for the actor to begin the ADR line. For example: beep beep beep "start speaking ADR lines." You can create these short audible beeps in any DAW by using quarter-second samples of a pure 1000 cycle sine wave. These quarter-second samples become the beep. Simply record one and copy it two more times. Assemble the beeps so that they are exactly one second apart, and you will have a perfect standard cue for any ADR session.

VOICE-OVER AND NARRATION IN AN ADR SESSION

Voice-over (VO) and narration are a very important aspect of an ADR session. Television and radio commercials, as well as feature animation and film trailers, live and die by having the perfect voice to represent their character, present their message, or sell their product. Voice casting is big business, and many actors will bend over backwards at the opportunity to lend their voice to a project or commercial. Narration is just as important, as it will guide you through a presentation or walk you through a timeline.

These sessions are based around getting the lines recorded in a certain amount of time. For example, the *copy* (text) for a 30 second radio commercial needs to be read in less than 30 seconds in order to fit in the time slot, and intelligibility will make or break the delivery/performance. As an engineer, your focus is to get a good clean level as you document the performances. And there will probably be many performances. The producer may also instruct you and the talent to get some "wild" takes as well. This means that you will record the talent with no reference at all to the spot, with the hopes that the voice talent will deliver a performance that is accurate and unique.

Documentation is key to being a good VO/narration engineer. The producer will most likely hand you a script at the end of the session and direct you to edit selections from the circled (best) takes into a complete and intelligible composite take. This may require grabbing different lines from different tracks/takes and combining them into a final "comp" track. It can be a little tricky, and you may find that even though you have comp'd all of the selected/circled takes into a complete track, the timing of each line may not flow like a natural delivery. You can remedy this by nudging lines earlier and later to make the flow appear much more natural.

All in all, recording and editing dialogue for radio, film, or television is a very important part of the post-production process. Most projects are dialogue driven, so capturing the dialogue and editing it so that it is intelligible and transparent are the main focus. There are numerous techniques that you can use to help a dialogue track or performance that is lacking in luster. But the key is to get it right the first time. Of course, this is easier said than done, and there are a host of obstacles that can get in the way of capturing and delivering a great dialogue track.

Now that you know the nuts and bolts of this process, you should be able to accurately address most dialogue situations in short order.

CHAPTER 8

Foley

The idea of sync effect acting came from Jack Foley in the early days of "talking" movies, in Hollywood. His technique of recording acted-out sound effects, such as footsteps and clothing movement, along with specific props, has developed into an intricate element in audio post production for both film and television.

One thing that the audience isn't always aware of is that, on a film or television set, most of the props and staging are often artificial. The ocean is really a large pool, the gun is plastic, and the front of the house is actually plywood. These makeshift props and set designs are often reflected in the production sound. So, splashing around in a pool will not sound like the ocean, setting down a plastic gun will not sound like setting down a 357 magnum, and closing the front door of a plywood set will not sound like closing the front door of your house.

Foley effects are added to help cover this up and add a more realistic layer of audio to make the soundtrack more authentic. These subtle acted-out human sound effects have a dynamic effect on the subconcious mind while watching a film or television show. They make the audience feel like they are in the same room or location while experiencing the human sonic presence of each character.

A *Foley artist* recreates these sound effects for film, television, and radio productions on a Foley stage in a post-production facility. Using many different kinds of shoes, surfaces, and props (car fenders, plates, glasses, chairs, etc.), the Foley artist can replace the original sound completely or augment existing sound to create a richer, smoother track. Almost every motion picture and television show that you have ever seen and heard contains a Foley track.

The focus of the location sound crew is almost always on capturing dialogue. However, it is common for the production sound to pick up additional effects (like the actual footsteps, clothing movement, body taps, etc.). This is what makes the production sound the first choice for dialogue when mixing the final soundtrack. Unfortunately, outside interference can mask the dialogue. In that case, the dialogue lines that are deemed unusable are re-recorded in ADR (see chapter 7).

The ADR process works perfectly to resolve any dialogue that is unusable, but the dialogue replacement is recorded in a dry and lifeless studio on an ADR stage. Therefore, it lacks the additional effects listed earlier, along with room tone and ambience. This is where Foley effects come into place: it fills in the gaps and breathes some life into the ADR lines.

Again, Foley is really addressing the subconcious mind. Footsteps are never very loud, and the sound of a coat or jacket is rarely featured in the soundtrack. But without a subtle bed of these Foley effects, along with the room tone, the listener will notice that a sonic shift is taking place and will inadvertantly become aware of the ADR lines.

Often, a film is rereleased in a foreign country to take advantage of its profitability in the world market. When this is done, all of the discernable English must be removed, so that the dialogue can be re-recorded in a foreign language. This process is called creating an M&E mix (or music and effects mix, see chapter 14).

The M&E mix is created to make it easier and more realistic for the dialogue to be replaced in a different language. But when the original dialogue (production track) is removed, so are the production effects that are captured along with it (footsteps, clothing movement, body taps, etc.). Therefore, the M&E mixers will be looking to the Foley track to provide the effects and fill in the gaps in lieu of the original production sound. Each element is added along with backgrounds and room tones, and the result is a naturally sounding scene with no dialogue.

A Foley track combines three types of sound elements:

- moves/clothing
- footsteps
- specifics

THE MOVES/CLOTHING TRACK

The moves/clothing track is created because, as human beings, we create noises all the time in our day to day activities. My pants make sound when walking from room to room, my jacket makes noise when raising my hand to say hello to someone, and I am constantly making random sounds as I scratch my head, reach into my pockets, or tie my shoes. All of this movement is subtle yet extremely important in authenticating a performance in a film or television program.

The moves/clothing pass addresses all of this. If you were to exclude it, the performance on screen would seem dry and lifeless. This track is placed low in the mix, more to imply its activity than to feature it as a big part of the soundtrack.

Most Foley walkers prefer to do this pass first, as it allows them to watch the scene, act, or reel, and get a good feel for what is happening in the project. They will notice other things going on and start to make mental notes as to what props they will need, as well as choosing shoes and surfaces.

When this track is completed, it should add a more human feel to the picture, as it provides a rich texture of sound to the characters on screen. It will be the foundation of the Foley track and set the tone for additional passes. This track also gives the Foley walker an opportunity to get a better feel for the film, the characters, and their intentions.

THE FOOTSTEPS/STEPS TRACK

The *steps track* is the one that most people identify as the Foley walkers' most prominent contribution to the film. This is the pass that gave them their title as Foley *walkers*. Often, the production sound will not have a good representaion of shoes, footsteps, and surfaces. So, this track is very important to authenticate that action. The Foley walker will be looking to see what shoes to use and the surface that they will be walking on. Matching these elements makes all the difference in a believeable performance and useable track.

A Foley stage will have numerous (sometimes hundreds) of different kinds of shoes to choose from for this pass. The stage will also have several different surfaces (often referred to as the *Foley pit*) to walk on, as well. These surfaces will vary from concrete to hardwood floors to stones, sand, dirt, makeshift grass, etc. The more diversity, the better. Every project will call for something different, and it is best for the stage and the Foley walker to be prepared for anything.

Foley walkers also need to be ready to change shoes and surfaces at a moment's notice. The actor that they are covering may be running from grass into a heavily planted garden and then onto a driveway, all in about twelve seconds. This requires good planning and focus on both the walker and the Foley mixer, as they change surfaces and watch out for any level changes in the performance.

Foley walkers also must be very sensitive to sync. They need to make sure that each step matches the movement of the actor. Watching the feet is not always the best option for this. The feet may not be included in the scene (depending on the angle of the shot), so it can be a bit tricky to use the feet as a reference. Interestingly, most Foley walkers will look to the shoulders as a guide for footstep synchronization. This is proven to be the best source for matching the movement of each actor.

Every character's steps are addressed in the steps track, as well as the intention of the performance. The skill of a Foley walker is often revealed in this pass, as it takes a lot of experience to pull this off. They are not just running across a room or field. The Foley walkers are almost always working in a very small area, often walking and/or running in place.

This can be fun to observe, too. Can you imagine a forty-year-old man in a pair of women's pumps, walking in place on a small slab of concrete to match actress Jennifer Aniston walking in a parking lot? It happens all the time. Most Foley walkers are quite worn out at the end of an 8 hour day, as their work can be very similar to going to the gym. That said, most Foley walkers are in great shape, physically!

THE PROPS/SPECIFICS TRACK

Once all of the clothing and footsteps are covered, the last thing is to address the specifics or props. This is an extremely broad range that could include anything from a book being set down on a table to a bicycle riding on a driveway to a car door being shut to a living-room door opening, etc. This is why a Foley stage often resembles an old and extremely cluttered garage, full of all of these props and more. These aditional props will provide a much more realistic layer of sound to the Foley track and ultimately to the final mix of the film.

Fig. 8.1. Foley Stage at Larson Studios in Hollywood CA 2710. Photo by Molly Quaid.

The specifics track will also include human actions, such as punches, body falls, jumps, or a pat on the back, along with simple and subtle sounds like handshakes and head scratches. It is paramount that the Foley actor and mixer work together, so that they capture all of this activity and get good recorded levels. It would be difficult for any professional to get all of this in one pass, especially if there is a lot going on. The Foley mixer and walker will often discuss how they will recreate the sequence and whether there is a good clean area for a punch-in, if that is called for.

RECORDING FOLEY

Here are some of the general practices for recording Foley effects.

- Each section (clothing, steps, and props) will be recorded separately. They are usually recorded on a single track, from start to finish. This allows the Foley walker to gather momentum and stay in pace with the character. The Foley mixer will set a good mic level and let the Foley artist do their work, but the Foley mixer will often need to ride the level so that they capture the sublty of a kiss along with the extreme level of a door slam.

- The mic is placed approximately three feet in front of the Foley walker to allow for a little room sound to be included. Occasionally, a second mic is placed further away, to capture more room ambience, and it is mixed in with the direct mic to create a fuller overall sound. The mix of the two mics is about 80 percent close and 20 percent distant (but this can vary). That said, a silent Foley stage is key to capturing a realistic and usable performance.

- Any fixes or punch-ins are done at a point in the action where a punch-in would be the least noticeable. This may mean going back a little further, but a smooth punch-in (usually accompanied by a seamless crossfade) needs to be done so that it doesn't call attention to itself. This could be a lull in the action or a picture cut on a scene change.

SPOTTING FOLEY

The process of spotting Foley is very similar to the spotting sessions that we have discussed in the past few chapters. Spotting is almost always done by the supervising sound editor. He or she will be looking and listening for opportunities to enrich the sound as well as to fill in the gaps that clean ADR will create. They will go through each reel/act of the program and make a detailed list (cross-referenced to SMPTE time code "ins and outs") of where they feel this needs to be addressed.

This process can take a long time when you are involved with a feature length film project; however, an episodic television show or short indie film can be spotted for Foley in a few hours or less. In some situations, the supervising sound editor will have the Foley mixer spot the Foley, as they may have a better, more experienced eye for that. Often, Foley cues are added in the actual Foley recording process, as the Foley actors notice opportunities that may have been missed. Of course, this is all budget and time dependent.

In the past, this process was thoroughly documented on a Foley cue sheet. It may be handwritten on blank templates or entered into a Word or Excel type of document. In that situation, it is common to start with a blank Foley cue sheet.

The Foley can be categorized/identified as (CM) Clothes/Movement, (FS) Footsteps, (S) or (P) Specifics/Props, etc. This helps the Foley mixer to plan and direct the session. They will divide the activities into groups to make the session more efficient. They will describe the action and list the duration. Being specific is key, so that there is no room for confusion.

Here is a Foley cue sheet.

Page 1
FOLEY LIST 1/15/12
Producer's Cut # TRT: 30:08

(FS) Footsteps (CM) Cloth Movement
(N) Noise (M) Movement

TIMECODE		DESCRIPTION	TIME PERMITTING	PRODUCER NOTES
01:00:12	FS	MC up stairs (carpet on wood)		
01:00:12	N	MC holding a tray with soup and silverware		
01:00:18	FS	MC walks across bedroom with tray (carpet)		
01:00:23	N	Noise: MC hands tray to Loretta on bed		
01:00:23	N	Gail moves tray and silverware		
01:00:25	N	Gail picks up spoon off of wood tray		
01:00:27	N	Gail sips soup		
01:00:29	N	Gail puts spoon back on plate		
01:00:34	N	Gail hands soup w/ plate & spoon to LD		
01:00:38	CM	Gail moves wood tray off of lap onto bed		
01:00:51	CM	Loretta adjusts in bed		
01:01:02	FS	MC toward Leon		
01:01:05	FS	Joe walking into room		
01:01:13	N	Gail bed cloth		
01:01:32	FS	MC exits room		
01:01:34	FS	MC walks down steps		
01:01:37	FS	Carol and kids walk in		
01:02:24	M	Carol brushes chest		
01:02:26	FS	Carol walking away		
01:03:02-01:04:33	N	John working on bicycle with wrench throughout scene (on and off)		
01:03:27	FS	Olly enters		
01:03:35	N	MC spins bike tire		
01:04:23	N	MC spins bike tire		
01:04:31	N	MC spins bike tire		
01:04:33	FS	MC Footsteps		
01:04:47	M	Carol and Lee handshake		
01:05:08	N	Lee opens bag		
01:05:09	N	Lee digs through bag		
01:05:22	M	Lee hand clap		
01:05:59	N	Lee's papers in his hand		
01:06:04	N	Lee opens fridge		
01:06:05	N	Lee pulls out can of lemonade		
01:06:09	N	Open can		
01:06:12	N	Pours can into glass		
01:06:17	N	Lee places can on counter		
01:06:24	N	Lee sips lemonade		

Fig. 8.2. Foley Cue Sheet

With the advent of technology and the vastness of extremely intricate DAWs, the supervising sound editors have begun to do the Foley spotting directly in the DAW. This process makes the spotting session go much faster and is equally, if not more, efficient than the previous method. This calls for importing and resolving a quick time movie of the film, reel, or episode into a DAW session and creating region lists for each Foley cue. This can be done very intricately, as you have the freedom to nudge in increments as small as a frame. This allows you to spot, identify, and locate Foley cues rapidly in both the spotting session and recording session by using markers to identify the regions/clips cued for Foley.

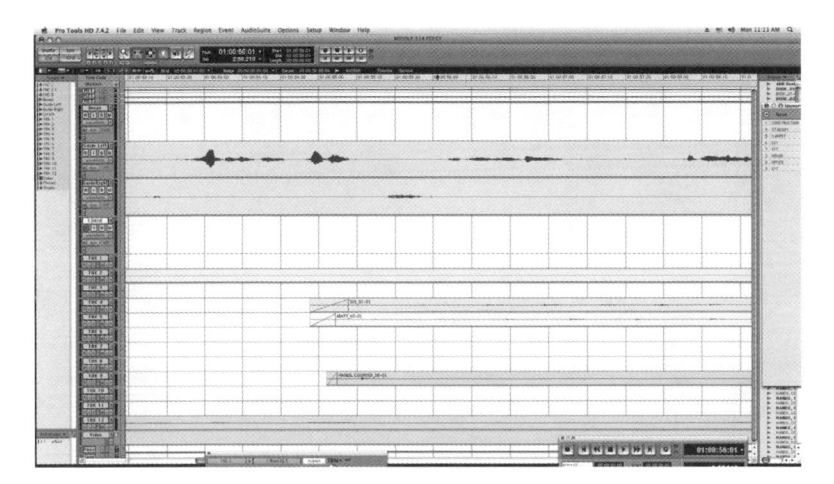

Here is a screen shot of cued Foley in a DAW.

Fig. 8.3. Foley Regions/Clips Cued in Pro Tools

RECORDING FOLEY

There are a few things that you can do to set up the session to make it more efficient with regards to time and activity. Foley is almost always recorded on a Foley stage in a post-production studio. These stages consist of at least two rooms: the control room and the actual Foley stage (recording area/studio).

THE CONTROL ROOM

The control room will resemble a typical recording studio. This is where the engineer works, and it hosts the gear usually associated with recording (mixing desk, outboard gear, computer, video monitors, etc.). The control room will most likely have multiple video monitors: one for the computer/DAW, one for the playback of the movie, and occasionally an additional monitor from a camera out on the Foley stage. There should be enough room to facilitate multiple clients and typical client needs (sofas, chairs, phones, Internet, coffee, etc.).

Here is a Foley control room.

Fig. 8.4. Foley Stage Control Room at Larson Studios in Hollywood CA 2715-2. Photo by Molly Quaid.

THE FOLEY STAGE

The Foley stage typically resembles an old garage that hasn't been cleaned in decades. It will have a variety of props, from car doors to wooden doors, from cowboy boots to pumps, from fold-up chairs to wheelchairs, etc. They are set up this way for a reason. You never know what kind of project will come through the door, so Foley studios need to be prepared for just about anything. It is not uncommon to see more than a hundred pairs of shoes, as well as a similar amount of old clothes that are made from a variety of materials. It could easily resemble a garage sale from hell.

Here are a few Foley stages.

Fig. 8.5. Foley Stage at Larson Studios in Hollywood CA

Fig. 8.6. Foley Stage at RH Factor Studios in Burbank, CA

The Foley stage will also have what is called a *pit*. The pit has sectioned areas with different surfaces for capturing realistic footsteps.

Here is an example of a Foley pit.

Fig. 8.7. Foley Pit at RH Factor Studios in Burbank, CA. Notice the variety of surfaces, from sand to carpet to granite.

In both examples we see different surfaces as well as some mic placement techniques to capture the Foley sounds. Foley actors need to be creative to create the sounds that are needed for the project. As a Foley mixer or artist, you will be using your imagination to create sounds that will impact the viewer.

FOLEY AT HOME

You may not have the opportunity or capacity to set up your home studio like a Hollywood Foley stage in a professional post-production facility, but here are a few ideas to make one that will be serviceable for small projects.

Monitors

If you have a separate control room, you will need to set up an additional monitor in your studio/Foley stage so that the Foley actors can follow the picture and create the Foley in sync with the movie.

Headphones

You will need some good headphones for the Foley actors, for reference and communication. These should be professional headphones that completely cover the ear so that there is no level leakage from playback in the headphones into the Foley mics.

Microphones

You will need some good shotgun mics, like the Sennheiser MKH 416 shotgun and a Neumann U87 for ambience. These are both condenser mics that will require phantom power (which is usually available via the console or pre-amp). You will also need good mic pre-amps for these mics (which are usually available from the mixing desk).

Props

This goes without saying. You will need a ton of props!

Surfaces

You will need to create or at least have access to a variety of surfaces for your steps. This can include hardwood floors, concrete, gravel, etc.

If you do not have an additional room or gear for recording, you will have to do your best to create your Foley in the control room with the gear that you have. This is not recommended, as it can get quite messy and is not conducive for sensitive and expensive electronic studio gear. If this is your only option, be very careful, and make sure that you have enough room to create your Foley. You may need to record additional passes to accommodate your limitations, but don't let that get in your way. Foley (like all audio recording) has been captured in some very unusual spaces.

THE FOLEY MIXER

Foley sessions are like most sessions in the sense that there is a list of tasks that need to be accomplished and a certain amount of time available to complete them. The Foley mixer and Foley walkers are aware of this and will create an efficient workflow to accomplish what is required. It is important that the Foley walker and mixer have a great rapport. Most professional teams have been working together for numerous years and are very close. They spend so much time working together in the recording studio that they often communicate like old married couples, as they finish each other's sentences or speak in terms of looks and nods.

The Foley mixer will take the lead as far as planning the session. They will direct the actors on what has been cued and what is coming up. They may comment as they preview the scene and suggest a process in which to get everything quickly and efficiently. They will also comment if something isn't working or if there is a mistake. The Foley mixer will be focusing with their eyes and ears throughout the recording process and responding to good and bad takes. The objective is to be as transparent as possible.

When they are ready to record, the mixer will set up the cues with beeps. This is common practice and very similar to an ADR session. The beeps are sent to the control room monitors and to the Foley walker's headphones, to cue them where to start. There will be three audible beeps one second apart from each other; at a fourth (silent/implied) beep, the mixer puts the DAW in Record, and the walker performs the cue. The Foley mixer often has these beeps available to insert at the beginning of each Foley cue at the touch of a button as a key command or a computer macro.

The Foley mixer will capture each cue and keep the session well organized. The final delivery track layout for the Foley can vary, but the idea is to make it easy for the mixer to interpret as they are mixing. In most television shows, the Foley mixer is given up to twelve tracks for the Foley: six for steps and six for everything else. The layout is character specific, and again, the main objective is that the tracks can be mixed easily.

Before the Foley session is delivered, the Foley mixer will clean it up a bit. They will go through the session and delete any unused regions/clips or files. This will help to keep the size of the session in check, so that it can upload and download to and from a server in fairly short order. There is no need to include anything that isn't needed.

The Foley mixer and walker are in close communication with the re-recording mixer, as well as the supervising sound editor. They will attend playbacks (if possible) of final mixes and encourage feedback from the mixers. The feedback is very helpful, especially in an episodic television show. This will help to create a workflow that extends beyond the Foley stage and makes the Foley process more efficient.

Here is Foley mixer Cecilia Perna in action.

Fig. 8.8. Foley Mixer Cecilia Perna at RH Factor Studios Foley Stage

CHAPTER 9

Music Editing

Music is used in film and television to help tell the story, and it speaks to the emotional context of the scene. *Music editing* is the process in which the music is creatively placed in key moments of a film or television show. The music editor is in charge of this, and communicates with the picture editor, director, composer, music supervisor, assistant editors, sound editor, and re-recording mixer, throughout this process.

Music for a film or television show breaks down into two categories: score and source.

score: The internal music within the film itself, written specifically for the film by a composer.

source: Music that is coming from a source in the scene by way of a radio, television, or jukebox in the background, etc.

In addition to these categories, here are some subcategories and terms:

song source: Songs that are placed in the film to project the emotional story line or scene montage.

pre-record source: Music that is simultaneously happening on-screen by way of a band performing live on-camera. This music will need to be pre-recorded (recorded ahead of time) so that it can be played back on location as the band/actors performs or mimes to it.

temp music/score: Placeholder music that helps to develop and focus the musical direction of what the director is looking for, before the actual score is ready. It is prepared by either the picture editor or music editor to use in creating the rough cut of the picture. It is usually taken from music scores to previously released film soundtracks. A temp score is meant to be a guide for the director and composer to create the final music score, or at the very least, form the basis of a conversation regarding music for the film.

soundtrack music: Music used to capitalize on a film's success, or to generate success from an otherwise unsuccessful film. Soundtrack music is all-encompassing music, which gives an overall view of the film. It usually includes the beginning- and end-credit songs, as well as full-length versions of any internal music in the film. This is often a tool to translate mediums and give the audience a sensorial memento of the movie experience.

music libraries: A source for *production music*—music owned by production music libraries and licensed to use in film, television, radio, and other media. These libraries own all of the copyrights of their music, meaning that it can be licensed without seeking the composer's permission, as is necessary in licensing music from normal publishers. This is because virtually all music created for music libraries is done on a work-for-hire basis. Production music libraries will typically offer a broad range of musical styles and genres, enabling producers and editors to find much of what they need in the same library. Music libraries vary in size from a few hundred tracks up to many thousands. The first production music library was set up by De Wolfe Music, in 1927, with the advent of sound in film. The company originally scored music for use in silent film.

THE PROCESS

Music editors place the music in the film or television show. They work directly with the composer, before, during, and after the scoring process, and often serve as the conduit between the director and composer to make sure that everyone is on the same page. Music editors are also likely to interface between the picture editor and the director, as well as the music supervisor, assistant editors, sound editor, and re-recording mixer.

The music editor prepares notes on the music based on the temp score and the spotting session. As with sound effects and Foley, the spotting session is key to the process and is one of the first things addressed when preparing the music. For spotting music, it is crucial to play the movie from beginning to end in real time. But, in a spotting session, they'll stop and start throughout the process, so as not to miss any specific concerns that the director, the composer, or the music supervisor might have.

The spotting session will include all of the key players in the project. They watch the film entirely, to decide where and what music should be placed and whether or not it should be score or source. The in and out points of each music cue are documented with an accompanying SMPTE time code address, and each cue is labeled with a numeric ID.

A music cue label will reflect its placement in the film. If it is the second music cue in reel 2, it will be called 2m2 (reel 2, music cue 2). If it is the fifth music cue in reel 4, it will be named 4m5, etc. If there is dialogue before, during, or after the music, the music editor will often take a key phrase from the dialogue to name the cue: 3m2 "looking for cover" or 5m4 "why is it so cold." This way, there is a SMPTE address along with a numeric and text name for each cue.

In addition to the cue name, the music editor documents whether it is score or source music. If the music is source, they discuss what kind of special preparation needs to be done for that music. If there is a live band in a scene, musicians and contractors must be hired for the performance and film shoot. In most cases, the music for that scene is pre-recorded in a studio, ahead of time, and fed to the musicians on set to play along with or mime to. Occasionally, the music is recorded live on set, but that requires additional preparation and gear for the location sound crew, as they are not normally set up for that.

The source music could be more straightforward, like using a song from a band. In that case, the music supervisor works with the band to secure a license in which that song can be used for that show. This can get more expensive, if you are dealing with a popular/successful group. It is usually cheaper to license songs from new/up-and-coming groups, as opposed to using tracks by more established artists, such as the Rolling Stones or the Beatles.

When the spotting session is complete, the music editor formalizes the music spotting notes, providing a detailed account of everything that was discussed and decided on in the spotting session. The notes are distributed to all key players, but most importantly, to the composer and director. The composer uses these notes as a guide for composing the score.

Spotting notes should be kept up-to-date throughout the post-production process and through the final dub and print master. Everyone will begin working on the music, upon completion of the spotting session. The composer starts composing and the music editor begins putting together or reworking the temp music/temp score.

Here is an example of some spotting notes from the film *Dream of the Romans*.

Dream Of The Romans   Page 1

Spotting Notes
Mon, Nov 10, 2008

Reel 1

1M01s v1   01:58   MAIN TITLE

01:00:08:11   Start
01:02:05:27   1st frame in black... over title credits..
Other   End
Main Title   Fade out through dissolve...natural tail..reverb out before DIA
Vid Ver: R1-v2-11/27 L   Comments
                     Song for open / last chord hits and holds as full screen of book starts dissolve and reverbs
                     out through dissolve / ?: maybe teddy to compose / T beateals.. / J : traveling song /
                     spontaneously get away for the weekend ! / T: nice vibe

1M02/1M3 v1   00:39   MEDITATION #1 F#*K THE DOOR

01:02:52:23   Start
01:03:31:14   CUT CU of unlit candles as camera pans to right revealing the back of Arlen..meditating / VO
SCORE   of agent still describing Arlen to visitor in her office.
Underscore   End
Vid Ver: R1-v2-11/27 L   Tails a bit and ends under Arlen DIA " ...shit mother fucker.." as the doorbell interrupts his
Status: To Be Apprvd   meditation / SEGUE into 1m03..comedy music
                     Comments
                     TEMP: "meditation music".. solo wood flute and some little bells /

1M04 v3   01:24   OPENING MAIL INTO THE KITCHEN

01:04:22:10   Start
01:05:45:26   After door slam and as Arlen sits down and opens his mail.
SCORE   End
Underscore   As Elizabeth is finishing the her drink at breakfast music accent her "face" and ring over next
Vid Ver: R1-v2-11/27 L   scene as she is driving her son to school.
Status: To Be Apprvd   Comments
                     TEMP: shifts from comedy feel as Arlen opens the monster figurine and segues to next scene
                     in the breakfast room with Elizabeth and Alex...Play through kitchen even though temp
                     stops...comedy in temp picks up again at: 01:05:22:22 / give her her own theme at
                     breakfast .. introduce her, T: becareful to not be tv style cues / L: we don't want to notice it
                     in & out / T: theme for her / T: be careful with short cues.

1M05s v2   00:36   -THE THIEVING MAGPIE-

01:05:46:06   Start
01:06:21:27   CUT to MS Elizabeth is in her car dropping her son off at school, listening to classical music
Other   to "educate" him.
Non Visual Src   End
Vid Ver: R1-v2-11/27 L   Elizabeth changes the channel on the car radio to R & R music
                     Comments
                     SOURCE classical from her radio. Overature to OPERA L "The Thieving Mac pie".. / cut for
                     persp

Fig. 9.1. Spotting Notes for *Dreams of the Romans*

Spotting notes supply all of the crucial data regarding any given music cue. Looking at the first cue, we see that it is called "1M01s v1 Main Title." The "s" in the number suggests that it is a source cue. It starts at 1:00:08:11 and plays until 1:02:05:27. It is 1 minute and 58 seconds in length, and it was cut to picture version R1-v2-11/27 L. There are some comments regarding placement and suggestions on the possibilities of the composer writing something or grabbing an existing track. These notes are imperative in getting the score to work with the picture, and the music editor will do everything possible to help the composer, director, and music supervisor achieve that goal.

TEMP AND SOURCE MUSIC

As discussed, the temp score may be assembled long before a composer is brought onboard. Often, a music editor will be working on the temp score while the picture is being cut and assembled. It is not uncommon for music editors to prepare three or four (or more) versions of the temp score, as they may be reporting to several different people (who all have opinions on the music). There may be one version for the director, one version for the picture editor, one version for a producer, and so on. This can be a bit maddening, but it is part of the process.

The temp score is refined as the picture starts to come together in the form of a rough cut or a temp dub. At that point, the picture gets screened for the producers, and perhaps a focus group, to test how well the film is translating to the audience. After the screening, many changes occur to both the picture cut and the temp score. These changes reflect the notes from the screening and the feedback from the focus group.

When all changes are complete, they will usually have another screening along with another focus group and another set of notes. This process may go on a few more times (depending on the budget of the project). Each screening adds a new set of changes to the temp score. The composer usually becomes involved after a few screenings, and the music editor will try to cut in some of the composer's demos, to get feedback on them as well.

The music editor works directly with the composer to help shape the score around what the director intended in the temp score. This can be a bit of a process, creating new music that sounds like the intention of someone else's music. Some composers struggle with coming up with new music to replace cues in temp scores, especially if the temp score was based upon music that the composer had originally written for a different project. Imagine Hans Zimmer creating a score for a new movie that used *Batman: The Dark Knight* (a film he originally scored) as its temp score. It must be odd trying to sound like yourself, yet be totally different, while bringing fresh new music to a film!

The Dark Knight is a great example of a music editor working overtime to make the score work. The first sequence filmed for *The Dark Knight* is the opening bank robbery scene. The studio executives decided that the opening sequence would make a great trailer (promo) for the film, so the director approached Hans Zimmer to compose music for the trailer. Hans had an idea that the musical theme for the Joker (lead character in the film) was to be based on a single sustained cello note.

Zimmer contacted the best cellist in Los Angeles to perform the part that he recorded in his studio in Santa Monica. He was looking for something unique in the performance and really worked this A-list musician for quite some time, as they tried to get him (perhaps the best cellist in the world) to alter his technique and play something that was rough and edgy. This was a long and tiresome process, and in the musician's frustration, he performed an aggravated attack on the note, which, in turn, thoroughly impressed Zimmer.

Hans took that single sustained cello note and built a score around it that included well over 800 Pro Tools tracks, which as we discussed earlier, were pre-dubbed down to 200 stems. The music editor took these stems and pre-dubbed them down to less than 100 stems. A *pre-dub* is like an additional sub mix with the focus on creating a more manageable track count (see chapter 11). This pre-dub allowed them to bring the music to the dub stage and mix it along with the other elements (dialogue, Foley, and SFX), to create a final mix to use for the trailer.

Often, these temp dubs and pre-dubs are created by the music editor in a DAW, and they include volume graphs and creative crossfades. The re-recording mixer may use these graphs and fades, depending on how the score is working along with the other elements. The music editor will do their best to keep a good communication going with the re-recording mixers to make sure that they have everything that they need for the final dub.

CHAPTER 9

CONFORMING MUSIC

As discussed in chapter 6, *conforming* is the process of editing an existing music cue to fit a newer-cut version of the film sequence. Often, the picture is still being cut after the scoring process has finished. Conforming scored music to a new picture cut creates a new set of issues for the music editor to address, beyond what must be dealt with when conforming sound effects or dialogue. Imagine a three-minute scene has been scored with music punctuating actions in the film. Now, that same scene has a few frames removed from minute 1, several seconds are removed from minute 2, and a few frames added to minute 3.

The music that was originally scored to that scene will now be out of sync, because the film length changed but the music is still three minutes long. Additionally, music has a regular pulse based on tempos, bars, and beats. Simply taking away a few seconds or frames here and there will interrupt that pulse and can make the music sound disjointed and choppy. It is the music editor's job to make sure that the music still flows flawlessly despite internal picture cuts, while making sure that any music *hits* (critical correlation between the music and picture) are in sync with the film's corresponding action.

Music editors will creatively grab snippets from alternate takes and cues to fill in the gaps, along with using crossfades to provide seamless transitions. It is common for music editors to draw from sound libraries (like Vienna Symphonic Library or L.A. Scoring Strings) to add to the score and help make an edit, fade, or transition sound smooth and transparent.

Another technique that composers and music editors use is to record alternate takes of music cues in the scoring sessions. These alternates are recorded without a melody, soloist, or featured performer, so that they can serve as a bed of music to be used if the solos are too pronounced or not working with a new picture cut. This also provides additional opportunities to use the music in other places in the film, for transitions, as well as for reusing it in other projects. This reuse is often called *repurposing* and is very common in the industry.

When the scoring sessions are complete and the score is mixed, the music editor will attend the final mix (also called the "final dub"). They are there to represent both the composer and the music, as well as help with the source music. They'll often make edits on the spot if more changes occur in the picture or if the director has new ideas about the music.

When the film is finally mixed, the music editor prepares cue sheets. Cue sheets list each music cue with its exact length (in minutes and seconds) and a description of how it was used in the film. The usage could be background instrumental, main title (opening credits), featured performance, or variations of each. Cue sheets also list who wrote/composed the music and that composer's respective performance rights agency (or "PRO," such as ASCAP, BMI, and SESAC). Cue sheets are used by PROs to assess performance royalties of the score and source music.

TECHNIQUES FOR PLACING AND EDITING MUSIC

There are many techniques used by music editors to make sure that the music is effective. Music is specifically chosen for a scene and reviewed in a DAW to assess whether it works. This instant feedback helps the editor to confirm the choices for certain scenes.

Here is an example of music edited and placed for an independent film:

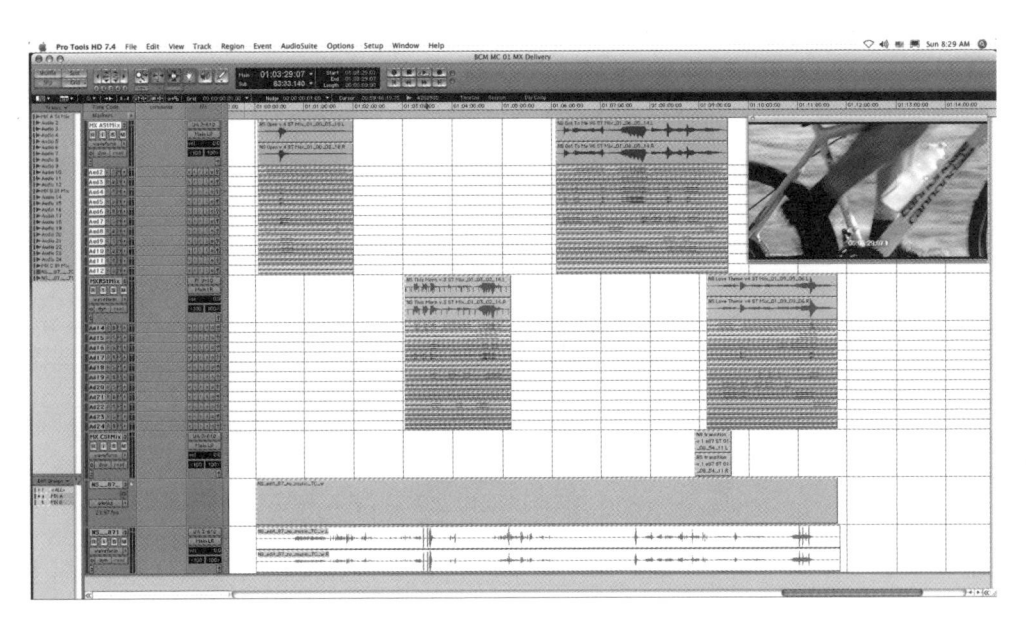

Fig. 9.2. Music and Video in a DAW

In the not-so-distant past, the music editor had to transfer the music from record/cassette tape/CD to mag film or multitrack tape and synchronize that medium with the picture (which was usually on a 3/4 U-matic Video Tape Machine). The process of synchronization was done by an external synchronizing device that would read the time code from both machines while controlling the transport of one to make sure that it constantly stayed in sync with the other. This was a daunting process. DAWs have really come a long way in helping the industry work more quickly and efficiently.

Score music is written in sync with the film, so placing it is not so difficult. The music editor references the spotting notes to see where the music should start and stop, as well as checking any possible sync points where the music is punctuating an action in the film. If the music track is in the form of a broadcast wave file (WAV), the file will be time-stamped, and the music editor can simply drag and drop the file into a DAW, to spot it to the original time stamp. This can save a lot of time.

The music editor may take liberties in nudging the music back and forth in time/placement, if they feel that it will be more effective. This won't work if you have a piece of music that has synchronized action in both the music and picture. These synchronization points are called "hits." A music editor may ask the composer, during the spotting session, whether they plan to hit any of the big moments in the scene. All of this information gets documented in the spotting notes.

The music editor devotes a great deal of time and energy on making songs (source music) work effectively in a television show or film. Songs are generally used during long montage sequences and can really help convey the story line. Music editors pay close attention to the key and tempo of each song to make sure that they don't rub against each other when placed back to back.

Music editors also pay close attention stylistically to the back-to-back songs. Obviously, a high-energy fast-paced punk rock song wouldn't work with a moderate paced polka following it. But composers and music supervisors are constantly pushing the envelope. An example of this is Danny Elfman's opening music to the feature film *To Die For*. The music goes from sweet orchestral to bombastic hardcore metal at the drop of a hat, and it works perfectly with the film!

Making sure that the keys are the same (or similar) and that the tempo and style are similar will help the songs work together. Music editors also focus on parts of the song that don't have too much going on lyrically or vocally. If the lyrics distract from what is happening on picture, the music editor will try to get instrumental mixes from the band/record company (if they exist) or try to find sections of the song (intro and solos) to use so that the vocal doesn't get in the way of the dialogue or story line.

Occasionally, they do just the opposite. A song is chosen specifically because the lyrics and feel actually help to tell the story. In this case, the music will include the vocal and is often mixed louder to help move the pacing of the scene or montage. This tends to be the case with dramatic/episodic television programs. Often, a song is featured over a montage of the characters involved in a story sequence.

There is no set way to use these techniques. Every show and every music situation is different. Knowing that these techniques are available and how to use them to your advantage is the key to working more efficiently.

CHAPTER 10

Mixing Music for Film and Television

The music score is essential in film and television. It acts as an emotional amplifier to magnify the mood in the story. Music can imply a subconscious element far better than dialogue or sound effects. It has a way of bypassing the human's normal, rational defense mechanisms. When used properly, music can help build the drama in a scene to a greater degree of intensity than any of the other elements. It is of little significance whether the scene involves an intimate relationship or a violent fight. Music evokes a gut reaction unobtainable in any other way.

Aaron Copland once said that "background" music is really the kind of music one isn't supposed to hear, the sort that helps to fill the empty spots between pauses in a conversation. This can sometimes be the film composer's most difficult task, as it calls for them to be at their most subordinate. At times, one of the functions of film music is to do nothing more than be there, as though it would exist as sound rather than as "constructed" music. Even though it is filling a rather subordinate role to other elements in the picture, using "filler" type music is in fact a very deliberate dramatic device.

Music can tie together a visual medium that is, by its very nature, continually in danger of falling apart. A film editor is probably most conscious of this particular attribute of music in films. In a montage, music can serve an almost indispensable function. It can hold the montage together with a unifying musical idea. Without music, the montage can, in some instances, become merely chaotic. Music can also develop a sense of continuity throughout the film as a whole, as well as help with its pacing.

MIXING FILM MUSIC

Mixing music for film can be quite delicate. The music has to stand on its own as well as sharing space with room tones, background/environmental sounds, sound effects, Foley, and, of course, dialogue. That said, great care must be taken both when recording and mixing the score.

The *scoring mixer* acts as the interface between the composer, the scoring stage, and musicians. Their main function is to record, mix, and deliver the music score within the parameters of the project and budget. A scoring mixer helps the composer to achieve their sonic vision, while understanding the needs of the film. The scoring mixer also provides the music editor and re-recording mixers flexibility in the score, in terms of changes and the final dub.

One of the first tasks a scoring mixer does is to sit down with the composer to discuss the film score and what the composer is trying to achieve. This includes listening to demos and trying to get a flavor for the score. It is through this meeting that they can start to prepare for the scoring session. Most of the scoring mixer's work is done in the planning process. A good plan will free them up to focus on the performance and balance of the orchestra.

Recording an orchestra requires a great deal of preparation in setup. The mixer and composer will discuss the floor plan for the orchestra based on the demos and the intent of the score, so that the sound complements the music. The scoring mixer uses that floor plan to determine mic selection and placement.

The orchestra is usually recorded as a group. However, current trends have included recording the orchestra in layers or sections. Recording in layers gives the scoring mixer a better sense of control. Sections are more easily dealt with, and the music editor will have more flexibility while preparing for the final dub. The downside of recording in layers is that it sounds different, with regards to intonation and dynamics. The timing suffers a bit, as well as the overall balance and impact. Orchestral musicians generally grow up playing with other musicians. They are more comfortable playing in groups and tend to use that interaction for their pitch, dynamics, and overall balance. Working in sections tends to throw that off a bit, and thus can introduce additional issues for the scoring mixer to address in the mix.

When the score has been completely recorded, the mix process begins. Mixing can take a great deal of time, depending on the scope of the project. When dealing with a standard orchestra or choir, the mix is straight forward. If you are using an orchestra along with numerous prelays of electronic synths, samplers, and virtual instruments, as well as alternate rhythm sections and percussion, the process can be time consuming.

The scoring mixer creates the final mix in a surround format so that it complements the film and how it will respond in a theater. The surround aspect is very important, as it gives the music the opportunity to fill the room. There is no set format as to what should be placed or panned to what speaker in the surround layout, but scoring engineers take great care in making sure that the music speaks clearly.

They are also aware of the reality of the theaters where the score will be played back. Not every theater is up to par, technically. Some may have damaged speakers, or one surround might not be working. The music mix shouldn't fall apart in the theater if one of the speakers is out. Therefore, the mixer will spot check the mix with and without the surrounds to make sure that the music will still speak, if a problem should occur. This is not necessarily defensive mixing—just something that a seasoned pro will consider while mixing a film score.

When the mix is complete, the stems are given to the music editor to prep for the final dub. These stems are organized in a DAW, synchronized to the final locked picture. The layout is time-based and is sometimes checkerboarded when the score overlaps. The music editor is always present at the final dub session and acts as a direct interface for the composer, music mixer, and re-recording mixer (who will mix the music for the final dub). Figure 10.1 shows a final mix of a music score for an independent film. You can see the individual stems for each cue, in a smaller size beneath the stereo mix.

130 CHAPTER 10

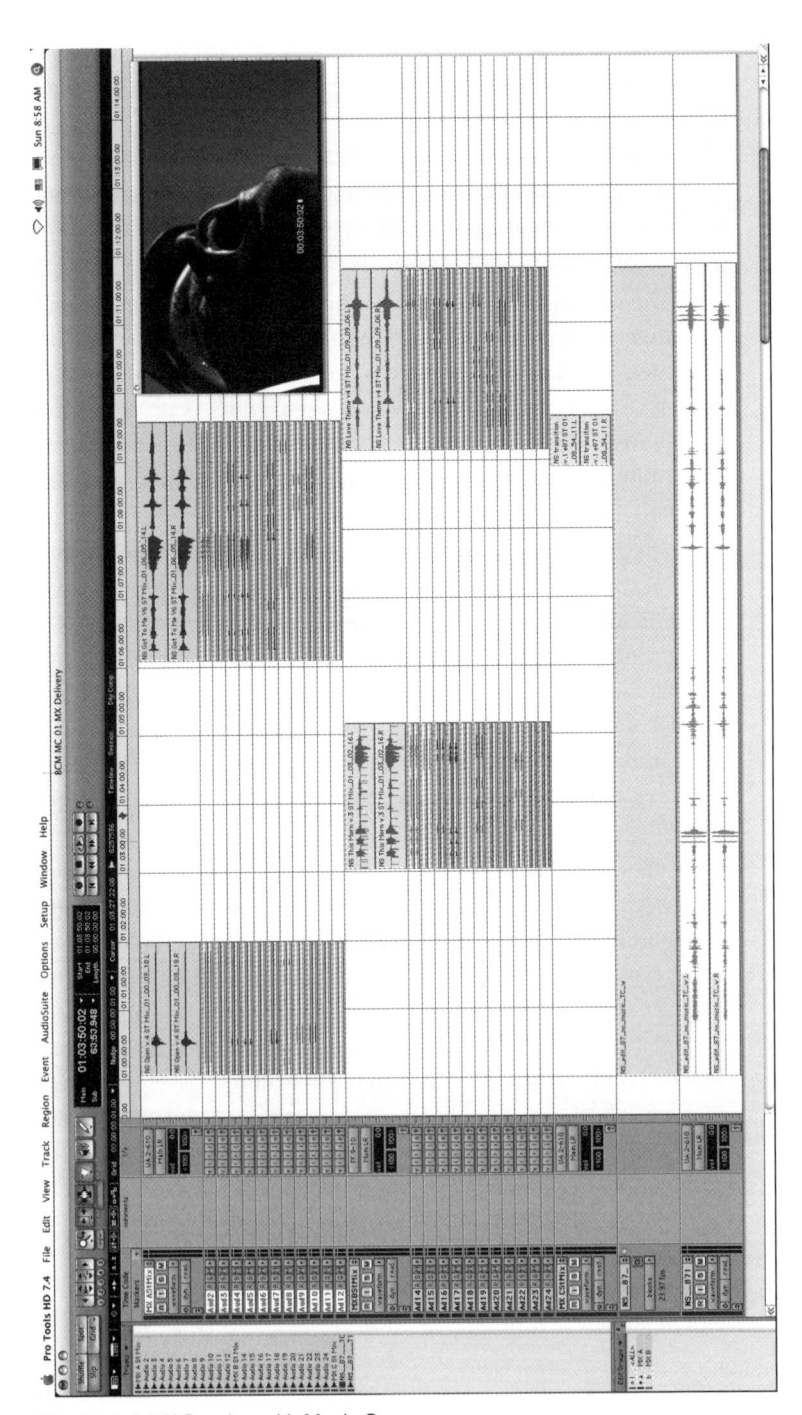

Fig. 10.1. DAW Session with Music Score

THE COMPOSER STUDIO

Contemporary composers use their own studios to create the music for any specific project. A studio might be as simple as a spare room or as elaborate as a dedicated multi-room facility for recording, mixing, and editing.

At its most basic form, the composer's studio will include a keyboard, microphone, and laptop computer with a computer-based music system designed to score music to picture. This system will consist of some form of sequencing/recording/DAW program with the ability to host a QuickTime/digital movie. There are many different applications available to do this (e.g., Pro Tools, Logic, Cubase), and most of them also include a vast array of virtual instruments that can cover the gamut of traditional and contemporary music. Often, composers augment the internal sounds with external sound libraries. There are many options available, and it is not uncommon for a professional composer to have most of them.

The studio gives the composer the ability to create and demo music for projects. The quality of each demo needs to be at a very high standard, as this will help the nonmusical film/television people to get a feel for what the final music will be like. This also helps get music approved quickly. Often, the composer has such realistic sound sources, along with a high level of craft as a composer and manipulator of electronic music, that the demos sound quite realistic—even sounding very close to an actual live orchestra. It is not uncommon for a director to fall in love with these authentic demos in lieu of the real thing.

132 CHAPTER 10

Here are a few shots from a composer's studio. These photos show that each room is set up to be as functional as possible.

Fig. 10.2. Composer Room

Fig. 10.3. Mix Room

MIXING MUSIC DEMOS

There are often opportunities for entry-level engineers and composers to work as general assistants at these studios and learn the craft of creating, preparing, and mixing music for film and television.

There was a movie that a big-name composer worked on several years ago where the sequence-based orchestral mock-ups sounded absolutely phenomenal. The composer had incredible electronic sound sources, along with a high level of craft, and the demos sounded unique and extremely realistic. The director was so pleased with the demos that both the studio and the director gave the "green light" for the music team to go to London to record the score with the London Symphony Orchestra at the famous Abbey Road Studios. They were there for several weeks recording and mixing at a cost of roughly one million dollars.

Upon their return, the music was brought to the final mix (final dub) where the re-recording mixers were creating the final mix of music, dialogue, SFX, and Foley. Halfway through the final dub, the director was starting to doubt the live-recorded score. He said that it had lost its emotional impact and couldn't understand why.

The music editor returned to the original demos that the composer had created earlier in his studio. The director exclaimed, "There's the score!" This "demo-itis" happens a lot in the music industry, and fortunately the music editor was a seasoned pro and knew exactly how to handle it: he used a combination of the two.

When everything was said and done, the film used over 90 percent of the original electronic demos in lieu of the million dollar LSO score. It wasn't because the LSO score wasn't fantastic. It was! But the director simply fell in love with the demos. His decision was based on how he reacted emotionally to what he was experiencing musically while watching the film.

The interesting backlash of all of this is that those demos were originally mixed by a young entry-level assistant engineer/ intern, hired by the composer to simply keep the studio clean and occasionally mix some demos, while learning more about scoring and mixing film music. The situation gave the assistant a huge screen credit and elevated him to scoring-mixer status almost overnight!

MIXING IN STEMS

Mixing music for film and television is a little different than mixing music for purely audio recordings. Most music soundtrack projects require *stems*, along with the surround or stereo mix. Stems are the individual premixed elements that make up the final mix. Stems are preferred so that the mix can be altered when added to SFX, Foley, and dialogue tracks in the final dub. Those elements may not be fully available when creating the final music mix. The scoring mixer might have a reference dialogue track with rough cuts, but it usually won't include all of those elements in their final state of preparation.

It is interesting how a room tone or background ambience can affect strings or synth pads in a mix. This can be said for many elements. With that in mind, the scoring mixer will need to provide stems of the music mix so that the re-recording mixer can adjust the music's level without affecting the integrity of the final music mix.

The scoring mixer must pre-analyze the music when creating stems for the final mix. If the music contains orchestra, synth pads, loops, guitars, drums, piano, and cello, will it be necessary to provide each of those stems to the re-recording mixer? This should be discussed in advance, and sometimes there is a limit to how far a mix can be split out.

LOCKED PICTURE

Locked picture occurs when the final film edit has been made and approved by the director. Then, the post-production team can finalize and conform their elements. This is slowly becoming more and more of a nonreality. Directors are sometimes cutting picture all the way up to the bitter end of the final dub.

Locked picture is very important when scoring is addressed, as the tempo-based score is synchronized and written to support— and even punctuate events in—the film. If a piece of music is written to support a certain film sequence, and the sequence is later edited, the timings will not hit the punctuations, and the music and picture will appear out of sync. Additionally, snipping a few seconds here and a few frames there will make the music sound disjointed and choppy. Therefore, the music scoring session has to be done to locked picture.

There are occasions when the score is done to locked picture and then the picture is edited again. In these cases, the music editor will come onboard and edit/manipulate the final mix stems to make it work with the new cut. I have experienced this, on occasion, working on the television show *ER*. We usually received a QuickTime movie for scoring of a finished episode that was marked "Final Locked Avid" (referring to the film editing platform they were using and indicating that the picture was locked). One day, I received an episode marked "Final Locked Avid," and began the process of scoring and mixing the show's music. The following day, I received a new QuickTime movie of the same episode marked "Final Locked Avid V. 2." I thought that it was a joke and wasn't sure how the studio was defining the word "Final." Sure enough, it was no joke: they were still editing—long after they announced they were finished!

PRE-RECORDS/PRE LAYS

Scores often morph together a live orchestra with electronic synths, samplers, and loops. When done correctly, this can be quite unique and complementary. In order to be effective, a substantial amount of preparation is in order. All of the electronic elements need to be pre-recorded, to both locked picture and the final click/metronome. This final click will be used in the scoring session, so that the conductor can reference the tempo and conduct the orchestra accordingly.

The synth/electronic elements need to be recorded first, individually, as separate tracks without effects so that the mixer can treat them when they are mixed with the live orchestra tracks in the final mix. Additionally, synths need to be provided premixed as stems (final mixes with effects, such as delay and reverb). The stems let the mixer easily reference them, as well as feed them to the conductor and the orchestra at the scoring date to help them hear what they are performing along with. Having these stems as final mixes gives the conductor, orchestra, mixer, etc., a reference for how the tracks will eventually sound when mixed together with the orchestra.

Accessing these premixed stems on just a few faders makes it easy for the scoring mixer to mix and reference them quickly. There is never time during a scoring session for an engineer to get a quick synth mix together for the orchestra to play with. Imagine having 110 people making triple scale on a high-dollar scoring stage, waiting for you to prepare a mix before they can start playing. That will never happen! So, *pre-records* are prepared in advance of the session, to make better use of everyone's time.

All of the pre-records must be thoroughly completed with locked picture and click so that the orchestra can play along and overdub to those tracks. These pre-records are located on a separate DAW that also hosts the video. When the orchestra is ready to record a pass, the DAW session begins, cueing the picture and playing back the click and pre-records. They are routed to the proper headphones and monitors for reference, and the orchestra performs along with them. The click, pre-records, and orchestra then record to a separate DAW, with the pre-record stems and click as references.

CLICKS

The click/metronome is just as important as the pre-record tracks. It is the tempo reference for the orchestra. When you have pre records with an orchestra, the actual scoring session is really an overdub session, with the mixer adding orchestra to the pre-records. The click is fed to the conductor's headphones to facilitate conducting the orchestra in sync with the picture.

If the orchestra is also hearing the click track, there will often be a specific engineer on the scoring stage mixing the clicks. This is to make sure that the headphone click level isn't too loud during soft/delicate sections and loud enough to be heard during intense/loud sections, but without being so loud that it leaks from the headphones into the mics. Film music is very dynamic and can go from a whisper to scream. Having a dedicated mixer available to ride the click level can make all the difference. The scoring mixer may have to do this while recording the orchestra on smaller budget projects.

RECORDING AND LIVE MIXING (ORCHESTRA)

Recording and mixing a live orchestra can be very demanding. The session can involve anywhere from sixty to a hundred or more musicians, along with the key players in the film (director, producers, picture editors, composer, orchestrators, etc.). It can get very tense. Having a calm and organized demeanor is often among the best attributes a scoring mixer can have. Everyone looks to them for feedback on how the session is going and sounding.

Recording the Orchestra, Demystified

When I was starting out in post production, I gravitated towards film music. The studio where I was working did a lot of score mixing but wasn't set up to score a large orchestra. As I worked with the mixers who came through, they noticed my interest, and one finally invited me to an actual scoring date at the Sony Scoring Stage in Culver City, California. This was one of the best sounding stages in the history of film music and had hosted numerous film scores, from *The Wizard of Oz* to *Titanic*.

I was very excited to be there, and upon walking in, I saw close to a hundred musicians and almost as many mics set up around where they were to perform. I had never seen a session of this size and caliber before, and it took me a bit by surprise. My engineer friend invited me to sit near the large mixing desk in the control room as the session began.

I wanted to ask him about mic technique for orchestras! How could one mixer balance all of that while capturing the orchestra and get a great playback mix simultaneously? There were so many questions that I wanted to ask. However, I decided to wait for a more appropriate time to address them. As he recorded the orchestra cue by cue, I observed that he was really only moving three to five faders, most of the time. He was very calm, despite a lot of chaos that was going on around him and kept the session flowing.

I started asking him about all of those mics during our lunch break. They all came up on the console (close to a hundred inputs), but he seemed to focus on the same three to five mic returns most of the time. He laughed and pointed to a large crane-type mic stand that held the three mics in question above the conductor. "That's the Decca tree," he explained. "I refer to that, along with a stereo pair of surround mics, for a majority of the sound." (More on the Decca tree in a moment.)

He then went on to explain that it is the conductor's job to balance the orchestra. That has been the case for hundreds of years. The conductor, along with the composer and orchestrators, make notes and suggestions to the orchestra on each performance until they perform it in a way that works best for the film.

He said, "I simply set up three great mics (in this case, three vintage Neumann M 50s) above the conductor's position in a great room, send them to three great mic pres, and get out of the way. These are some of the best musicians on the planet, playing music written and orchestrated by some of the best composers in the world." It is really hard to screw that up.

That made complete sense. Later that day, he suggested that I go out into the room where the musicians were to get a better feel for the actual sound. I was blown away at what an incredible sound they made. He was right. The conductor and the musicians do all of the work. He simply captured it and got out of the way. He was able to combine those three mics along with another stereo pair for a wide left and right to create a perfect balance of the orchestra. He then sent the mix to a high-end digital reverb, and the result was a lush and rich-sounding film score, walla!

But what about all of those other mics? The scoring mixer used them at low levels to add some depth to the overall sound, but mostly they were there in case he needed to feature a soloist or section of the orchestra that wasn't speaking very well. This can happen from time to time, and it is nice to have individual as well as section control to add to the sounds when needed.

THE DECCA TREE

The *Decca tree* is a technique that involves a special mic stand (also called the Decca tree) that is sturdy enough to hold three mics. A Decca tree setup includes three omnidirectional microphones in an upside down "T" pattern. The left and a right mics are placed about six feet apart, and the third is placed three feet out and centered in front. To mix, the side mics are panned hard left and right, and the middle mic is panned center to build in the stereo center image.

The Decca tree was originally used in orchestral situations, fitted on a tall boom and placed above and around the conductor. It is set up roughly thirteen feet above the conductor, and the mics are equally spaced from each other.

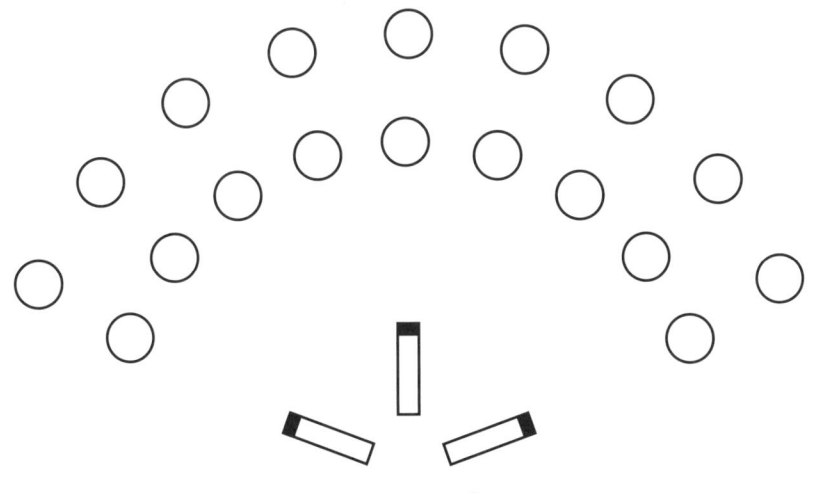

Fig. 10.4. Decca Tree

The theory behind the Decca tree is that the conductor is actually mixing/balancing the orchestra, and the engineer is simply capturing that sound. Given that, this is the optimum mic placement for recording the best possible overall sound. The engineer will often complement these mics with sectional spot mics. This is so they have the ability to raise the volume of a certain section (the strings for example) or to bring out a soloist (flute, cello, or percussion). About 90 percent of the orchestra sound will come from the Decca tree, and the rest will be available through these spot mics.

Here is a Decca tree setup for stereo (no center mic):

Fig. 10.5. Decca Tree Setup

The orchestra tracks are sent (along with the click and the pre-records) to a separate Pro Tools rig—likely a maxed out HD rig to facilitate numerous inputs. The track count can get quite large when you add up all of the spot mics, the Decca tree, the wide left and wide right surround mics, and the pre-records, along with the click. You may be adding a choir to this, as well as an alternate rhythm section.

THE MIX/DELIVERABLES

When all music is recorded and overdubbed, the scoring engineer will prepare a lush surround (5.1) mix that complements the film. Often, the film's dialogue and effects will be monitored and referenced throughout the mix to make sure that all of the elements are working well together. The mix is almost always stemmed out. The track count of the stems is often based on the track availability for music at the final dub.

The mix is printed to an additional DAW (depending on the track count). If the track count is small, it may be printed directly to a few newly created tracks for delivery. If the track count exceeds your availability, a new system will be used. Regardless, it is good to be organized and keep track of what is going where. Organization at this level makes all the difference.

Here is an example of a final film music stem mix:

Orchestra	5.1
Choir	5.1
Perc Hi	LCR
Perc Mid	LCR
Perc Lo	LCR
Drums	LCR
Rhythm Sect.	5.1
Synth Pads	5.1
Loops	LCR
E. GTR	LCR
ACG	LCR
Solo 1	LCR
Solo 2	LCR
Solo 3	LCR

Capturing and mixing music for film and television is a very involved process. This is mainly due to the nature in which it will eventually be combined with the dialogue and effects. There are many different factors in play throughout this part of the process. That said, it is a great career to pursue if you have a passion for both mixing music and audio post production.

CHAPTER 11

The Pre-Dub/Temp Mix

THE PRE-DUB/TEMP MIX IN FILM

The *pre-dub* process is usually the mix engineer's introduction to the material that they will be mixing. The main goal of the pre-dub is to combine and submix any common elements into stems to create a more manageable track count for the final dub. The pre-dub session will make all the difference in the pace of the final dub. A feature film may consist of hundreds of tracks of Foley, sound effects, dialogue, and music, and it is a daunting task to mix all these different elements. To streamline this process, the sound supervisor or co-producer will schedule a pre-dub session. At that session, the pre-dub mixers sift, sort, organize, and become familiar with these tracks. In a feature film, they will also create a *temp mix* for the project—a quick rough mix of the pre-dub's stems.

As a film matures from the dailies and becomes the first rough cut, the sound evolves too. The sound at this stage is usually rough and unedited production sound. This rough cut is a very important milestone in the post-production process, as it allows the key participants (director, producers, picture and sound editors, etc.) the opportunity to see the film in its embryonic state. The rough cut acts as a barometer for the project's progress.

Often, the rough cut will include a rough mix of the audio as well. This rough audio mix is called the *temp dub*. Like the rough cut, it is edgy and raw. There is usually a small amount of time set aside for producing this mix, and no one expects it to be as slick and as balanced as a final dub. Those viewing it focus more on the big picture than the roughness of it. There are techniques in understanding how to view a rough cut, but mostly, it involves looking past the subtle inadequacies and visualizing all of the possibilities in creating the finished product. More importantly, it helps everyone make decisions on how to proceed.

A feature film may have several temp dubs that morph and mature in form. Each temp dub provides a template on which to improve the next temp dub. The audio quality gets better and better as more and more of the final elements become available. A screening session follows each temp dub and will include all of the key participants, and occasionally, an independent focus group. The focus group's purpose is to give an alternate and objective point of view as to what the film is doing emotionally and how it is being perceived.

Re-recording mixers refer to temp dubs as "preliminary" rather than "temporary." The DAW sessions and the resulting mix data become part of the next temp dub, and they eventually go on to become the pre-dub and final dub. Early on, the mixers try to get an overview of the mix's status and the possibilities of where it can go. At this stage, the dialogue stem(s) should be pretty close to finished.

Temp dubs often serve as a vehicle in which to start pre-dubs. Pre-dubbing is an integral part of the mixing process. In feature films, some sequences, such as action sequences, commonly have hundreds of tracks of effects and dialogue. Since the number of tracks far exceeds the capabilities of a mixing console, a premixing session is in order. By doing a pre-dub, the mixer can more easily control the different audio elements during the final mix, making the process much more cost effective and time efficient. Separate pre-dub sessions are usually done for dialogue, music, and effects. Pre-dubs facilitate the final mix by reducing the number of source tracks and by bringing all the various audio sources closer to their final mix levels.

THE PRE-DUB/TEMP MIX IN TELEVISION

In television, pre-dubs are even more important because of the time factor. Without a pre-dub, the re-recording mixer has to mix many tracks and make decisions for the sound mix on the fly. It's very difficult to not be familiar with material and yet be expected to nail a mix session while creative executives sit behind you. The pre-dub gives the mixer time to focus on any aspect of the mix and establish a consistent sound and level for that element, like the dialog is smooth, balanced, and intelligible, and has an overall continuity from scene to scene. That said, all of the various audio sources are brought closer to their final mix levels. Some productions can afford a sound supervisor. This person acts as the liaison between the production's creative executives and the sound house. The pre-dub allows the sound supervisor to work on the sound mix with the re-recording mixer prior to getting input from the creative executives.

When talking about pre-dubs, you need to remember one equation: pre-dubs = more time. The more time a re-recording mixer has with the material, the more familiar they will be with it, be able to perfect it, and be able to provide more options to the creative executives, who will attend the mix session. I have found that pre-dubbing cuts down on the hours spent in the mixing session. Most creative executives don't have hours and hours to figure out the sound of their show, so the faster the better. Also, the re-recording mixer's ears are trained through this process, and it is to the production's advantage to rely on and trust that skill. Plus, it is the best use of money that will increase production value of the show itself.

With 5.1 surround being a home staple now, audiences expect the sound mix to enhance the programming. I think of the show *24* and how different the experience of the show would be if they didn't spend money on pre-dub and sound mixing. The post supervisor on that project spent a week and a half prepping each episode, a day and a half doing pre-dubs, and then half a day reviewing and attacking notes from the creative executives. This is the best example of useful pre-dub time. You can see that the creative executives are mixing for less time than the pre-dub, which is cost efficient.

Creative teams have less and less time to sit through the tedious process of pre-dubbing with the goal of putting their mark on the soundtrack. The picture editor traditionally likes and wants to do this, but it is often a budgetary issue to keep them on full pay to monitor pre-dubs, as opposed to editing picture. Since it is all virtual, with DAWs, they can all put their mark on it in the final dub without it costing more, because it is all a virtual pre-dub. Mixes used to be more written in stone, with analog pre-dubs that then had to be revisited off-line to affect significant changes—with a big collective sigh, as the forty old-school analog dubbers had to be reloaded (with all of the dialogue, music, and SFX) to even listen to the suggested change.

Pre-dubs affect the final mix by speeding up the process and allowing the mixers and producers/clients to focus on creative decisions, instead of technical ones. They can do this in several ways.

Pre-dubs allow the post producer and mixer to build options for effects. Although an effects editor will initially prepare the effects, sometimes there is a need for choices. With an improv or reality series, a pre-dub allows the mixer and the post producer to triple check the dialogue. In these dramatic formats, people are usually talking over one another. The work-print reference cut is a QuickTime movie that will come to the mix with the export of the audio elements. However, this reference is a stereo mix of the dialogue, effects, and music. So, the pre-dub is the time to decide the levels of each track of dialogue, attempting to hear the lines that the creative team intended. With all the characters talking at once, it takes time to set that rhythm in the sound mix.

Quite often, when a creative executive or music editor uses needle-drop music for score, they present two or three alternate music cues. The final decision on that cue will be made in the mix session. But the re-recording mixer needs to properly mix each cue for presentation. This can happen five or six times in one episode.

Also, the overall sound of each scene is checked in relationship to the episode and the precedent of the sound mix of the already established series. Once a show has aired, it has a sound identified with it. This motif needs to be consistent for the viewer, but the mixer also needs to mix each episode and each scene in a way that makes sense creatively as its own piece.

Mainly, the re-recording mixer needs to get the tracks down to a manageable number so that he can navigate through the mix quickly. An effects editor might build six or seven tracks for one moment, but the re-recording mixer needs their tracks simple—only the essentials. They may choose to mix the effects editor's tracks down. The main effect is that it allows the final mix to happen in fewer days. You can have twenty minutes of the show mixed per day, if you use pre-dubs.

Sound supervisors will schedule as much time as possible for pre-dubs, since it's the least costly part of the process. Of course, this depends on the nature of the material, the length of show, turnaround time, and the client's budget. Everything about budget depends on the format of the show. But for comedy television, usually an eight-hour day is budgeted for pre-dubs. If a producer has a tighter budget, then a pre-dub can be accomplished in four hours. This would allow the re-recording mix to at least have a pass at the episode before he or she needs to present it to the creative executives. Dramas can take up to a week of pre-dubbing, depending on the style of the show.

You need a sound stage for a pre-dub, and preferably a *Dolby certified* stage. It is always best to pre-dub in the same room that you mix, if you can. You don't want to pre-dub in a smaller stage with different speakers, because when you move to the stage that your creative executives will hear the mix on, it will sound very different. More importantly, the choices you, the sound supervisor, or the re-recording mixer made in the pre-dub studio might not sound the same. In that case, the pre-dub time was wasted.

In television, a pre-dub session will usually start with anywhere from 8 to 32 tracks, depending on the show. The pre-dub should bring that down considerably. As an example, for *The Hills*, there are 6 to 8 dialog tracks, 4 mono hard SFX tracks, 6 mono BG (background) SFX tracks, 8 stereo BG SFX tracks, 2 stereo-score tracks, 2 stereo source-music tracks, and no Foley. For *Curb Your Enthusiasm*, there are 12 to 16 dialog tracks, 4 to 8 mono hard SFX tracks, 4 mono BG tracks, 8 stereo BG tracks, 2 stereo score tracks, 2 stereo source music tracks, and 16 Foley tracks. The number of tracks varies, depending on the show's format. Typically, the dialogue will stay the same at 4 tracks, with ADR on a fifth track. Effects can expand the most—anywhere from 2 to 10 tracks, depending on whether a lot of action is taking place.

There have been situations where there wasn't enough time for pre-dubs, but mostly for short form projects (promos or trailers under 5 minutes long). *However*, I have been in a situation where the pre-dub wasn't budgeted. Since that experience, I pitch very hard for there to be pre-dubbing time before we even start shooting. The ideal situation is to know a creative executive's expectations for the sound mix so well that the re-recording mixer and sound supervisor can nail the mix. Then, after one playback and some notes, everyone can be out of the dub stage on time.

When the pre-dub isn't budgeted, I ask the creative executives to start their mix at 11:00 A.M., so that I can have time with the episode from 9:00 A.M. to 11:00 A.M. It helps to cut down on the hours of mixing for the creative executives, but ultimately, we will expect to still end up with a lot of overtime on the sound stage on that show.

Also, one thing to keep in mind is that the better sound houses have clients scheduled every day of the week. If you run out of time in the mix session, you won't necessarily be able to return the next day to finish. And if the sound house does have a stage available the following day, you may end up with a different re-recording mixer.

There are many things that you do to prepare for the pre-dub process, beyond simply making sure the mixer has the absolute best source tracks laid out in efficient and intuitive ways. As a post supervisor, the most important thing is to know the cut. You need to communicate, or even sit down and watch the locked cut, with the editor and assistant editor. Review all the sound notes and expectations of the creative executives. Those notes should be conveyed to the re-recording mixer. Then, ask the assistant editor for the cut on DVD, with time code. Give that DVD to the creative executives, and ask for notes from them as well. This forces them to think only about the sound mix and explain their expectations.

THE PRE-DUB SESSION

The *pre-dub session* is the re-recording mixer's first opportunity to get familiar with the material that they will be working with. In this process, they carefully and thoroughly go through each audio track. This can be a long, tedious process, but it is essential to getting the most efficient and best sounding final dub. This initial review also helps in making decisions on how to approach the mix.

Throughout this session, the mixer will organize the tracks, as far as layout, color-coding, naming, and routing, as well as getting a feel for what types of processors will be used. Going through the project and seeing what there is to work with will help to determine if the required reverbs will be tight rooms or wide-open spaces, if your EQ technique will be radical effects or simply employing filters to fine-tune the sound, and if your dynamic range processors will be subtle or extreme.

The pre-dub session also provides a chance to get comfortable with how the location sound mixer and dialogue editor prepped the tracks. Sometimes, there is absolutely no prep.

Trimming

A Trim tool is a great editing feature in DAWs. They usually have several modes: Standard, Time Compression/Expansion, and Loop. Standard mode (which is most common in post) allows you to expand or trim the audio regions/clips. If you have a fade at the end of the region/clip, the Trim tool can be used to shorten or lengthen that too. Time Compression/Expansion allows you to change the duration of an audio region/clip by making it faster or slower based on your grid settings.

Handles

There are many tools and techniques that you can use to clean up tracks. Fortunately, almost all of them can be achieved in DAWs by using any of the stock tools, or by utilizing a plug-in/processor to reshape the sonic characteristics of the sound. We also want to be aware of the available handles.

As discussed in chapter 7, handles are the extra audio available in any given audio region/clip. You can access the handles by utilizing the trim tool to expand the region. This is done by simply dragging the file start or end past the original start or end points in the session. Handles are usually given to you in an OMF or DAW session, especially when that is professionally prepared for you. This is considered standard operating procedure when exporting OMFs, as most systems allow you to choose how long the handles are on each audio region.

Handles are very important. You may find yourself needing more dialogue, music, SFX, etc. in a region when you get an updated cut of the film. You may also want to go into the handles to find elements that you can use for alternate situations, such as re-editing what was prepared for you and needing an additional sound byte to make it work.

Here is a picture of a dialogue region/clip, as it was prepared in the session.

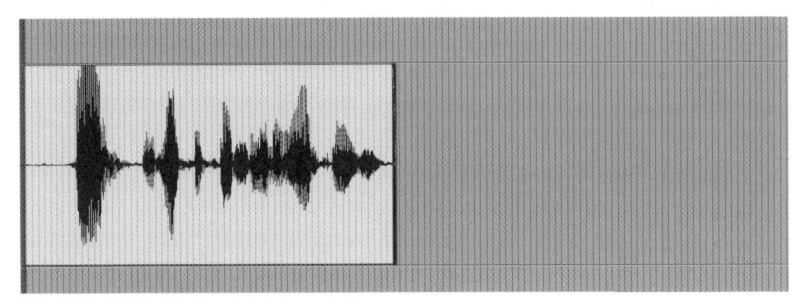

Fig. 11.1. Audio Region/Clip, as Originally Prepared

Here is the same region/clip, utilizing handles, expanded to reveal additional dialogue.

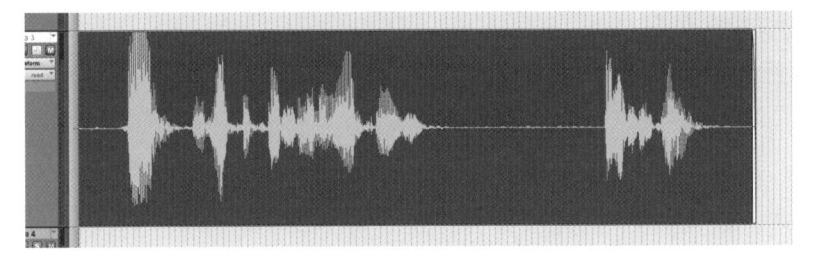

Fig. 11.2. Audio Region/Clip, Expanded

Fades and Crossfades

Some DAWs render each fade and crossfade as a separate, small audio file and store them all in a special folder within the Session folder called "Fade Files." Not all DAWs work like this; most actually calculate fades and crossfades in real time and play them from RAM, as required. Using fades is key in post production. Often, the audio region's/clip's entrances are abrupt. This can cause clicks and pops in the audio. Hopefully, the sound editor has trimmed and applied fades and crossfades to the project. If not, or if you are the sound editor, it is in your best interest to spend the extra time to trim and apply them to each region/clip. This can be time consuming, but it will make everything sound much smoother in the final mix.

Here is a screen shot of a few dialogue units before the pre-dub. You'll notice that they often overlap and have no fades.

The Pre-Dub/Temp Mix **151**

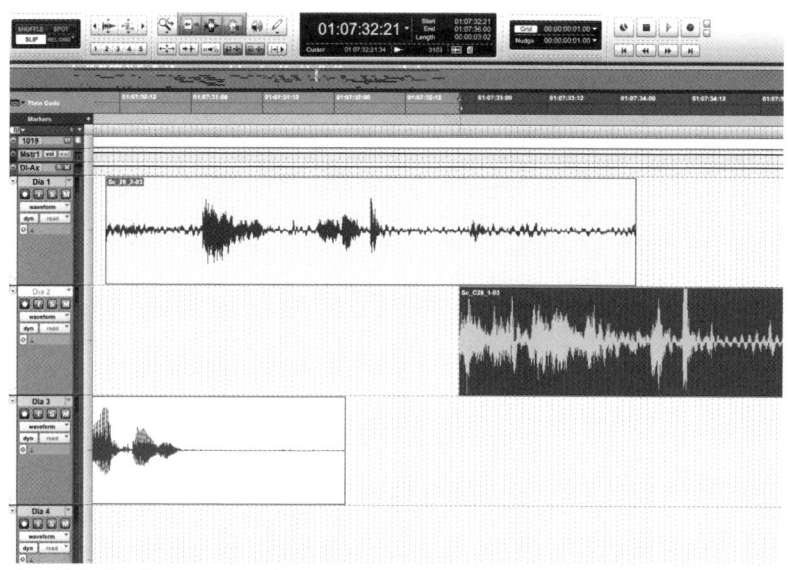

Fig. 11.3. Pre-Dub Regions/Clips without Fades

Here is how it looked after I pre-dubbed the tracks and cleaned them up a bit. Notice how the audio has been trimmed, with fades used to get in and out of each region/clip.

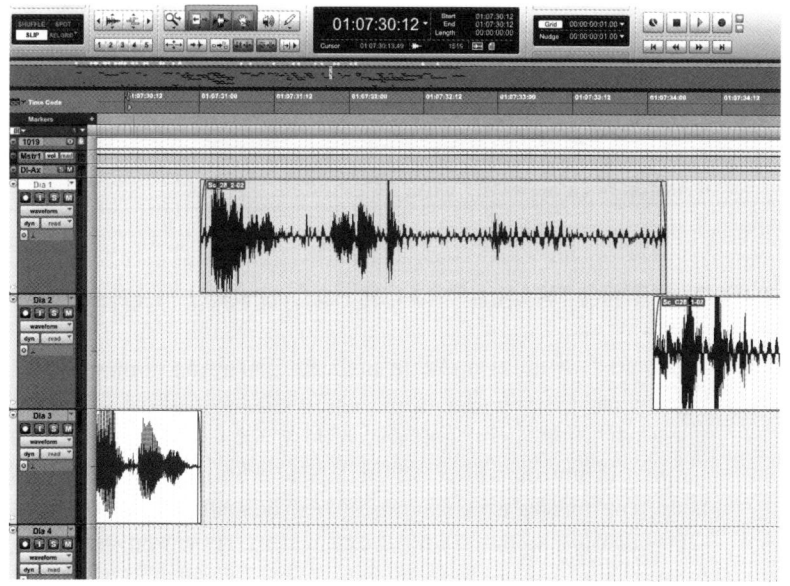

Fig. 11.4. Using Fades

Conforming

As discussed in previous chapters, one of the biggest hurdles faced by sound editors is dealing with picture changes. Every time a picture editor moves clips or changes edit durations, the sound editor must conform the sound mix to the new picture cut. All sound editors, music editors, composers, and re-recording mixers face picture changes on a regular basis.

Here is a common scenario:
- temp mix, preview, change picture
- temp again, preview again, change again
- temp again, preview again, change again

The cycle repeats over and over. Updating sound elements to stay in sync with picture is a laborious and tedious process that steals days and sometimes weeks from the more creative aspects of our work.

When manually conforming a sound mix to a new picture cut, a sound editor imports the picture editor's new picture, along with a stereo mix reference from the new cut into an existing DAW session. Next, the sound editor has to walk through the new edits one by one, comparing the old placement of clips to the new ones (as they reference the new stereo mix from the new cut). Clips in the old mix must be adjusted so that they line up with new cuts in the video. Clips may also need to be deleted or added because a shot was cut or added.

PRE-DUBBING TRAILERS FOR RADIO AND TELEVISION

Let's look at an example of how the pre-dubbing process can go. A few years ago, I mixed some television-show trailers at a post facility here in Hollywood. All of the production was done in-house: video editing, SFX editing, dialogue prep, etc. The trailers were a series of weekly spots, which would be broadcasted on both radio and television. They went something like this: "Next week on show x, this week on show x, tonight on show x...." The spots were 60, 30, 20, and 10 seconds long.

Each clip usually had a separate spot for radio (because the visual effects were no longer relevant). Often, I had to create this radio spot and determine which SFXs were usable.

The picture editor and the producer spent a few days assembling and preparing each cut on either an Avid or Final Cut Pro video editing system. They would grab both video and audio clips from the shows, rip the dialogue and theme music (from either the stems or DVD), and add a series of sound effects to punctuate hits or video transitions and resolves (reverse cymbals, whooshes, and big drum hits). When each spot was finished, they exported the session from their DAWs as an OMF (open media format) file. I could then find it on their server and import it into my DAW session along with the accompanying QuickTime movie.

When a batch of these spots was ready, I would either record the voice-over/narration copy or edit and pre-dub the elements that I was given.

It was very clear to me that the schedule was hyper-accelerated, as the audio prep that I had to deal with was quite rough, and more often than not, it was out of sync. I knew that pre-dubbing this was essential to making it work, because of the stems and splits that were required for final mix delivery.

Our delivery spec was to stem out the audio elements as dialogue, music, and effects. I spent a considerable amount of time simply going through the project, track by track, to edit, clean, and move the audio, as well as trimming and adding fades, as I got familiar with the content. There was no labeling, and there were no track sheets. Often, I would find music, dialogue, and SFX on the same track. At times, it was a bit maddening.

This process would always begin by making sure that I knew the delivery and technical specs of the projects. I had to be certain of the file type, sample rate, and bit resolution, along with the correct time code format and QuickTime codec. With that information, I would start my DAW session (with those specs) and import the OMF. From there I would start my pre-dub process as I soloed and listened to each clip, identifying the elements, while I dragged them to the respective pre-assigned unit tracks that I had created in the template that I created for the project.

As soon as I knew what each region/clip was, I would trim it and put a subtle crossfade on it, so that there were no clicks or pops. Once I had everything where it needed to be, I would mute the SFX and music and start balancing the dialogue. This is a pre-dub technique that I often use to help get the dialogue close to the final mix levels while considering any treatments that may be needed for each element.

When the dialogue was in good shape, I would add the music (in trailers for radio and television, the music is usually very low in comparison to the dialogue). At that point, I would simply start un-muting the SFX and balance them. In television and film trailers the audio is usually ripped directly from the show stems (or DVD rerelease) so there really isn't that much need for treatment as far as EQ, compression etc. I often found that the less processing that I did, the better and more realistic the spot sounded.

I found that the extensive pre-dubbing that I had to do was essential to this situation. With no track sheets, labeling, or roadmaps, I was pretty much on my own. No problem. I was there to mix and the pre-dubbing made all the difference in my mixes. Fortunately, the producers could see what I was dealing with and were very supportive. The end result was that they just kept calling and calling, and I think at the end of the summer I calculated that I had mixed over a thousand radio and television trailers.

In conclusion, pre-dubbing makes all the difference when prepping for the final dub. Whether you are on a feature film, episodic television series, movie of the week, trailer, or small indie film, the pre-dub will make the final mix more streamlined and cost efficient. Fortunately, the big DAWs can handle a large amount of tracks, but it is still a time-consuming and daunting task to sift through all of that material in the final mix. Some of the smaller (consumer/LE) versions of the DAWs have a limited amount of tracks, so pre-dubbing is essential to actually attempting to do a final dub on a smaller system. With these tools and techniques, your pre-dubs will most likely be more focused and ultimately save you time and money in your final dub.

CHAPTER 12

The Final Dub

The *final dub* of a film refers to the final mix of its soundtrack. It is where all of the final audio post-production elements (dialogue, Foley, music, and sound effects) are brought together for this final mix. This mix is also referred to as the "print master." This mix is done on a dub stage—a theater-like environment with a mixing console, in which the mix is created. The final dub and dub stage can vary in size, depending on the project. More on that in a minute.

Creating the final dub is considered one of the final stages in the post-production process. This is the last opportunity to make any changes in sound before theatrical or mechanical release. The people involved in the final dub are aware of this and are constantly monitoring its progress. If something isn't working, this is the last opportunity to fix it.

DUB STAGES

The dub stage for a feature film emulates a movie theater environment with a large-format mixing console in the middle of it. This allows the mixers to accurately assess the mix in the environment in which it is intended to be presented. A final dub for a television show or independent film may be mixed in a smaller version of this or in an edit bay/suite by a single mixer, depending on budget.

The dub stage facilitates monitoring in a surround environment featuring either 5.1 or 7.1 monitoring speaker systems. They are mostly constructed in accordance with the THX specifications for the monitors, screen, projector, and mixing-console placement. A dub stage is by far the best environment to mix in, as the walls, floors, and ceilings are acoustically treated to eliminate standing waves and room echo. As discussed, the basic concept is that a mix created in a THX or Dolby-approved dub stage will sound the same in a THX or Dolby-approved theater.

Dub stages come in all shapes and sizes (bigger for films and smaller for television shows). They are mainly set up to facilitate an environment in which the final viewing is done. Feature films are normally dubbed at bigger stages. For example, a film like *The Dark Knight* would be mixed on a large dub stage (similar in size of a large scale movie theater), because of the length of the film and the large amount of elements to mix in a fast-paced/action movie. However, a popular episodic television show like *Grey's Anatomy* would be mixed on a dub stage a quarter of the size of that, because the project is shorter in length and has fewer elements. Film and television projects also vary in schedule. The episodic television show may take a few days to dub, whereas a feature film may take more than a month. How long it takes is always based on the scope of the project.

Fig. 12.1. Large Dub Stage at Larson Studios in Hollywood, CA. Photo by Molly Quaid.

Television shows and low-budget independent films are often mixed on smaller dub stages. A large feature-film stage would simply be overkill for this, and most of the gear and console would never be used. Also, a medium-sized dub stage would translate better when the program is broadcast and experienced on your home television in your living room. These rooms are smaller but still focus on creating a true atmosphere for mixing audio for film and television. The key to having a great mixing atmosphere is accurate monitoring systems and levels. You want your mix to translate from room to room, and good monitors at nominal levels are a great start. Of course, the studios need to be acoustically treated, but the monitors and levels are key.

Here is a medium sized dub stage, suitable to mix a television show:

Fig. 12.2. Medium Dub Stage at Larson Studios in Hollywood, CA. Photo by Molly Quaid.

Fig. 12.3. Small Dub Stage at Gray Martin Studios in Santa Monica, CA

THE RE-RECORDING MIXER

The *re-recording mixer* is in charge of the final audio mix for a film's soundtrack. This could be a single engineer or a team of two or more, depending on the budget. If there is more than one mixer, they will divide the mix duties, such as one mixing dialogue and music and the other mixing Foley and sound effects. In many cases, the re-recording mixer is also the supervising sound editor and doing the pre-dub as well. This means that they have been involved in the soundtrack throughout the entire post-production process. This is favorable, as they are then intimately familiar with the soundtrack.

Sometimes, re-recording mixers are brought in fresh, at the last minute. In these cases, they must review the most recent temp dub to get a feel for what they are about to mix. The new re-recording mixers might also have a spotting session with the director. This could be as simple as a conversation regarding the demands of the project, though a more elaborate spotting session would be in order if there are special needs and key moments in sound that will benefit from a specific treatment.

These conversations and spotting sessions help the re-recording mixer to create a plan, schedule, and budget to complete the final mix. Preparation is key to making this work, both creatively and within the scope of the schedule and budget. They often act as an interface between the director and the dub stage to create the best sonic presentation of the film's soundtrack. The re-recording mixer will keep all of this in mind when choosing a dub stage that will best suit the project.

The re-recording mixer(s) balance and treat every element of audio. Creating the print master is the last stop before broadcast, theatrical, or mechanical release, so it is important to be detail orientated and thorough. If there are any issues with a sound, the mixers will try to resolve them themselves or reach out to that department head to take care of it. With the advent of DAWs, this is a lot quicker and much more efficient than how it was done in the not-so-distant past.

When a problem comes up, the *recordist* (assistant to the re-recording mixers, equivalent to a first or second engineer) will contact the department head directly and have the solution sent back via the Internet in relatively short order. In the past, the conversation might happen on the phone, and the fix would have to be delivered via messenger. When the fix arrived, it had to be transferred to a medium so that it could be synchronized and included in the final dub. This all required significant time, and it was especially critical then that any fix had to be as close to a perfect solution as possible, or they would have to try again. Timing could be especially problematic if the dub is in a remote area or in a different city, state, or country.

The dub stage should provide a recordist who knows all of the gear on the dub stage thoroughly and can make sure that the stage is working at full capacity throughout the dubbing process. The recordist is there to receive, prep, and load elements into DAWs and to keep the work flow of the dub on schedule. If there is a problem that is beyond their scope, they should reach out to the stage tech (or an outside source) for more help. The stage tech is the chief engineer for the studio and/or facility. They most likely designed the stages and are there to troubleshoot any technical problems that may occur.

The recordist is also in charge of renting, setting up, and resolving any additional gear that is needed for the mix. A good recordist will have a background in electronics, mechanical engineering, as well as an overall knowledge of audio engineering and post production. Recordists interface with the department heads with regards to the dub, so having a good balance of those skills along with the ability to navigate through the different areas in post production is to their advantage.

Today, most mixing is done entirely in a DAW. This gives re-recording mixers options that they never had before, thus allowing them to do some of the editorial-type fixes right there on the spot. The tools available in DAWs allow them to re-edit, replace, or completely rework a sound or sequence quickly and efficiently in the mix. Despite the ease and flexibility of the DAW and skills of the mixer, these extra tasks do take time and can really eat into your mix schedule and budget.

A good film mix will be dynamic in nature, with a good balance. The best film mix is one that never calls attention to itself. It should be thoroughly transparent so that the audience doesn't even know it's there. At least, that is the main goal in most cases. This is what the re-recording mixer is shooting for when mixing final soundtrack for any project.

MIXING WORKFLOW ON PRO TOOLS

Today, the majority of my mixing is accomplished with Pro Tools and the Icon console in 5.1 digital audio. I love these new tools. Here are some insights to describe workflows while mixing with Pro Tools. Although I use an Icon console, this workflow could be used with any Pro Tools mixing surface. I am going to focus on the dialogue portion of a temp mix.

Goals

The workflow is designed so that the individual units of the temp mix can be conformed and incorporated into the next temp mix and so on up to final mix. This process enables the filmmakers to retain any components of a particular mix that they would like to keep, remix what they don't want to keep, and add or delete material as the picture evolves. A Pro Tools mix can be entirely virtual, and therefore automation for equalization and plug-in settings can be conformed in the session, just as audio regions are conformed. Let's look at how we set up, mixed, and turned over this first temp mix.

Session Setup

The first thing to do when mixing on a Pro Tools system is check the state of a very important option, "Automation Follows Edit," under the Options menu. If I move a region with Automation Follows Edit (AFE) checked, the automation moves with the region. If I move the region with Automation Follows Edit unchecked, the automation is left behind. The need to turn AFE on or off is determined by the task. For example, if, during the mix, I want to paste a re-edited region to replace a region that was already mixed, I will turn AFE off before I replace the region. This replaces the audio but retains the mix automation. Conversely, if a picture change is made and an editor wants to delete ten frames from the session, they will turn AFE on, so that the automation will move up ten frames along with the audio region.

Next, I copy my personal Plug-in Settings folder into the mix system. For example, this folder contains custom default settings for the plug-ins I use. To copy my plug-in settings folder, I open the Library folder within the computer's system drive and then select Application Support > Digidesign > Plug-in Settings. I copy my folder into the Plug-in Settings folder. Next I need to point the Pro Tools temp mix session to my plug-in folder. I open any plug-in window within my session and select Settings Preferences. I conclude by selecting my folder "plug-in settings_ project x."

CREATING THE MIX SESSIONS

I have a variety of Pro Tools/Icon mixing templates that I use to build different kinds of mix sessions. These templates define the mixing console, including I/O routing, aux sends and returns, output assignments, VCA structure, and plug-in defaults. Let's focus on how to create a basic dialogue track for a template.

I begin by creating a new mono audio track. At the minimum, we will need an equalizer. I like the Digidesign 7-Band EQ 3, as it sounds great on dialogue and maps well onto the Icon control surface. Create an instance (instantiate) of the EQ 3 plug-in. Next, automate all the parameters of the plug-in. Open the plug-in window by selecting the plug-in and then select AUTO in the upper right-hand side of the window. Now, add all parameters to the ADD list. I have an EQ3 default setting entitled DIA.EQ.default that I recall from my plug-in settings folder. Pro Tools will revert to these default settings *only* if we set two anchor points for all settings at the very beginning of the session. The first anchor is automatically created at the beginning of the session, when the session is created. To set the second anchor point, call up the automation settings window, enable all Write Enable options, and then Suspend Automation. This guarantees that Pro Tools will not play back automation but instead will write the new settings. Press Return to take the cursor to the beginning of the mix, and then make a selection one frame in length by typing 1 frame into the Length field of the Transport window. Set all your default settings and then write your default settings with the Write to All Enabled command. This creates the second anchor point and thus functional default settings. Although I have only illustrated a simple template track, this technique is used to create defaults for all automated parameters of the Pro Tools mix template.

The next task is merging the mix template with the dialogue session to create the mix session. Start by copying the dialogue edit sessions to the mix system into their own folder, in this case PRX_DialogEdit_Temp1_091412. PRX stands for Project X. Next, we create a new folder to contain the mix sessions: PRX_Mixd_Temp1_091412. Copy the mix template session into this folder, and rename the template to the project: PRX_R1_DX_Mixd_Temp1_091412. Open this mix session, and bring in the dialogue editor's tracks using Import Session Data. Link to the audio in the

DialogEdit folder, instead of copying it. This avoids duplicating the editor's original audio files. Only newly created audio will be saved into the mix session's audio folder. Copy and rename unit tracks from the template to match the track layout and naming scheme of the imported tracks. Next, copy all the regions and volume automation from the editor's tracks to the template tracks (with AFE turned on!). To do this, select all the regions on the editor's track and use the Grabber tool to Control Drag the regions to the new tracks. Finally, carefully delete the original edit tracks. Check that all session I/O routing is correct. Be sure to check all session attributes (frame rates, audio file formats, pull-up, etc.) under Session Setup, and Save the mix session.

MIXING THE REEL

One of the things I love about mixing on the Icon with Pro Tools is that I can mix with faders or I can mix using the Pencil tool to draw automation graphs. Sometimes, I can mix a musical phrase more accurately by drawing the volume automation up on the first note with the Pencil tool, rather than pushing up the fader. In any case, temps are fast, so I pick the technique that is the best compromise between speed and quality.

TURNING BACK OVER TO THE EDITOR

Once the mix is complete, my mix tech and I prepare the mix session to turn back over to the dialogue editor for the next conform and mix. First, we create a turnover session folder for the sessions we are about to create, naming it: PRX_Turnover_DX_Temp1_091412. Then we open the mix session from within the mix folder. We set all mix session automation to Read and then select "Show All Tracks" and "Sort Tracks by Type" under the Tracks Bin on the far left of the Edit window. Sorting makes it easier to view the different flavors of tracks in the session. We choose to delete all unused tracks and then clear unused audio from the session. To clear audio, we go to the Region List Menu and choose Select Unused Regions, and then Clear Selected (choosing the option to Clear from the session rather than from the drive).

It is important to make sure the session will open on the editor's system and can be easily monitored. For example, the editor's Pro Tools system does not have the DSP power to open a mix session until I deactivate all my plug-ins. Therefore, I deactivate my plug-ins, one insert row at a time, by selecting all tracks. Deactivated plug-in names are italicized. It's in the mixer's interest to disable the 5.1 monitoring paths in the I/O setup and create a monitor path for the editor before he or she turns the mix over to the editor.

If mix routing is changed by the editor, it could cause the deletion of all pan automation. I create an editor's monitor path by going to **Setup > (I/O) > Bus > New Path/Stereo** and naming the new path **Edit Mon**. While I/O is open, I also deactivate all 5.1 outputs by unchecking the associated paths. Then I go back to Mix view and instantiate the Edit Mon aux send in each aux return, such as the dialogue return, reverb return, etc., thereby creating a post-fader stereo editor's monitor.

Next we initiate a "Save Session Copy In," making sure to keep the "Copy Audio Files" box *unchecked* (to avoid duplication) and choosing the Turnover Session folder as our destination. We finish by copying the Audio Files folder from the mix session (all the *newly* created audio from the mix) into this turnover session folder. We *don't* copy the original Edit Audio to the turnover session, because the editor already has this audio. We then copy all the turnover sessions to the editor's drive and open it up on the editor's system, making sure everything will open, all the audio regions link, and the headphone monitor works.

What I have described here is a recipe that I offer for you to follow, modify, or reinvent as you see fit.

CHAPTER 13

Templates

With all of the advances in sound and workflow in DAWs, it is very common to do the entire dub "in the box." Today, mixers frequently work on projects where a number of different sessions are required. There is often a lot in common between each of these sessions, and in these situations, you can save a lot of time by creating mix templates within DAWs, as a starting point.

Templates are sessions created in DAWs that are set up to deal with the similarities in the work that you are doing. These similarities can include advanced routing, plug-ins, and auxiliary and audio tracks. It is common for a mixer to have several different templates for mixing alone. And it is certainly common to create dedicated templates for recording ADR, Foley, and/or pre-dubs.

In a post-production mixing template, the mixer sets up a routing scheme that will accommodate the deliverable requirements for the project. Each project will have a different set of deliverable requirements. That said, we can create a basic template that covers the most common requirements.

I/O ROUTING IN A FINAL DUB TEMPLATE

The best place to start in creating a final dub template in a DAW is the routing (also known as the I/O). I/O refers to the input and output assignments for each track in the session. The I/O section of the DAW should allow you to set up specific pathways to route the signal for a complex mix. In the final dub, you will need to set up to record a final mix (print master) of the project, as well as separate stems for dialogue (DX), music (MX), sound effects (FX), and Foley (FO). Prepare at least one separate reverb for each element, as well as a separate final aux track bus for overall EQ/dynamic-range processing before the signal reaches the final stem.

CHAPTER 13

In the following example we will prepare a stereo template for a final dub. After setting up a monitor path, go to the bussing/routing area to create busses to facilitate a separate stereo reverb for each element, along with a stereo bus (for group dynamic range processing) for each element, as well as a stereo-record track for each element and a final stereo print master track.

Here is a screenshot of the I/O section of a DAW setup for exactly that.

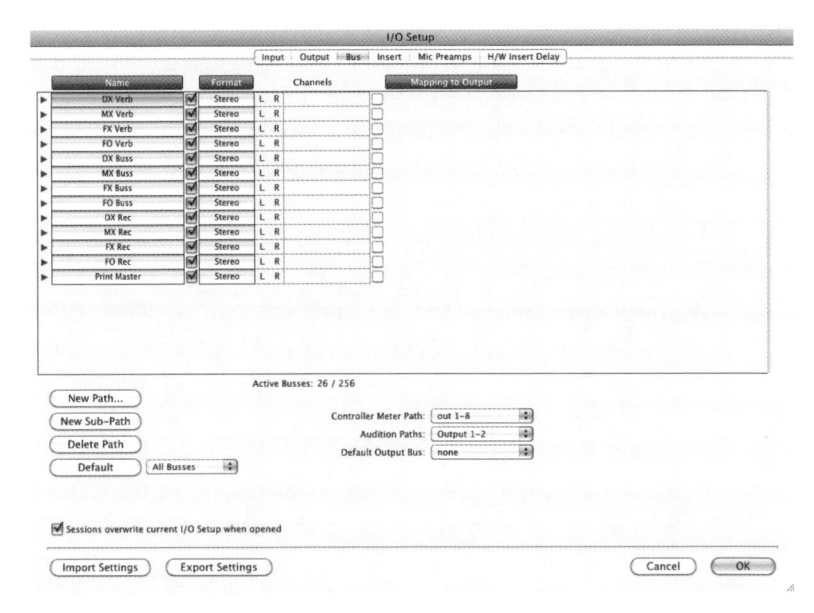

Fig. 13.1. I/O Setup for Final Dub

Looking at the Mix window (figure 13.2), you'll see eight stereo auxiliary tracks (one for each element's reverb and bus) as well as five stereo audio tracks (to record the stems and final mix), along with an additional mono auxiliary track used to test it.

Each track is labeled, and each group is color-coded. This will help you navigate through the session and locate these tracks if the track count gets excessive.

The I/Os of each track are routed as follows:

Reverbs: Input to the reverbs is from the associated reverb bus in the I/O so that it can be easily assigned from the Sends section of an audio track.

Outputs of the reverbs go to the respective groups/busses so that any final group dynamics will cover all elements in that path.

Busses: Input to the busses is from the respective busses routed in the I/O for group EQ or dynamics processing.

Outputs from the busses are routed to the respective track inputs of the stem record tracks.

Stem Record Tracks: Input to these tracks is from the respective record busses created in the I/O. This will be the final recording of each stem/element and the level (fader) will always be at unity gain (0), and there will be absolutely no inserts/plug-in (so that the stems are a mirrored refection of the audio that makes up the print master).

Outputs will be routed directly to the print master track for the final mix.

These tracks will always be in Input mode so that we can monitor through them:

Print Master: Input of the print master is from the print master bus created in the I/O. This is the output of all the stems for the final stereo mix.

Output of the print master is to the monitor path created in the I/O. This is how we will monitor the mix.

The Print Master and Stems will always be in Input mode so that we can monitor through them.

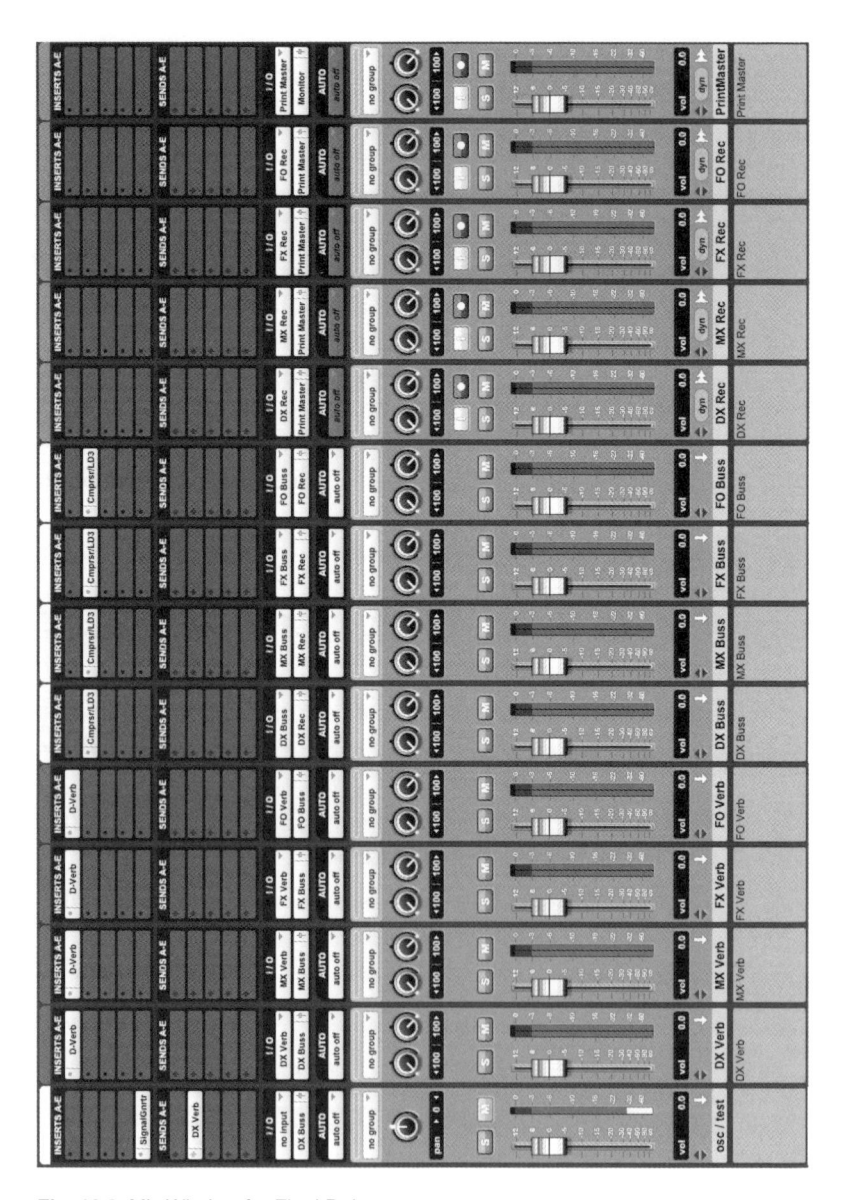

Fig. 13.2. Mix Window for Final Dub

This template includes a few plug-ins as a starting/reference point. These will vary based on the types of plug-ins available in the DAW and to what the project needs. That said, these are basic examples of where you could begin.

The reverb plug-in (D-Verb) is set to "Large Hall Bright." Again, this is not the best actual choice for dialogue, sound effects, or music. However, it works great for initially testing a new session made using a template, as the decay of a massive 6-second reverb is easy to hear and helps verify that the routing is correctly set.

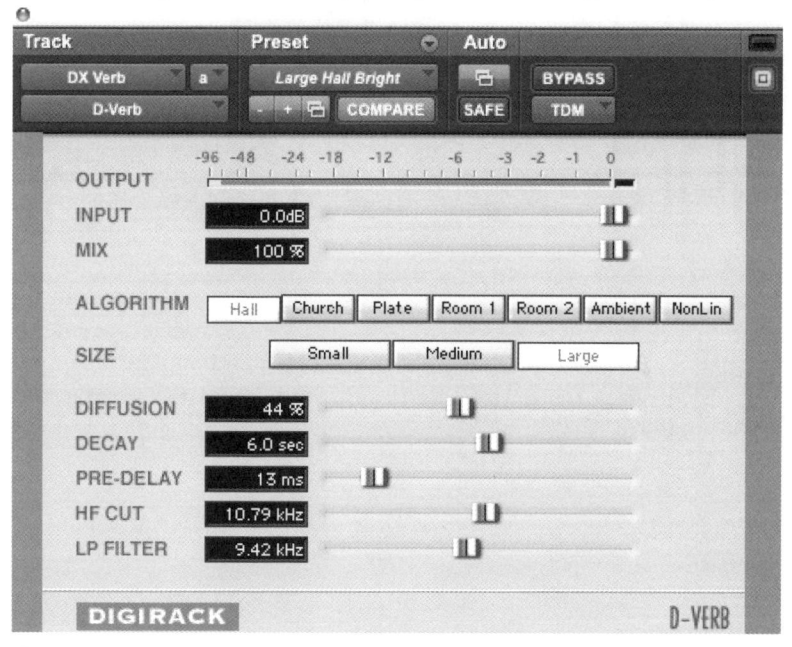

Fig. 13.3. Reverb Settings for Template

The limiters in my template are more in step with what I would use on the final busses. This stage is the last opportunity to do any processing before the signal goes to the Record stem. (The stems can't have any processing on them so that they remain true stems of the final mix.) Therefore, I will use a brick-wall limiter to make sure that there are no audio level peaks that will distort my stems or print master.

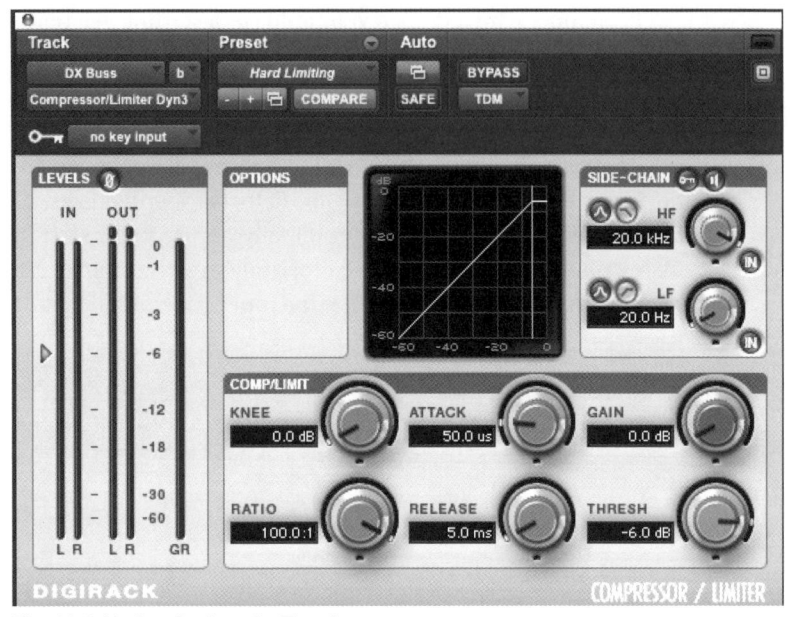

Fig. 13.4. Limiter Settings for Template

The last track that I recommend for your template is a mono auxiliary track. Use this to test your template's routing and effects.

Fig. 13.5. Mono Aux Track for Template

The mono aux track includes a signal generator plug-in set to white noise. Use this to test the template by routing it to a bus and setting up a reverb send to make sure that the routing is correct. Check your session every morning before you begin mixing to make sure that the routing is correct. It is very important to confirm that when you pan something to the right, it goes to the right (visually and sonically). Sessions can get corrupted for no apparent reason, and it is always better to be safe than sorry. This can get more complex in 5.1 mixes.

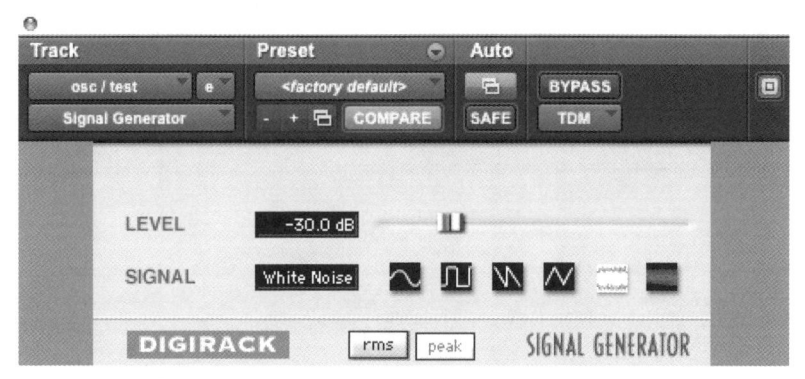

Fig. 13.6. Test Signal

There is nothing worse than mixing for hours and then finding out that something is routed incorrectly. It can be a drag (on many levels) to interrupt the creative mixing process to perform some extensive troubleshooting. Additionally, you may then find that while you have identified and corrected your routing issue, the solution changes how your mix sounds. This adds more time and headache to your mixing, while you correct all of the work done up to that point. This is why I recommend that you check and recheck your routing often.

Figure 13.7 shows a session set up to test the Send to the Dialogue bus, Reverb Send, Stem, and Print master track. You can see that the aux track is routed to the DX bus, along with a send set to unity gain, which sends to the DX Reverb. The levels are clearly visible. You can simply pan the aux left or right to make sure that you both see and hear the results. Check the reverb by simply muting the aux track, listening for the 6-second reverb tail (as well as seeing it in the DX Verb meters).

CHAPTER 13

Fig. 13.7. Template Session Setup

When the session has been accurately tested and is working properly, save it and store it as a template in your DAW.

PLUG-INS AND PROCESSORS FOR MIXING DIALOGUE, SOUND EFFECTS, FOLEY, AND MUSIC

Templates commonly include dedicated tracks for dialogue, sound effects, Foley, and music. These tracks (also referred to as "units") will have dedicated plug-ins inserted and ready to go. For example, a dialogue unit may have a de-esser inserted, with a workable preset waiting to be engaged. A music unit might have a Trim plug-in preset with a volume decrease for importing full-level CDs or MP3s. A sound effects unit might have a compressor/limiter set up to handle the massive peaks of a loud explosion effect.

This is par for the course when setting up a mixing template for post production. This sort of preparation can save you time and money. Your templates get built up over your years of experience. You will find yourself constantly modifying them, as each project that you apply them to will be different in its own unique way. That said, let's take a look at some generic units and relative plug-ins.

DIALOGUE UNIT (DX)

The DX track is set to deal with most dialogue situations. Duplicate this track for however many dialogue tracks that you'll need for the mix. Then, when you import the elements that you'll be mixing (from either a separate DAW session or OMF files from an AVID or Final Cut Pro video editing session), you can simply drag and drop those audio files/clips to these template units, which are pre-bussed and have related plug-ins ready for mixing. When you have moved all of your audio files to the units, all of your routing will have been pretested, and all of the unit related plug-ins will be set and ready at your fingertips.

Fig. 13.8. Dialogue Track Template Settings

The DX unit shown in figure 13.8 has three plug-ins inserted on the track: compressor/limiter, de-esser, and EQ. This set of plug-ins is sometimes referred to as a *DX chain*, a reference from back to the analog days when you would set up a chain or series of processors to help you process the dialogue and make it more intelligible. It is routed to the reassign for additional dialogue processing and then to the dialogue stem. (We will discuss reassigning later in this chapter.)

Compressor ⟹ De-esser ⟹ EQ

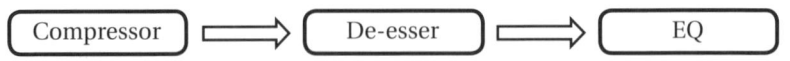

Fig. 13.9. Dialogue Chain

DX Compressor

The dialogue compressor helps smooth out the levels that can fluctuate in a performance. It can also be a starting point for a series of compressors that will follow in the reassign path. Figure 13.10 shows the standard Digirack Compressor/Limiter Dyn3. It is set up for a conservative application with a ratio of 3.4:1 and a threshold that you will set for each character or track.

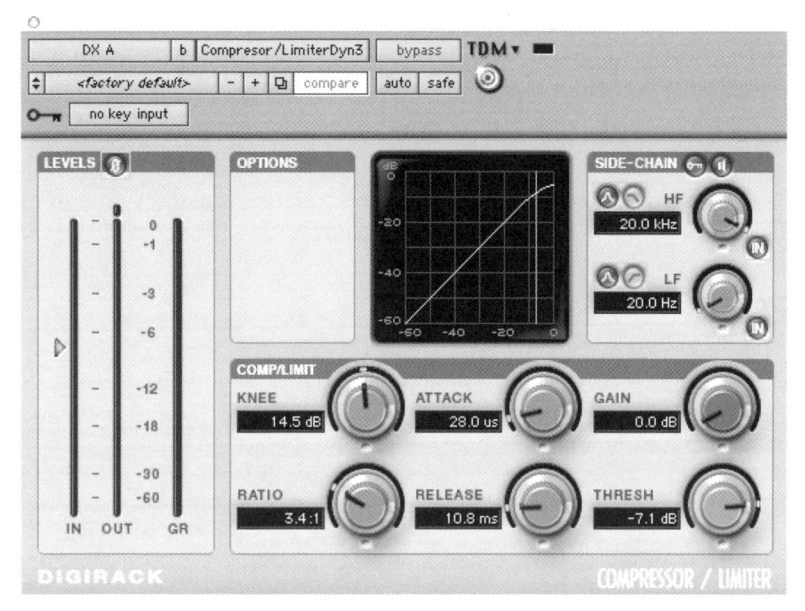

Fig. 13.10. Dialogue Compressor/Limiter

DX De-Esser

The next plug-in used in this path is the Digirack De-Esser, which helps control dialogue that is very sibilant. The S's can be very annoying, and the de-esser helps reduce the effect.

Fig. 13.11. Dialogue De-Esser

In figure 13.11, the de-esser is set to compress the troublesome S's in the 7 kHz range with a gain reduction of 3.6 dB. It is engaging "HF Only" (high frequency) in the Options box, so that the gain reduction is frequency specific. This initial setup should be sufficient—or at least, act as a good starting point—for each character. Sometimes, I will use a frequency analysis plug-in to see what the frequency of interest truly is.

DX EQ

Figure 13.12 is the standard Digirack 7-band EQ plug-in. It is a nice EQ for dialogue, and it can be easily found on any Pro Tools system.

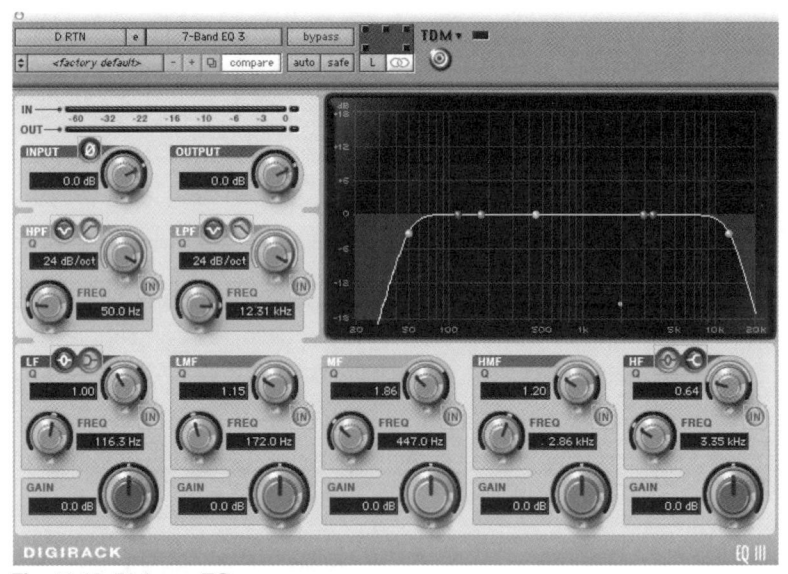

Fig. 13.12. Dialogue EQ

There are a few points of interest with these EQ presets. First, the filters are engaged at 60 Hz and 12 kHz. This is because there are really no useable dialogue frequencies above 12 kHz. Anything below 60 Hz (on a dialogue track) is probably hum from a bad electrical ground or noise from a power generator on location. Engaging these filters will usually improve the sound of the dialogue. Dialogue certainly sounds best and most transparent when treated the least. However, there are situations where EQ can help clean up poorly recorded dialogue, or dialogue with a lot of extraneous interference.

The biggest issue with dialogue is intelligibility. This can be improved in various ways. The subtractive approach is one of the best techniques for EQing a problematic DX track. If the track has too much low end, simply go to the LF (low frequency) section, and lower the preset's gain at 116 Hz—a good starting frequency for dealing with low end. If the track is too boomy or boxy, try reducing the LMF (Low Mid Frequency) or MF (Mid Frequency), depending on where the boominess is, in the spectrum. Both of these preset frequencies are great starting points for dealing with that issue. A frequency analysis plug-in will help you to determine what the frequency of interest truly is.

Intelligibility is the exception. You might try adding a little HMF (High Mid Frequency) at 2.86 kHz. and/or HF (High Frequency) at 3.35 kHz to help the dialogue to be a bit more transparent. Be conscious and conservative in this, because too much EQ will make the dialogue too edgy.

Reassigns

Also, in the chain of the dialogue path are two additional auxiliary tracks with the same compressor, de-esser, and EQ, for further group processing. This is called the *reassign*. The dialogue unit is bussed into Reassign 1 (allowing you to take advantage of this additional processing in series), and then bussed to Reassign 2 (also for further processing). The output of Reassign 2 will then go to the Dialogue bus (that has a brick wall limiter on it) and then to the Dialogue stem.

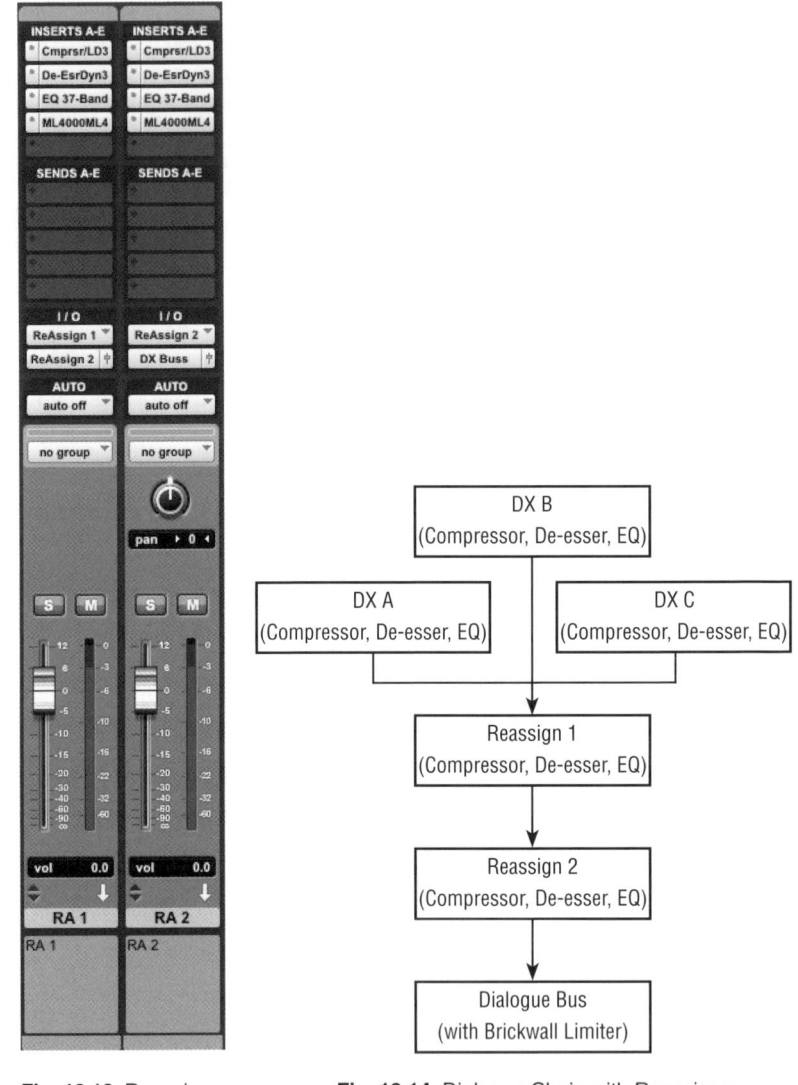

Fig. 13.13. Reassigns

Fig. 13.14. Dialogue Chain with Reassigns

The reassigns are where you can shape the overall sound of your dialogue. Here, you might add an additional and more sophisticated multi-band frequency-based compressor/limiter (like the McDSP ML4000 or Cedar Box). This allows you to get much more in depth with your dialogue processing. All of this dynamic range processing is very common in a dialogue chain.

Fig. 13.15. McDSP ML4000 Multi-Band Limiter

The Cedar Box is modeled after the famous Dolby Cat 43/Cat 4300 analog dialogue processor. It was an industry standard back in the day, and the Cedar faithfully recreates it along with additional features.

Fig. 13.16. Cedar Dialogue Noise Suppressor

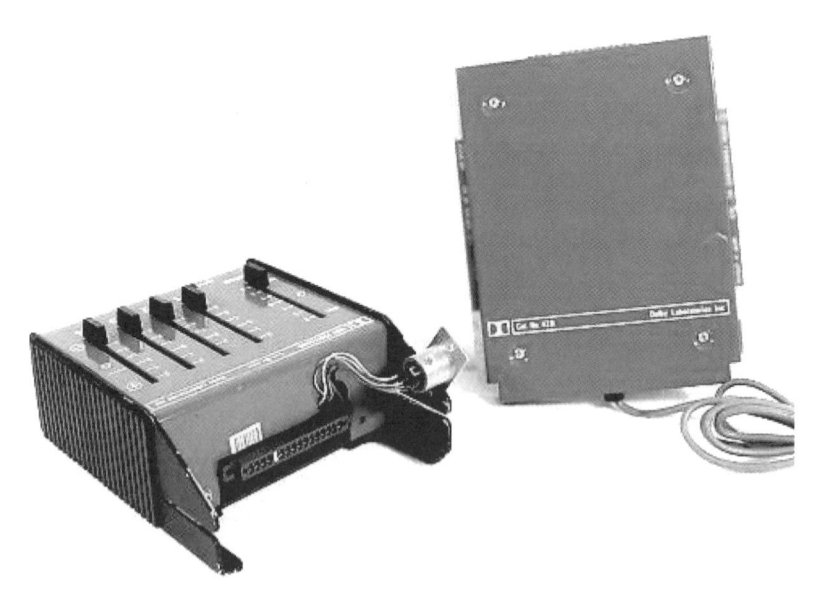

Fig. 13.17. The Dolby Cat 43. This is what the Cedar was modeled after (rarely used today).

FUTZ TRACK

The *futz* track is a Hollywood post-production mixing term for dealing with elements that appear to be coming from or through a telephone, car radio, or another altered sound source. We have heard this many times in television shows and films. Two characters are having a conversation on the phone, and the sound perspective is how one of the characters is hearing the voice through the phone. "Futz" is a reference to old school German directors who would ask the mixer to "futz up the sound" (loosely translated as rough/dirty up the sound to appear that it is coming through a telephone that has a limited frequency bandwidth).

The futz is created by a series of processors (compressor, de-esser, and EQ) like the DX unit. There is an additional lo-fi plug-in (to dirty up the sound) as well as a more radical EQ (to limit the frequency bandwidth along with a boost in the 2 kHz range, as you will see in figure 13.18).

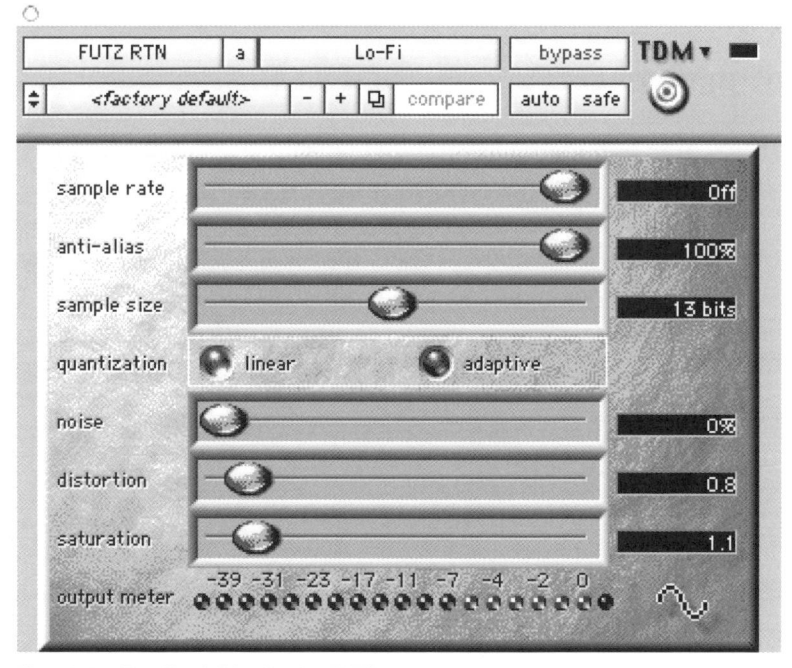

Fig. 13.18. Futz Track Plug-ins Lo-Fi Effect

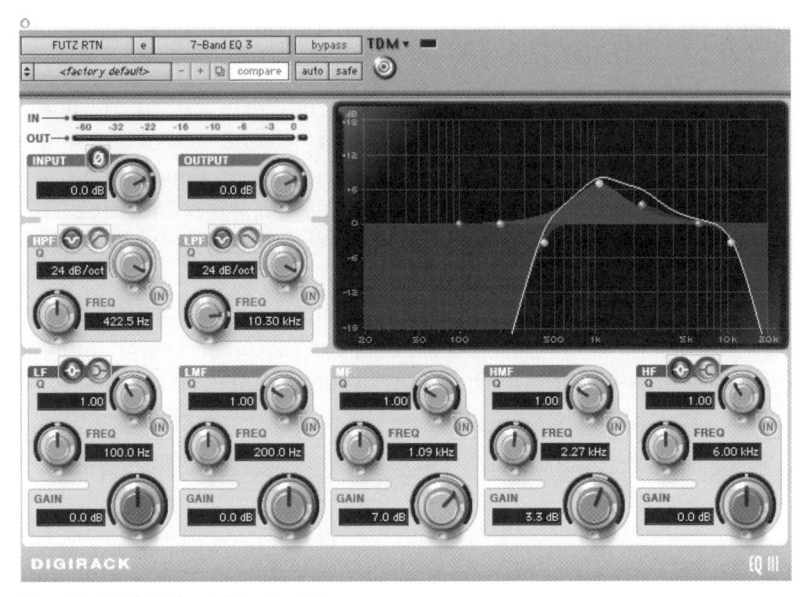

Fig. 13.19. Futz Track Plug-in EQ

DX REVERB

Let's look at a few useful reverbs for the dialogue units. The first is to simulate dialogue in a small wood room. For this application, we can see the Reverb One plug-in using the "small wood room" program in the Rooms section. The key to making this work is the send amount, which should be mixed to taste.

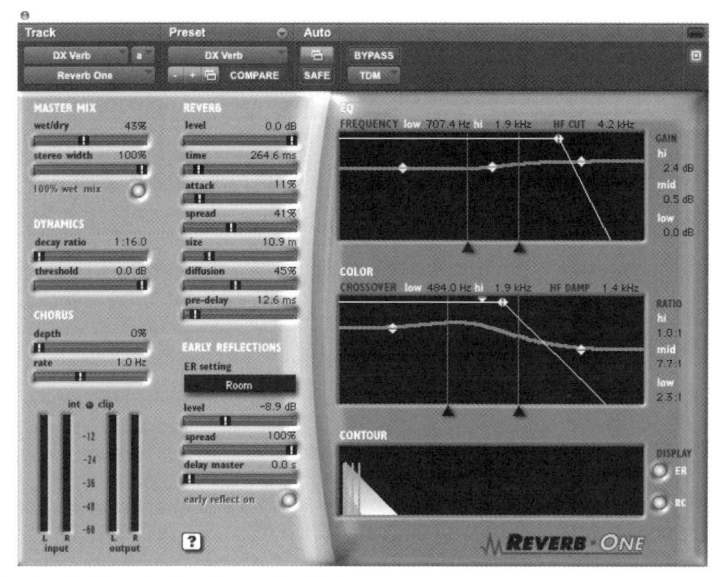

Fig. 13.20. Reverb One Preset for Dialogue

    Next, consider this second dialogue verb, set up to simulate dialogue in a kitchen. For this application, we can see the Revibe plug-in using the "small kitchen" program in the Film and Post section. Again, the key to making this work is in mixing the send level to taste.

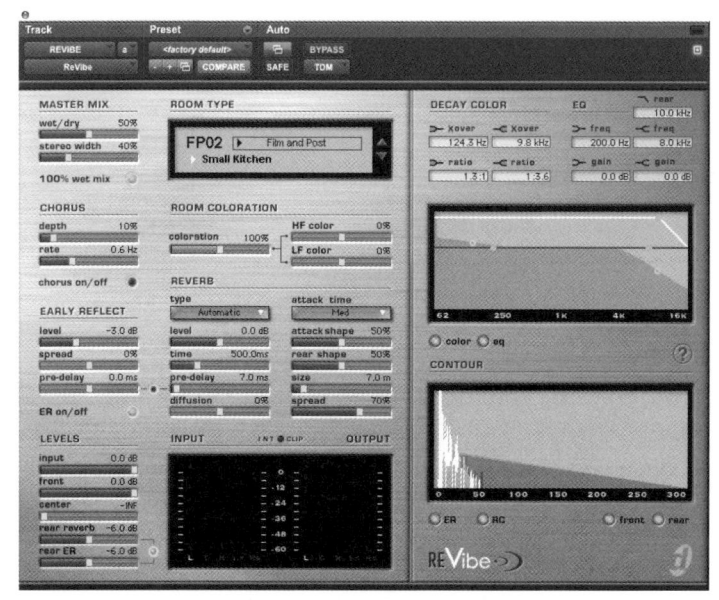

Fig. 13.21. Reverb Preset to "Small Kitchen"

SOUND EFFECTS UNIT (SFX)

The SFX track is set to deal with most sound effects situations. You can duplicate this for however many effects tracks you receive from the SFX editor. The template has two separate tracks: one for mono and one for stereo. There are two plug-ins inserted on each SFX track: compressor/limiter and EQ. This set of plug-ins is sometimes referred to as an SFX chain.

Fig. 13.22. SFX Presets

SFX Compressor

Figure 13.23 shows a preset for an SFX compressor. This will help smooth out audio level peaks that may occur in dynamic sound effects. Shown is the standard Digirack Compressor/Limiter Dyn3. It is set up for a conservative amount with a ratio of 3:1 and a threshold that you will set for each sound effect.

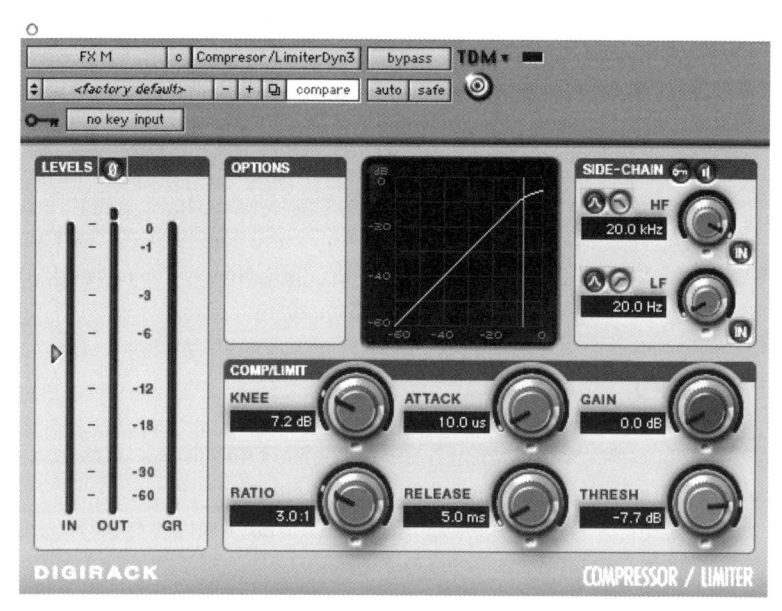

Fig. 13.23. FX Compressor/Limiter

SFX EQ

The next plug-in is the standard Digirack 7-band EQ plug-in. This is a nice EQ for sound effects, and it can be easily found on any Pro Tools system.

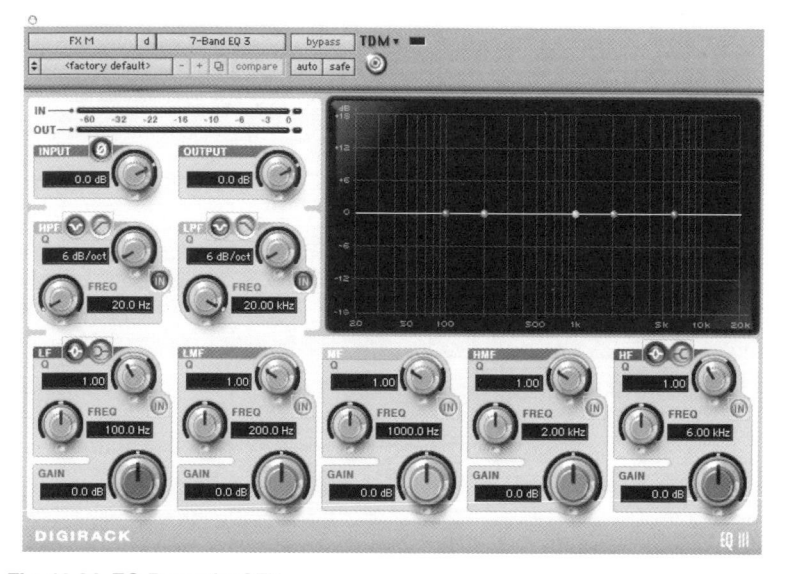

Fig. 13.24. EQ Preset for SFX

Sound effects are usually from libraries and are often premixed with volume graphs (from the pre-dub), when the mixer receives them. The effects often sound realistic, and much of the processing (if any) will be for levels and dynamics.

There are a few points of interest within the preset shown in figure 13.24, if we need to add any EQ. Here, we have the LF set to 100 Hz and LMF set to 200 Hz to boost any low end. Next, we have the MF set to 1000 Hz for any midrange boost. At the top end, we have 2 kHz and 6 kHz, set to boost any high end.

SFX Reverb

The SFX reverb shown in figure 13.25 is the ReVibe plug-in, set using the "Large Natural Studio 1" program in the Studio section. Again, the key to making this work is in mixing the send level to taste.

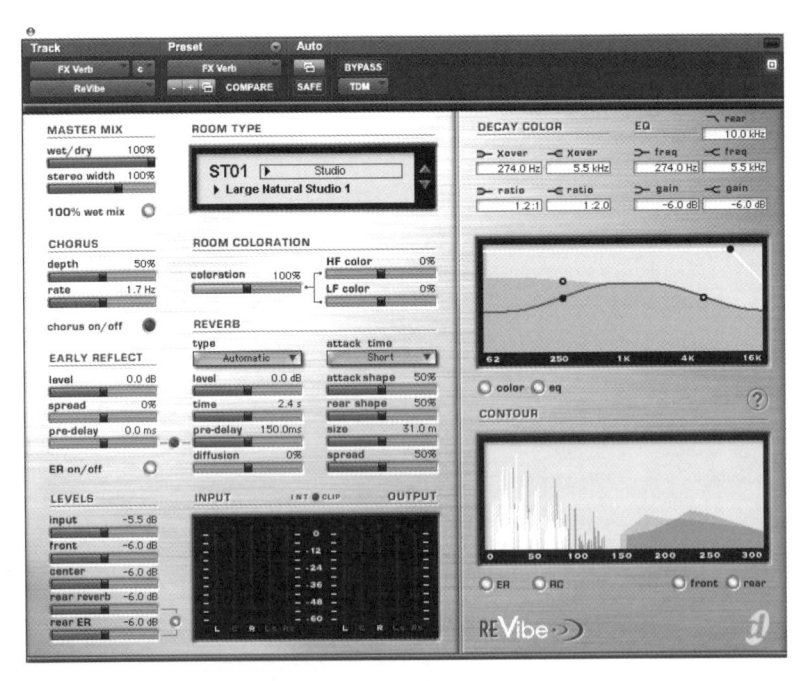

Fig. 13.25. SFX Reverb Preset

FOLEY UNIT (FO)

The preset shown in figure 13.26 is set to deal with most Foley situations. Duplicate it for the steps pass, the clothes pass, and the props pass. There are two plug-ins in this Foley chain: compressor/limiter and EQ.

Fig. 13.26. Foley Preset

FO Compressor

Here is the FO compressor. We will use it to help smooth out audio level peaks that may occur in dynamic Foley effects. This is the standard Digirack Compressor/Limiter Dyn3. It is set up for a conservative amount with a ratio of 3:1 and a threshold that you will set for each sound effect.

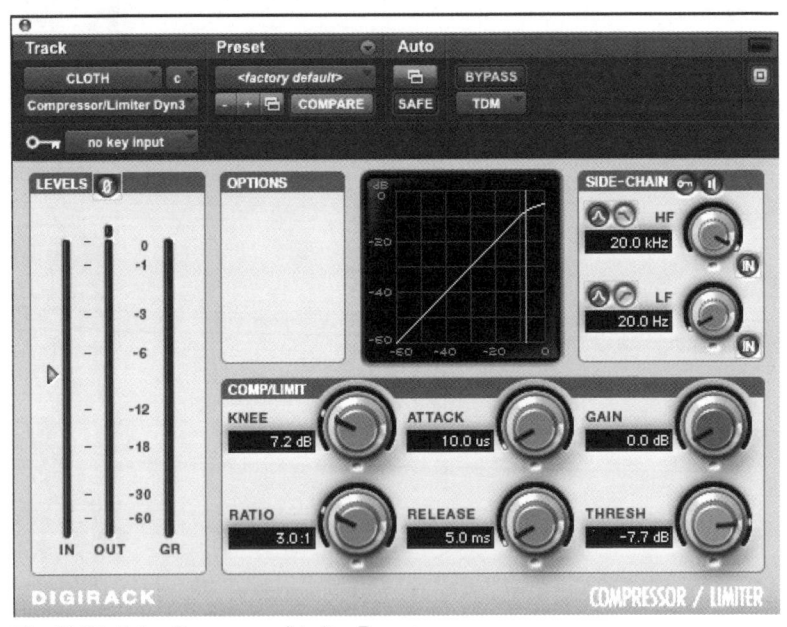

Fig. 13.27. Foley Compressor/Limiter Preset

FO EQ

The first plug-in is the standard Digirack 7-band EQ plug-in.

Foley tracks are often premixed with volume graphs (from the pre-dub) when the mixer receives them. The effects often sound realistic, and many of the processing modifications (if any) will be for levels and dynamics. There are a few points of interest within this preset, if we need to add any EQ. In figure 13.28, we have the LF set to 100 Hz and LMF set to 200 Hz to boost any low end. Next we have the MF set to 1000 Hz for any midrange boost. At the top, we have 1.9 kHz and 6 kHz set to boost any high end.

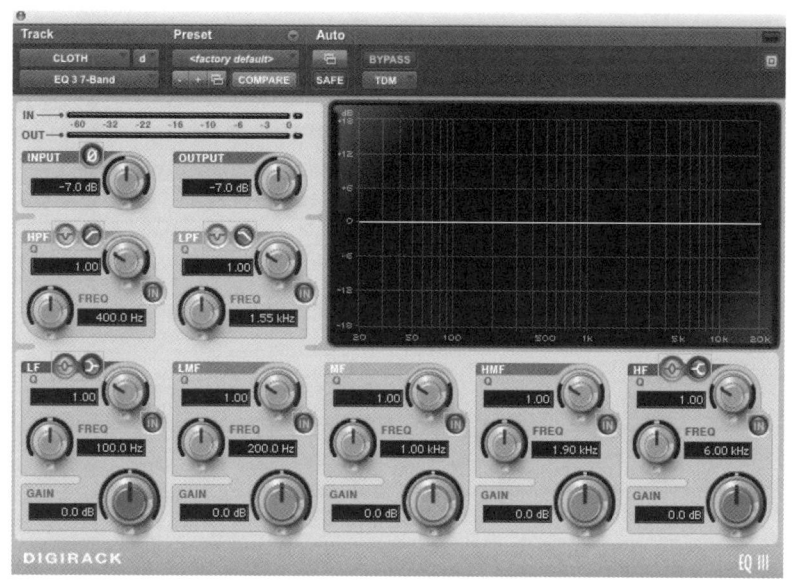

Fig. 13.28. Foley EQ Preset

FO Reverb

This Foley reverb preset includes a medium wood room with a 3-second reverb time rolling off the high end EQ of the reverb. Mix the send level to taste.

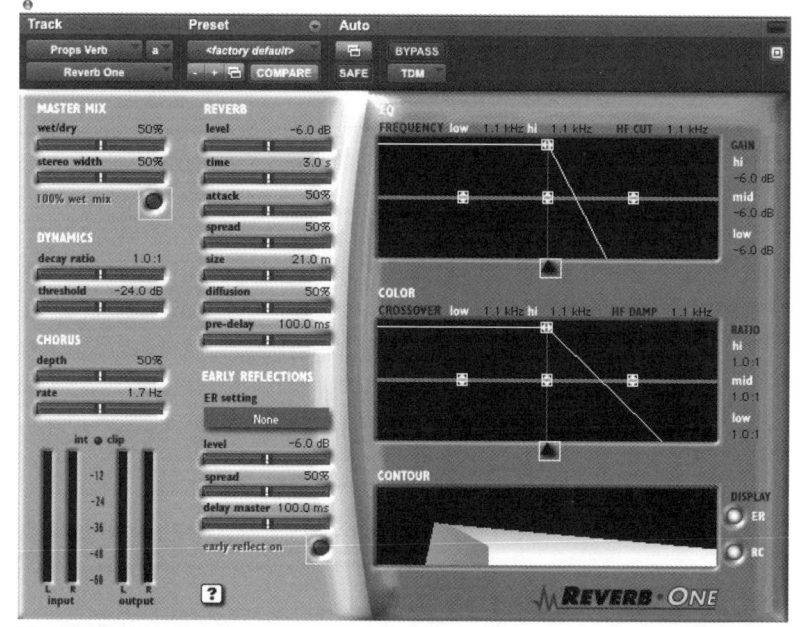

Fig. 13.29. Foley Reverb

MUSIC UNIT (MX)

This track is set to deal with most music situations. You may duplicate this for score and source. It has three plug-ins (Trim, Compression and EQ) inserted on the track. This set of plug-ins is sometimes referred to as a music chain.

Fig. 13.30. Music Preset

MX Trim

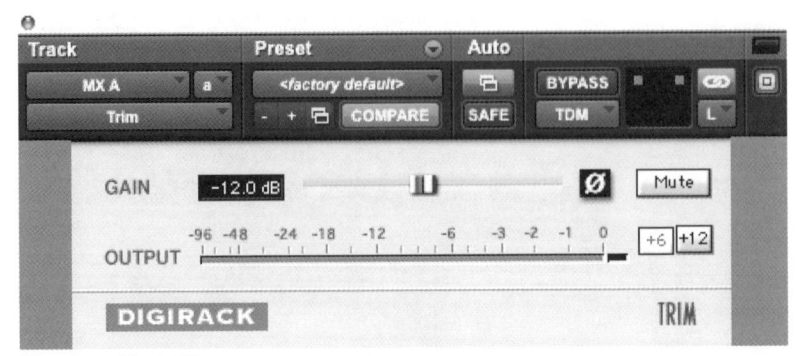

Fig. 13.31. Music Trim

The Trim plug-in is unique, simply allowing you to boost or cut the gain in variable increments. This is very useful in dealing with music. Often, we are dragging and dropping music source from CDs, iTunes, etc. These files are usually full volume and can really jump out at you when first auditioning them. With this plug-in set to –12 dB, the output is substantially lower, so the imported music is in a more workable volume level, compared to the rest of the mix.

MX EQ

The first plug-in is the standard Digirack 7-band EQ plug-in.

Music tracks are often premixed with volume graphs when the mixer receives them. There are a few points of interest within this preset, if we need to add any EQ. Here we have the LF set to 100 Hz and LMF set to 200 Hz to boost any low end. Next we have the MF set to 1000 Hz for any midrange boost. At the top end, we have 2 kHz and 6 kHz set to boost any high end, if needed (not active in figure 13.32).

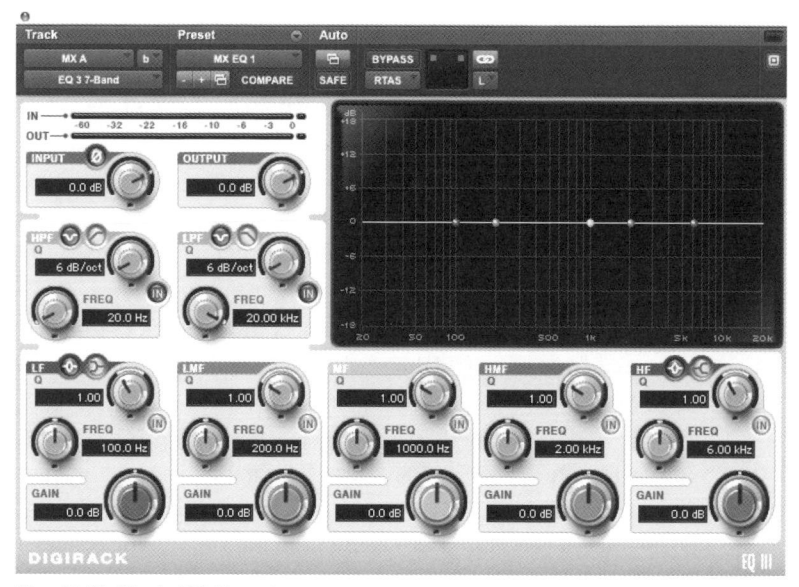

Fig. 13.32. Music EQ Preset

MIX WORKFLOW

Creating an efficient workflow is important in achieving a good overall mix while utilizing the best of your time and efforts. You will need to know how many dialogue, sound effects, Foley, and music tracks you'll be dealing with, so that you can duplicate your respective units accordingly. To save time, in advance of the session, ask the editor who has prepared the OMF that you will be mixing, or simply import the OMF into your DAW session, to see exactly what it is.

Once you understand the project's requirements, you can launch your mix template and save it as a new session. Incorporate the project name and the word "mix" into the session's name, and store it on your hard drive.

If you have 6 DX tracks, 12 stereo FX tracks, 4 FO tracks, and 8 stereo MX tracks in your OMF, you would duplicate it as follows:

- Duplicate the DX unit 5 times (so that you end up with 6 DX tracks).
- Duplicate the stereo FX unit 11 times.
- Duplicate the FO unit 3 times.
- Duplicate the stereo MX unit 7 times.

The amount of units/tracks should match what you are about to put on them.

When the tracks are set up, drag the elements that you've imported into your session onto their respective units. Make sure that the files/regions do not move either left or right in the timeline as you move them to their new location.

Once this is complete, you can select the new tracks that you imported from your OMF, and choose to Hide and make them Inactive. Hiding tracks reduces screen clutter.

Now you are ready to begin your mix. I recommend that you start with the dialogue first. Especially if this is your maiden voyage on a final dub. Most projects are dialogue driven. Dialogue is a very important element in the storytelling process, and dialogue is usually placed at a healthy and intelligible level, front and center. Therefore, setting the dialogue level first will be a perfect guide for adding music and FX.

LEVELS

Each project has its own set of deliverable requirements. There is no standard here. The levels, sample rate, bit resolution, deliverable requirements, etc., are variable and project specific. It is always best to address these technical specifications before you get started.

That said, we will mix this using 0 (unity gain on the stereo fader/meter) as our mix reference level. Therefore, the final mix level (on the print master track) should not exceed 0 VU on the meter. If it does, the audio will distort and our meter on the print master VU will go into the red. You will constantly be referencing this level to make sure that you don't go over it!

You may choose to insert a meter plug-in on the print master track. Keep this plug-in on the desktop as a constant reference, and try not to surpass –3, so that you have at least 3 dB of headroom in your mix. You may recall that earlier, we inserted brickwall limiters on the DX, FX, FO, and MX busses with a threshold of –3 dB. This will work to our advantage, as it controls the final levels before they hit your stem tracks (which ultimately feed your print master).

CHAPTER 13

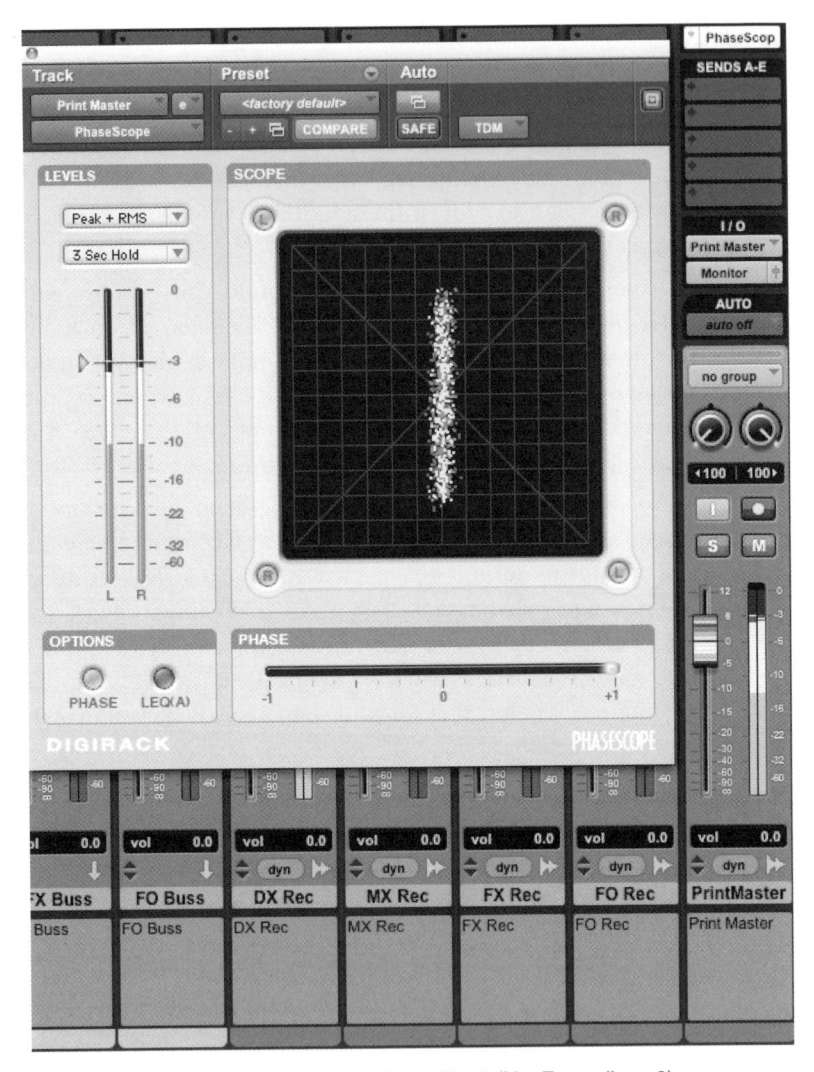

Fig. 13.33. Meter Plug-in on the Print Master Track (Not Exceeding −3)

Get the dialogue at a good level, and automate your fader rides to make sure that you have an even dialogue level. Using the −3 dB as a reference will allow you to have some headroom to add the music and effects.

Remember that the dialogue needs to be intelligible at all times. This may mean adjusting the music and effects at lower levels than you may be used to. If you have any questions, turn on your television or check the Internet to reference a similar show or program. Listen to how the mix sounds. Where is the music volume in relation to the dialogue? Where is SFX volume in relation to the dialogue? Where is the Foley (perhaps more implied than heard)?

Use these guidelines as starting points for your own projects.

CHAPTER 14

The Music and Effects Mix

Every successful television show and feature film is destined to have a prosperous second life when it is made available worldwide. This means that the program will need to be prepared and dubbed in a foreign language (dialogue redone) for multiple worldwide markets. In order to achieve this quickly and efficiently (while the iron is still hot), the program will need a separate music-and-effects-only mix (M&E), without the dialogue. This makes it much easier to dub the project in a foreign language and begin the process of international release.

M&Es are important because a larger portion of income for film is from international sales. The M&E enables a project to be revoiced in any language, and all text can be read in local language with voice-over. Also, local culture can be respected by putting questionable material in an optional 5.1 master—for example, kissing sounds.

THE M&E

The deliverable specs on most professional projects include an M&E. Many films are picked up for distribution in foreign countries first, requiring dubbing dialogue in different languages. This is how studios use and reuse the shows that they produce. International distribution is an important element in how the studios make back their investment in a project.

The main goal of the M&E is to identify and remove any and all discernable English dialogue in the project while maintaining the overall sound of the film. This includes *all* dialogue, seen and unseen. The dialogue spoken by the actors is obvious, but we need to identify everything else as well, like group dialogue in crowd scenes, as well as any offscreen shout-outs and chatter. Every bit of discernable language must be removed.

Once the M&E is created, it must be recorded to the final format. In most cases, it is in the form of broadcast wave (WAV) digital audio files, as well as a DAW session, but the required final format varies between projects.

Studios sometimes wait to do the M&E until after the film is picked up for international distribution. Accessing the original mix elements can make the M&E go faster. Alternately, you could start with mix stems and go from there. But the project may not originate as a DAW session. It could be a rerelease of an older film or television show that was created in an entirely different format. Current standards and trends lean towards using DAWs as a platform for recording, mixing, and backup. Therefore, if the project is in a different format, such as tape, a transfer would take place so that the M&E could be created in a DAW.

It is common to have some of the most popular American television shows running simultaneously in other countries, dubbed in foreign languages. People around the world watch many of the same popular television shows as Americans do, yet in their own country and dubbed in their own language. The foreign versions of these shows generally try to be as close to the original as possible. Voice casting is key to making them realistic.

In some cases, the voice casting for the dialogue replacement is not that great, and the show's presentation falls short. I have a friend who grew up in Mexico and often watched foreign dubs of popular American television shows. He was so sensitive to the poor sync, as well as the subpar voice casting, that he forced himself to watch the original English versions. Ironically, this helped him to learn to speak English (as a second language) fluently.

M&E SCENARIOS

Each project genre has its own set of challenges, so some M&Es can be more complex than others. An M&E for a documentary can be as simple as muting the narration, whereas an M&E for a feature film or television show can be much more involved. In the case of a documentary, the narration track is turned off, and the mix is output without narration. Also, it is not customary to dub dialogue for interviews. Subtitles are more common, which makes documentary M&Es quicker and easier.

A feature film or television show is more complex. All dialogue must be removed. Re-recording mixers need to do everything they can to make these M&E mixes as lively as possible. They'll listen with big ears, knowing that the dialogue replacement may not have the same production value. A lot of production effects that are married to the production dialogue track (such as original backgrounds and room tones, along with the actual steps, clothes, and effects) will disappear while muting the dialogue track, so the mixers will be looking to fill any gaps in sound in the M&E process.

Ambience must be edited in to smooth out those gaps. Foley may be added or pushed, to make it all sound more natural, once the foreign language is dubbed in. Adding additional Foley is not part of the normal process, but it is an option for high budget features. An M&E for a feature takes a week or so of editing, so Foley and mixing and can add significantly to the budget of a modest project.

Spoken dialogue is obviously in the dialogue and ADR tracks. But it can also be found in the backgrounds, walla, and music. Consider a scene filmed at a baseball park during a crowded ball game. There will be spoken dialogue from the actors, but there will also be dialogue in the backgrounds and walla. There may be a concession stand guy yelling to sell popcorn and hot dogs, people in the crowd shouting cheers for their favorite team, and another group of people in the background having a completely separate conversation.

Such situations are quite common and can get to be a little tricky in the M&E mix. If you simply mute the dialogue from your scene, it will be dry and lifeless. It would look like a silent movie shot at a very busy ballpark. There are a few techniques that will help breathe some life back into the M&E mix.

The first option is to bring in a professional loop group to create non-discernable group dialogue replacement for the scene. Although this may be a bit costly, it is the most effective way to fill in the gaps created by the loss of the original group. This would be spotted along with the ADR early on in the pre-production process and already created for you as an alternate background.

An alternate option would be to do some careful editing. You could find a section of the original group dialogue that has absolutely no discernable dialogue in it and create a long loop to play underneath the scene. You may look for a few different sections to loop so that it doesn't sound repetitive. This may also be an option in a SFX library, although those options are likely to be rather generic and may not match the scene perfectly. However, it may work well at a lower volume beneath the loop, to help fill in any gap created by removing the original dialogue.

Another problematic situation is having dialogue in the music tracks. I worked on a television show where the storyline had the actor in an old church singing traditional hymns with an organist and choir. Unfortunately, no one remembered to get an alternate shot or recording in the church of just the organ playing. The M&E required that they have that sequence in the show but with no discernable language (even as they sang the traditional hymn in the church). Therefore, I was asked to recreate the organ performance and mix as if it were the exact organ performed in that exact location. The singing was redone in different languages along with the dialogue replacement.

This kind of stuff happens all the time. Production could be running behind schedule, key people may not be on set to make sure alternate takes are done, and mistakes happen. Fortunately, the post-production process usually has opportunities to address these situations.

Another scenario is when you have a movie like *Hairspray* or *Almost Famous*, where music and songs play a big role in the film—especially when it includes a live performance. That requires additional music stems: one music stem for the instrumental tracks of the band and another stem for the vocals. This facilitates someone resinging the songs in another language.

M&E MIX TECHNIQUES

Backgrounds

Backgrounds are there to add more ambience to your production sound, as well as provide realistic filler for ADR lines. Hopefully, the location sound crew has provided original room tones and ambience tracks. As you may recall, one of the things that the location sound crew is responsible for is recording the room/location at rest. These tracks will work the best, as they reference that actual room tone or location ambience from the scene. If that is not available, you can look to a library for a variety of backgrounds and room tones.

Most M&E mixers begin mixing the background tracks first, bringing them up in increments. They may start by making a background group, raising the level of the overall backgrounds 3 dB, and then listening to the mix. If this is not enough, they repeat this process. This has to be finessed a bit, because what works well in one area or scene may not work very well in another. The benefit of this technique is that it will put you in the ballpark level-wise as far as how the M&E should sound, while allowing the option to make additional adjustments along the way.

Some backgrounds will work better than others. If you have several backgrounds/room tones to choose from, you can simply rebalance them to add some ambience into the M&E mix. Repeat this process until the scene is more realistic without the dialogue.

Foley

Just as the backgrounds are adding atmosphere to the production sound, the Foley is there to enhance the movements that the actors make in the scene. When you mute the production dialogue, you lose all of the natural sound of the actors' movement (footsteps, clothes movement, grabs and downs, etc.). Foley is rarely redone for an M&E mix, but you could look to the existing Foley to add more realism to the mix.

Start by using the same technique that you used with the backgrounds. First, group the Foley tracks, raise the level 3 dB, and listen back. Repeat this process until the track sounds more full again. Of course, simply performing an overall volume raise to the Foley track is not the instant solution, and it will only get you in the ballpark. Fine-tuning the Foley level will ultimately make the M&E more realistic and transparent.

Again, you are mixing and referencing with big ears. The new dialogue will be recorded in a controlled studio environment and lack all of the ambience and movement from the original production track. While you mix the M&E, there will be no dialogue present, and you have to make mixing decisions based on the dialogue that you anticipate will be there eventually.

The goal is to create an M&E mix that will need little tweaking when the new dialogue is added. Anything that you can do to help this will make the project more real and more interesting to view in the international markets for which they are targeted.

Mixing the M&E

The final mix will be the starting point of the M&E in terms of reference. In most cases, the final mix is "the bible" for M&E. All pans, balances, treatments, etc. are to be duplicated. Since the music will not be remixed for an M&E, the levels of the music in the final mix will stay the same in the M&E. What becomes a variable are usually the background SFX and Foley.

For example, if the production track in a scene picked up some of the actors' footsteps along with the dialogue, and those footsteps from the production track are left in the mix, chances are, the footsteps for that character that were recorded in Foley will not be put into the final mix, to avoid any doubling or extraneous SFX. Once the dialogue tracks are taken away for the M&E, so go those footsteps from the production tracks. The M&E mixer now has to be sure that they put those footsteps back into the M&E from the Foley tracks, so that the scene is complete with all sound elements.

Sound effects that were captured within the original production sound recordings and are not tied to dialog are called *production sound effects*, or PFX. These PFX should be included, if they were in the original mix, unless they are too noisy or unusable in some way and can be convincingly replaced by effects and Foley.

M&Es should be mixed in the room where the final mix was done, and by one or all of the original mixers. These are the people who did the original mix and have the best perspective on filling out the soundtrack for the M&E. Anyone mixing an M&E needs to pay close attention to choices made in the original mix. For example, it would be a serious mistake to fill in a scene with Foley and effects when the original mix was done as a montage with just music. What to play and what not to play, as well as perspective, are vital in matching the original mix.

There are a few things that you can do to prepare for the M&E process. As stated earlier, it helps to be the person who did the final mix. Then, you are already aware of any Foley you may have not mixed in or any backgrounds you mixed low. However, this isn't always the case, so taking a little time to get to know how your tracks are laid out is a good way to start.

Taking notes as you mix the domestic version helps. On a recent project, the mixers spoke in advance with the music department about needing "minus vocal" tracks for an M&E of a film about a band that featured numerous live performances, so they were budgeted and prepared. This took one day away from final mix because of extra time needed for the M&E.

When I am not the original mixer, it is very helpful for me to see and hear the original mix before doing the M&E. If there is no time for that, then I will at least preview each scene or segment and then go back and mix it. Again, the goal of an M&E is to match the mix choices that were made in the domestic mix.

The original print master is used for reference and the stems (minus dialogue, of course) are used to keep as much of the original mix as possible. The M&E production process usually starts with the original stems, and I use those stems for the music and the SFX. For the background SFX and Foley, use the original mix. This way, you can have complete control over the volume of each individual sound from those two elements. A majority of the time, it is the Foley and background SFX that end up either low level or completely taken out in the final domestic mix, depending on how much extra sound the production tracks pick up in addition to dialogue. The following is a breakdown of the approach:

Dialogue: All production sound effects (PFX) are separated from English and are isolated so they can be used in the M&E. General walla, without discernable English, is retrieved.

Anything questionable, like television broadcast or other languages, is sent to an M&E optional master (often 5.1 or 5.1+lcr).

Sound Effects: Backgrounds are often remixed for the M&E to make it fully filled.

Foley: Foley is often remixed for the M&E to make it fully filled.

Music: The music stem is used, except if there are separate vocals, in which case a vocal stem is created.

Fill the gaps when production dialogue is removed, and make sure that you hear something! This is my rule of thumb. Bring up the clothes track from the Foley to give scenes a little bit of life. Generally, the remaining production SFX are infrequent, and so, if the remaining production SFX are faded in and out, the existing backgrounds from the sound effects will be sufficient. Listening is critical! Use your ears, and listen to the original mix. Use all of your knowledge of the tools at your disposal (EQ, reverb, plug-ins, etc.) to match the sound.

The M&E delivery format should be defined in the original sound contract. Typically, both 5.1 and any additional stems are created to accommodate the formats needed to maximize foreign sales. It is possible and not uncommon for the M&E to generate more income than the original release.

Most of the time, the M&E is done in both 5.1 and stereo. The only exception would be if a 5.1 version of the project was never created; then a 5.1 M&E won't be needed either. Standard delivery requirements are usually to provide a 5.1 M&E, a mono dialog guide track, and a mono track with optional material. Often, a 5.1 version of this optional material is also provided. The 5.1 M&E is usually folded down to stereo or a Dolby encoded 2-track (LTRT).

It is the usual case not to have enough time for the M&E, just as there is usually not enough time to do the final. Of course, this is for budgetary reasons. As a mixer, I find it rare to have "enough" time for most any mix! I always wish I had a little more time to tweak the sound. The trick is to adjust your pace in order to maximize as much quality as possible in the time allotted. I feel like every mix I do is a compromise between time and quality. I pay as much attention to detail as I can, within the time frame of the mix. It can be frustrating when there just isn't the kind of time needed for a "proper mix." You are forced to prioritize the source material you have for its value to the storytelling on-screen.

If there is not enough time allotted for the M&E, we might end up just recording the SFX stem and the music stem from the final mix and call it an M&E. It's not the most ideal way to go, but if it is for reality television shows, then you can probably get away with it.

Time allotted for M&Es is determined by the budget of the show and complexity of the soundtrack. A week is a generous amount of time for the completion of a feature M&E, while you may only get half a day for a typical one-hour television show. With small budget indie films, usually one day is budgeted for an M&E. Often, just one day is enough.

The producer or director rarely attend these sessions. I personally haven't been involved in any M&E where someone else attended. Usually, the producers and directors put all their time and effort into the final mix, and then their job is pretty much done. As far as final approval goes, as long as the M&E passes any technical quality controls, then it's an approved M&E. As far as creativity goes, it's sort of on an "I'll take your word for it" basis. The best situation is when producer sends an international representative to consult and approve or disapprove of M&E choices. There are people at the production studios whose job it is to QC the M&E. They will listen and compare it to the original mix. If there are discrepancies, they may reject the mix until changes are made and approved.

The future of the M&E process is leaning towards Better, Faster, Smaller, Cheaper. It seems like there is less time, less money, and higher expectations with each new mix. The trick is to maximize and refine your skill set and keep your passion for sound intact. M&Es will always be an important factor in the sound industry. It may not be the most glamorous part of the job, but it's an important one. There have been a number of occasions where small indie films didn't do too well in the United States, but foreign countries loved them. So, they buy the movie for their country, and, all of a sudden, the film makes money. In a nutshell, people in Germany wouldn't be able to enjoy *Avatar* if an M&E was never created. The global market is constantly growing, and it is a major source of financing, so the M&E process will be provided more resources, in the future, but it will always remain second priority.

CHAPTER 15

Delivery and Archiving

A professional delivery of assets is key to success in post production. These archives are what the studio will use and reuse for the shows that they produce. Preparing them is an important step in the process, and it will enable studios to make their money back on their initial investment in the production.

Throughout this book, we have addressed the audio post-production elements in a film or television show. We have also seen how those elements (dialogue, SFX, Foley, and music) have evolved with the film over time. You can easily see that audio post production is very technical, and that identifying your specific objectives early can make all the difference.

Now, we will explore the final process in audio post production: deliverables and archiving. Creating professional, clearly labeled and accurate deliverables (whatever the format may be) is what we are paid for, and these deliverable units are clearly defined before we begin our work. Once the deliverables are received, the studio can begin their process for the material to be archived and vaulted.

DELIVERABLES, FORMATS, AND DEADLINES

Deliverables and deadlines are very important. We could be the best mixers in the history of man, but if we don't give the client what they requested, when they requested it, we haven't truly completed our job. Therefore, you want to make sure that everyone is on the same page early, so that you can plan accordingly.

CHAPTER 15

Specifications for the deliverables are addressed and determined in pre-production. There is a conversation between the studio (which is financing the production) and the post-production supervisor regarding exactly what the studio requires for the specific production. Deliverable formats and elements may vary between projects and studios. Most studios employ the CRAM (Consolidated Re-recording Audio Masters) method for deliverables and archiving. This is a way for the studios to organize what they are archiving, as well as a way to let the mixers know what they need to supply.

It is best to spec the deliverables early on, so that the mixer can prepare and set up the mix routing and bussing to facilitate what is needed. This is something that you could easily do by augmenting one of your mix templates in your DAW. Simply add tracks to your mix session (along with related bussing/routing) to accomplish this. Once your bussing and tracks are in order, you'll be able to accommodate the deliverable request. Creating the final deliverable stems is quite easy when the mix bussing/routing is set up correctly. You simply arm the tracks that are set up to facilitate the deliverable requirements and record them when your mix is complete.

Here is an example of a CRAM sheet:

DOLBY 5.1 DIGITAL CRAM CONFIGURATION

Trk.				Trk.		
Trk. 1	DOMESTIC 5.1 PRINTMASTER	LEFT		Trk. 34	DIALOGUE STEMS	LEFT
Trk. 2		RIGHT		Trk. 35		RIGHT
Trk. 3		CENTER		Trk. 36		CENTER - DIALOGUE
Trk. 4		LFE		Trk. 37		CENTER - ADR
Trk. 5		LEFT SURROUND		Trk. 38		LEFT SURROUND
Trk. 6		RIGHT SURROUND		Trk. 39		RIGHT SURROUND
Trk. 7	DOMESTIC Lt/Rt PRINTMASTER	Matrix & Encoded - LT		Trk. 40	MUSIC STEMS	LEFT
Trk. 8		Matrix & Encoded - RT		Trk. 41		RIGHT
Trk. 9	M&E 5.1 PRINTMASTER	LEFT		Trk. 42		CENTER
Trk. 10		RIGHT		Trk. 43		LFE
Trk. 11		CENTER		Trk. 44		LEFT SURROUND
Trk. 12		LFE		Trk. 45		RIGHT SURROUND
Trk. 13		LEFT SURROUND		*THESE DISKS TO BE MADE ONLY IF APPLICABLE MATERIALS EXIST*		
Trk. 14		RIGHT SURROUND		Trk. 46	MUSIC VOCALS	MUSIC VOCALS
Trk. 15	M&E LT/RT PRINTMASTER	Matrix & Encoded - LT		Trk. 47	(IF SEPARATE)	MUSIC VOCALS
Trk. 16		Matrix & Encoded - RT		Trk. 48	CLEAN MUSIC STEMS (NO PROFANITY) (IF NEEDED)	LEFT
Trk. 17	FX STEMS FOR M&E ONLY (Fully Filled)	LEFT		Trk. 49		RIGHT
Trk. 18		RIGHT		Trk. 50		CENTER
Trk. 19		CENTER		Trk. 51		LFE
Trk. 20		LFE		Trk. 52		LEFT SURROUND
Trk. 21		LEFT SURROUND		Trk. 53		RIGHT SURROUND
Trk. 22		RIGHT SURROUND		Trk. 54	ALTERNATE MUSIC FOR M&E ONLY (e.g., BACKGROUND TV) (IF NEEDED)	LEFT
Trk. 23	FX STEMS 5.1 (Domestic Mix)	LEFT		Trk. 55		RIGHT
Trk. 24		RIGHT		Trk. 56		CENTER
Trk. 25		CENTER		Trk. 57		LFE
Trk. 26		LFE		Trk. 58		LEFT SURROUND
Trk. 27		LEFT SURROUND		Trk. 59		RIGHT SURROUND
Trk. 28		RIGHT SURROUND		Trk. 60	OPTIONAL MATERIAL & ALTERNATE M&E SECTIONS (IF NEEDED)	LEFT
Trk. 29	FOLEY STEMS (Domestic Mix)	LEFT		Trk. 61		RIGHT
Trk. 30		RIGHT		Trk. 62		CENTER
Trk. 31		CENTER		Trk. 63		LFE
Trk. 32		LEFT SURROUND		Trk. 64		LEFT SURROUND
Trk. 33		RIGHT SURROUND		Trk. 65		RIGHT SURROUND

Fig. 15.1. Sample Deliverables: Dolby 5.1 Digital CRAM Configuration

Delivery Item	Notes	Format
Sound Track Negative	Formats: Dolby SR, Dolby SRD, DTS, SDDS	ESTAR NEGATIVE
6 Track PrintMaster	Made From Final Mix Track Layout: L R C S Ls Rs	FW DRIVE, LTO, MAG
2 Track Printmaster	Made From Final Mix Dolby Encoded Lt Rt	FW DRIVE, LTO, MAG
6 Track Dialogue Stem Master	Made From Final Mix Elements Track Layout: L R C S Ls Rs	FW DRIVE, LTO, MAG
6 Track Music Stem Master	Made from Final Mix Elements Track Layout: L R C S Ls Rs	FW DRIVE, LTO, MAG
6 Track Effects Stem Master	Made from Final Mix Elements Track layout: L R C S Ls Rs	FW DRIVE, LTO, MAG
6 + 2 Track M & E Master	Made from International Music and Effects Mix Track Layout: L R C S Ls Rs Ch7 & Ch8 will be instructed by Paramount International Rep.	FW DRIVE, LTO, MAG
Optional Material for M&E	Made from International Music and Effects Mix Track Layout: L R C S Ls Rs	FW DRIVE, LTO, MAG
6 Track D M & E Master	Made from Final Mix Elements Track Layout D D M M E E	FW DRIVE, LTO
Pre-Dubs	All Pre-Dubs, Pro-Tools Session	FW DRIVE, LTO
Production Sound Dailies	Un-Cut Production Sound Masters	DEVA DVD-RAMs
Sound Reports	Production Daily Sound Reports	PAPER OR ELECTRONIC

Fig. 15.2. Sample Deliverables: Delivery Items

Each studio has a different process for receiving audio post-production materials. It is very important for the studio to create archives. Unless audio engineers make these archived files platform agnostic, we cannot guarantee that the project will survive and be supported in future wares from DAW manufacturers.

The studios are well aware of this. They will need to use the archive files to create international releases, syndicated rebroadcasts, as well as mechanical rereleases. Repurposing their content is ultimately how studios make money. They invest a lot of time and money in producing their shows, and it usually isn't recouped in the initial broadcast. So, they will take great care in making sure that their archives will be ready for future opportunities.

QUALITY CONTROL AND QUALITY ASSURANCE

Studios rely on mix engineers to output to the spec that they have designated. Today's trend is to ask mixers to supply the deliverables as broadcast wave files. WAVs are preferred mostly because of the fact that they are time-stamped within their metadata. Additionally, the files should all be the same length and clearly labeled so that they can be easily identified.

I worked with a very successful music producer for a few years on a variety of albums. Upon completion of each project, it was my task to prepare it for the record company. It was at this point that he would always say to me, "Give them all the formats that they've requested, and please label it so that even dumb people know what it is."

This seemed peculiar and a bit funny, at first. But I then realized how important it was to make sure that everything was completed, labeled, and delivered correctly. Not everyone at a studio/record company/business understands the technical terms and language in the studio, so it is in everyone's best interest to make this as clear and precise as possible. That was probably one of the keys to his continued success as a producer. I often remember that day, when I am in the process of preparing deliverables for a project.

The production studio will go through extensive quality control before they transfer the files to be archived. A series of highly trained professional engineers will go through each stem to make sure that everything is where it's supposed to be, as well as looking for any level peaks or dropouts. The quality control process is very important because the archives must be complete for future reference. If they find any issues, the studio will have the re-recording mixers correct them. This is a poor reflection of the mixer's work, and the correction is usually done on their dime.

The studio's archive department will then transfer these files to multiple formats. They will initially be stored on a dedicated hard drive, as well as being doubly backed up on DVD RAM.

There are a variety of formats that have been used throughout the years (some with great success; others, not so much). It is very difficult in today's ever-changing technological environment to know what is going to survive in a hundred years. However, the one thing that studios believe will survive is film and audio recorded onto mag film stock. Film has a proven shelf life and is a great medium for storage. Unfortunately, film stock is slowly disappearing. More and more films and television shows are shot digitally, so the need for film stock is slowly decreasing.

Studios also use gold-plated DVD RAM discs, which are said to have a shelf life of at least one hundred years (yet to be proven). This is also the format that most production sound mixers are delivering the initial production sound on, because they find it to be the most durable and reliable.

When the archives are created, they are shipped to off-site facilities. In the world of data, a file is not truly considered archived or backed up until it exists in three separate locations, as well as on multiple forms of media, preferably in separate buildings. It would make little sense to have three backups of the work stored in different parts of the same building, only to lose them all to a fire.

The material is bar coded and fed into an extensive database. The archives are then stored in a climate-controlled room. They will remain there until they need to be checked or migrated to a different medium, or to be rereleased or rebroadcast.

SESSION MANAGEMENT FOR DELIVERABLES IN DAWS

Session management in DAWs is very important in all aspects of recording. The post-production process is a continuing chain of events, and you will almost always be passing your session on to the next person in the chain to use your work. You want to make sure that even the most inexperienced person can open your DAW session and have a basic understanding of what it is (or at least, how to explain what they have to someone in charge of their department).

It is in everyone's best interest to create sessions that are clean and easy to comprehend. The last thing that you want is to have someone wasting time trying to navigate through your session and possibly altering it in the process.

Creating clean and efficient sessions in DAWs is quite easy. There are a few things that you can do to make sure that the session is easily understandable.

- Delete all of the tracks (audio, aux, etc.) that are *not* being used. Make sure that you don't delete the movie. Keep it there for reference.
- Go to the Region/Clip List, and delete the unused regions/clips.
- Save a copy of this new "cleaned" session, and include only those audio files that are in use. Rename this new session so that you know that this is the one that you will be using as the deliverable.

This will make for a better deliverable that only includes the elements for the final specifications.

FINAL IMPLEMENTATION AND DELIVERY

Final delivery can be done in a variety of ways. The deliverables can be saved to a separate/dedicated hard drive (or set of DVD-RAM discs) and hand-delivered to the client. It can also be uploaded to an FTP site. The uploading option is project and size specific. This may not be an option if this is a feature-length film and your deliverables consist of many large audio files. A project of that size will take too long to upload and download.

It is best to check with the client, as to how they wish to receive the deliverables. It may vary from project to project, and this may be done by the mix tech, if you are doing this in a post-production studio. The main issue is to make sure that everyone receives exactly what they need exactly when they need it (if not sooner). Doing a good job and doing it on time makes a great impression on a client. It will likely come back to you in the form of a referral or repeat business.

Afterword

You may be interested in exploring audio post production as a career or as an alternate business. In this age of cost effective DV cameras and interest in creating more and more low budget independent films, the opportunities in audio post production are expanding. This is also true in the constantly growing cable television, Internet, and gaming industries. All of these outlets need good audio, and you can start in a few different ways.

You may decide to relocate to an area where audio post production exists and is in great demand. Hollywood is an obvious option. There are more feature films, television shows, industrial training films, commercials, promo videos, games, etc. created there than anywhere else in the world. You could easily inquire within human resources at any given audio post facility for an entry-level position.

Entry-level positions are great because they provide the opportunity to experience a variety of activities. Often, these positions include delivering elements and getting coffee, so you will be learning how to navigate around town as well. Additionally, it gives you the chance to meet other people with similar interests in the industry. Nobody stays in an entry-level position for an extended period of time, and it's fun to see where your friends and colleagues end up. People that I used to prepare fruit baskets with (in my entry-level days) are now receiving Grammy and Emmy awards!

AFTERWORD

If you do not have an interest in relocating, you can look to your local television, cable, or radio station for opportunities. These are great places to learn the basics of day-to-day production chores. You may be surprised to find out how much audio post production is going on in some of the sleepiest little towns across the country. A good way to find these places is to search the Internet.

Film and television career opportunity websites are changing all of the time, but they are a great resource for finding opportunities from people who are making their first film and have a need for better sound. You may find that these entry-level positions pay little money up front, but will pay off in the long run, as you develop and refine your skills in audio post. Experience is priceless! This will also make you more desirable in the work force as you move forward with your career.

You will also acquire credits along the way. Credits are very important. It shows your project-related experience within the post-production industry. This was a key point for me, as I was developing my career. I made a conscious decision to dedicate my first few years in post production to positioning myself in a series of high profile/low paying gigs. I knew that it would it help me in the long run. I was clearly focused on creating a long-term career, and clients acknowledged and respected that dedication.

Good Luck!

About the Author

Mark Cross is an award winning producer, composer, mixer, engineer, author, and educator, with an extensive career in audio post production that spans over two decades. He has been a composer for several seasons of the NBC prime time hit show *Last Comic Standing*, as well as contributing additional music for *American Idol* and *The CBS Evening News*. Other projects include composing for NASA and the X-Prize Foundation, and working with James Newton Howard, Martin Davich, and Youssou N'Dour on the score for *I Bring What I Love*, a documentary on Youssou's career, focusing on his controversial Grammy-winning album *Egypt*.

Additionally, Cross has created musical themes for Nickelodeon's *Wow Wow Wubbzy* and the *Seinfeld* season 8 DVD, as well as producing and performing with Grammy-winner John Legend on HBO's *Curb Your Enthusiasm*. He has worked on numerous albums, film scores, and television episodes, including the Grammy-winning *I Am Shelby Lynne* and Randy Newman's Oscar-nominated and Grammy-winning *Cars* and *Meet the Parents* scores and soundtracks, along with mixing hundreds of episodes of the NBC series *ER*, for over ten years.

Mark has been a voting NARAS (The Recording Academy/Grammy Awards) member since 2000 and serves in the NARAS Producers & Engineers Wing (Los Angeles Chapter). He was the P&E Wing Committee Chair from 2008 to 2011. Mark is also a two term Governor on the NARAS Board of Governors, serving from 2008 to 2012.

Index

Italicized page numbers indicate figures.

A
actor, 3–4
AD. *See* assistant director
ADR. *See* Automated Dialogue Replacement
Altman, Robert, 23
ambience, 199
Apocalypse Now, 72
archiving
    CRAM method for, 208, *208*
    formats used in, 211
    I Love Lucy, 28
    in post production stage, 28
    quality control and assurance in, 210–11
    separate locations in, 211
    studio, 210–11
artist. *See* Foley artist/walker
aspect ratio, 40
assistant dialogue editor, 53
    auto-assembly application employed by, 89
    DAWS employed by, 88
    demuxing by, 89
    EDL use by, 89
    items gathered by, 88
    role of, 88–89
    sound reels addressed by, 88
assistant director (AD), 31
audio path, 55
audio post production
    basic elements of, xi, 1
    budget, 213
    career in, x, 213–14
    contributors to, xi–xii
    DAWS basic setup in, 6–12
    DAWS driving, xi
    digital technology impact on, xi
    DX in, 1, 2, 83
    entry-level positions in, 213, 214
    evolution of, 1
    location for, 213, 214
    overview of, 1–12
    for PA, 23
    7.1 technology development in, 20, 21
    SFX role in, 71
    as team effort, xi, 1
    in visual presentation, xi
audio production, 2
auto-assembly application, 89
Automated Dialogue Replacement (ADR)
    actor, director, and post-production supervisor involvement in, 3–4
    cues and cue sheet for, 84, *85*, 97
    DAWS use for, 4, 97
    documentation and time in, 98
    film example requiring extensive, 95–96
    FX filling in gaps in, 100
    microphone for, 97
    nature and process of, *3*, 3–4, 84
    principal and group, 91
    production dialogue replaced by, 83
    reality TV, 95
    room tone/filler impact on, 90, 91
    stage, 86, *86*, *87*, 96
    studio space creation requirements for, 96–97
    terms glossary for, 84–86, *85*, *86*, *87*
    in TV dialogue editing, 90–91, 92
    VO and narration in, 98
AVI Codecs (Audio Video Interleave), 41

B
background sound effects (BGs)
    benefits of, 75–76
    buzz-tone in, 76
    common terminology for, 76
    in M&E, 201
    SFX use of, 75–76
    sound effects editor using backgrounds pass and, 77
    sound types included in, 75
backgrounds pass, 77

Index

backup systems, 66
Becka, Kevin, x
BGs. *See* background sound effects
black and white format (B&W), 40
boom operator
    equipment of, 50
    fisher boom used by, 48
    in location sound crew, *48*, 48–50, *49*
    microphone placement, 49
    nature and function of, 48, 49, 50
    tasks, 50
boom poles, 63, *64*
budget, 147–48, 213
busses, 167, 208
buzz-tone, 76
B&W. *See* black and white format

C

cardioid microphone, 57–59, *58*
career, x, 213–14
cavity microphone, 95
Chase, Josh, 78, *78*
checkerboarding, 92, *92*
cleaning, 87
clicks, 136
comments, 52
composer. *See also* music, in television and film; music editing
    demo mixing, 131, 133
    music editor relationship to, 120, 133
    music mixing for film and television and studio of, 131–32, *132*
    scoring mixer relationship to, 128, 133
compressor/limiter
    DX, 174, *175*, 179, *179*
    FO, 188, *188*
    SFX unit, 185, *186*
conductor, 138
conforming
    DAWS applications for, 79
    defined, 79, 122
    music editor and, 122
    in MX and music editing, 122–23
    in pre-dub session, 152
    repurposing through music, 122
    in SFX, 79
    sound effects editor, 79
    soundtrack shortening in, 79
co-producer, 30–31
CRAM (Consolidated Re-recording Audio Masters) method, 208, *208*

Cross, Mark, x
CSI, 81
cue sheets
    for ADR, 84, *85*, 97
    FX, 105, 106, *106*
    music editor preparing, 123

D

dailies, 25–26
The Dark Knight, 156
    King as supervising sound editor on, 74–75
    as music editing example, 120–21
    sound design for, 74–75
    track count in, 27
DAWS. *See* digital audio workstations
deadlines, 207
decca tree technique, *139*, 139–40, *140*
deliverables. *See also* mix/deliverables
    CRAM method for, 208, *208*
    DAWS session management, 211–12
    deadlines and, 207
    final implementation and delivery, 212
    pre-production for specifications of, 208
    quality control and assurance for, 210–11
    routing and bussing for, 208
    sample, *208*, *209*
    studio receipt process for, 209, 210
    as WAV files, 210
delivery
    deliverables final implementation and, 212
    post production dependent on professional, 207
    Pro Tools TV dialogue editing, 94
    SFX dub stage, 80
demo mixing, 131, 133
demuxing, 89
development, 24
DFTC. *See* Drop Frame Time Code
dialogue (DX). *See also* Automated Dialogue Replacement; production dialogue
    ADR, or re-recording, 3
    in audio post production, 1, 2, 83
    compressor/limiter, 174, *175*, 179, *179*
    De-Esser, *175*, 175–76
    defined, 2
    EQ, *176*, 176–77
    film and TV sources of, 199

film examples, 2
  intelligibility as issue in, 177, 195
  location sound crew focus on, 100
  M&E TV/film removal and
    replacement of, 198, 199, 204
  mix session through merging mix
    template and session for, 162–63
  in mix workflow, 192
  plug-ins and processors for mixing,
    173–77, 182–83
  post production and process of
    editing, 98
  production dialogue editing and
    mixer of, 2
  reassigns and unit of, 177, *178*, 179
  reverb in units of, 182–83, *183*
  templates, equipment used, and unit
    of, 173–79, *179*, *180*
  track and template settings for unit of,
    173–74, *174*
dialogue (DX), editor
  assistant, 53, 88–89
  checkerboarding by, 92, *92*
  cleaning done by, 87
  DAWS use by, 91–92
  final dub role of, 163–64
  handles region extensions by, 93
  patchwork, 92
  for production audio, 2
  production dialogue role of, 87
  role of assistant, 88–89
  session layout, 91–92
  in sound crew, 32
  sound logs employed by, 53
  sound supervisor and director
    relationship with, 90
  TV dialogue editing role of, 90–94
  X track use by, 91
dialogue editing, television. *See also*
  reality television
  ADR in, 90–91, 92
  DX editor and location sound editor
    relationship in, 90
  DX editor role in, 90–94
  PFX track creation in, 93
  plug-ins for, 93
  Pro Tools as standard delivery
    platform for, 94
  reality TV production dialogue in,
    94–95
  room tones/filler in, 90
Dickson, W.K.L., 13–14
Digirack 7-band EQ plug-in. *See* EQ

digital audio file formats, 160
  audio file types, 39
  DAWS and conversion of, 39
  in post production media, 38–39
digital audio workstations (DAWS), 1
  in ADR work, 4, 97
  assistant dialogue editor employing,
    88
  audio post production basic setup,
    6–12
  audio post production driven by, xi
  conforming applications for, 79
  deliverables session management in,
    211–12
  digital audio file format conversion
    on, 39
  DX editor checkerboarding with,
    92, *92*
  DX editor use of, 91–92
  final dub use of, 159, 160
  functions of, 6
  FX and spotting through,
    5, 106, *107*, 112
  M&E format transfer to, 198
  music editing and mixing in,
    124, *124*, 129, *130*, 141
  platforms, 6
  pre-dub/temp mix use of,
    149, 150, 153, 154
  properties for session setup in, 10
  resolved system for, 6
  session setup, 7, *7–10*, 10
  session synchronization criteria, 12
  SFX work in, 4
  sound effects editor employing, 76, 77
  spotting using, 5, 106, *107*, 112
  templates created using,
    165, 166, *166*, 173
  time code for video synchronization
    with, 11–12
  video importation in, 11
digital formats, 41. *See also specific types*
digital-multitrack field recorders and
  mixers, 52–53
digital technology, xi
digital theater sound, 21
director, 120
  ADR work of, 3–4
  DX editor and sound supervisor
    relationship with, 90
  in film crew, 31
  M&E mixing involvement of, 205
director of photography (DP), 31

Index

Disney
    Fantasia as traveling production for, 16
    Garity as chief engineer at, 17
    sound evolution techniques of, 16, 17
distribution, 28
Dolby
    certified sound stage, 147, 156
    MP Matrix from, 18
    A noise reduction, 18
Dolby Laboratories, 18
Dolby Motion Picture Matrix, 18
Dolby Stereo
    Digital system, 21
    mechanics of, 18
    sound evolution and development of, 18
DP. *See* director of photography
Dream of the Romans, 118, *119*
drop-frame/non-drop-frame rates
    color/black-and-white TV compatibility and, 37
    DFTC in, 38
    NTSC frame rates in, 37
    SMPTE time code, 37
    standard frame and sample rates, 38
    in synchronization, 37–38
Drop Frame Time Code (DFTC), 38
dub. *See* final dub; pre-dub
dub stage
    film and TV differences in, 80, 155, *156*, 156–57, *157*, *158*
    in final dub, 155–57
    nature and functioning of, 80, 155–56
    SFX and delivery to, 80
    sound effects editor role during, 80
    surround environment monitoring, 155–56
DV camcorder audio, 66
DV Codecs (Digital Video), 41
DX. *See* dialogue

E

Eastman Kodak, 18
Edison Company, 13
EDL (Edit Decision List)
    assistant dialogue editor use of, 89
    events, 54
    in film-to-video transfers, 53–54, *54*
effects, 146. *See also specific topics*
Engel, Josef, 14
EP. *See* executive producer

EQ
    DX, *176*, 176–77
    FO, 188, *189*
    MX, 191, *191*
    SFX, *185*, 185–86
equipment. *See specific topics*
executive producer (EP), 31

F

fades and crossfades, 150, *151*
Fantasia
    Fantasound in, 16
    mono optical sound recording and multitrack playback in, 15–16
    multi-channel surround-sound playback and, 16
    theater sound impact of, 15
    as traveling production, 16
    Volkmann as recording engineer for, 15–16
film. *See also* music, in television and film; sound evolution, for film and television
    crew, 30–31
    dub stage differences between TV and, 80, 155, *156*, 156–57, *157*, *158*
    DX sources in, 199
    extensive ADR example required for, 95–96
    film/video format and use of, 39
    M&E DX removal and replacement in, 198, 199, 204
    mix, 160
    pre-dub/temp mix in, 143–44
    SFX categories in, 72
    sound design for, 1
    Telecine process and frames of, 42
filmmaking, process
    development stage in, 24
    distribution and archiving in, 28
    film crew in, 30–31
    organization, *29*
    players in, 28–29
    post production stage of, 26–27
    pre-production stage of, 24–25
    production stage in, 25–26
    sound crew in, 32–33
    stages of, 23
film-to-video transfers. *See also* Telecine machines and process
    EDL in, 53–54, *54*
    equipment for, 55
    location sound recording and, 53–55

220 INDEX

nature and process of, 53
SMPTE time code in, 54
sound logs in, 53
synchronization need in, 53
film/video formats
  film use in, 39
  in post production media, 39–41
  video quality standards within, 40–41
  video use in, 40
final dub
  DAWS use in, 159, 160
  defined, 155
  dub stage, 155–57
  DX editor role in, 163–64
  final mix and stems required in, 165
  I/O routing in template for, 165–73, *166*
  mix session creation in, 162–63
  mix window for, *168*
  in post production, 27, 155
  pre-dub impact on, 154
  Pro Tools and mixing workflow in, 160–61
  reel mixing in, 163
  re-recording mixer in, 158–60
  stages for, 155–57
  stereo template instruction example, 166–73
final mix
  final dub required stems and, 165
  levels, 193
  in M&E mixing, 202, 203
  pre-dub impact on, 146
fisher boom, 48
FO. *See* Foley unit
Foley, Jack, 99
Foley artist/walker, 5, 99, 104
  footsteps/steps track for, 101, 102
  FX mixer relationship with, 112
  in sound crew, 32
Foley effects (FX)
  ADR gaps filled in by, 100
  control room, 107, *108*
  cue sheet, 105, 106, *106*
  in DAWS, 5, 106, *107*, 112
  fake props covered up by, 99
  footsteps/steps track, 101–2
  at home and equipment/environment needed, 110–11
  identification and categorization of, 105
  in M&E process, 199, 201–3, 204
  moves/clothing track, 101
  nature and process of, 4–5
  props/specifics track, 103
  recording, 104, 107
  re-recording mixer role in, 113
  spotting, 104–6, 112
  stage and pit, 102, 103, *103*, 108, *109*, 110, *110*
  supervising sound editor role in, 104, 106, 113
  sync effect acting or, 4
  track sound elements, 100
Foley mixer/editor, 5, *113*
  in FX recording, 104
  FX role of, 112–13
  FX walker relationship with, 112
  props/specifics track for, 103
  in sound crew, 33
Foley unit (FO)
  compressor, 188, *188*
  EQ, 188, *189*
  plug-ins and processors for, 173, 187–89
  reverb, 189, *189*
  template for, *187*, 187–89
foreign language, 100
formats, archiving, 211
Forrest Gump, 2
424 matrix, 18
frame rates, 42–43
"Frankenbits" dialogue editing, 94
futz track, 181, *181*, 182
FX. *See* Foley effects

G

Garity, William, 17

H

handles, 93, 149, *150*
headphones
  distributor for, 97
  as location sound equipment, 69–70
  purposes and needs for, 69
  recommended, 70
High Definition (HD), 40, 41
Holman, Tomlinson, 19, 20
hypercardioid microphone, 57–59, *58*

I

IATSE. *See* International Alliance of Theatrical and Stage Employees
I Love Lucy, 28

intelligibility, 177, 195
International Alliance of Theatrical and Stage Employees (IATSE), 51
international distribution, 197, 198
I/O routing
 busses in, 167
 in final dub template, 165–73, *166*
 print master in, 167
 reverbs in, 166–67
 stem record tracks in, 167

J
The Jazz Singer, 14

K
Kinetephone, 13
Kinetescope, 13
King, Richard, 74–75

L
lavaliere microphone, 49
 as location sound equipment, 60, *60*, *61*
 nature and use of, 60
 omnidirectional and unidirectional lav in, 60
 as plant microphone, 60
 wireless, 61
levels, 193–95
Lights of New York, 14
line producer, 31
location audio mixer, 64–65, *66*
location recordist/mixer, 32
location scouting, 55
location sound crew
 boom operator in, *48*, 48–50, *49*
 DX capturing focus of, 100
 location sound recording by, 45–53
 production sound mixer in, 45–46, *47*
 production sound process for, 51
 production sound report for, *52*
 sound assistant in, 50–51
 sound logs for, 52–53
location sound equipment. *See also* microphone
 backup systems in, 66
 boom poles as, 63, *64*
 DV camcorder audio as, 66
 headphones as, 69–70
 location audio mixer as, 64–65, *66*
 in location sound recording, 57–70

microphones, 57–63
mixing and routing devices as, 64–65, *66*
monitoring system in, 69
multitrack hard-disk recorder as, 67–68
routing, 67
location sound recording, *56*
 audio path visualization in, 55
 continued evolution of, 56
 crew for, 45–53
 equipment, 57–70
 film-to-video transfers and, 53–55
 location scouting in, 55
 principles for, 55–56
 professional help in, 56
 sound check in, 56
 summary of, 70
locked picture, 134–35, 136
Logic, *8, 9*
loop group, 86
LTRT (Left Total, Right Total), 18
Lucas, George, 19, 20

M
Macpherson, Bill, *47*, 55
Martin, Earl, 94, 95
M&E. *See* music-and-effects-only mix
microphone
 for ADR work, 97
 boom operator placement of, 49
 decca tree technique, *139*, 139–40, *140*
 distance, 59
 lavaliere, 49, 60, *60*, 61
 location sound equipment, 57–63
 in orchestra recording, 137–38
 patterns, *58*
 reality TV and use of cavity, 95
 shotgun/hypercardioid and cardioid, 57–59, *58*, *59*
 wireless system, 61–62
 zeppelins and windsocks for, *62*, 62–63, *63*
mix/deliverables
 film, 160
 in music mixing for TV and film, 140–41
 stem mixing and, 140–41
mixer. *See specific topics*
mixing and routing devices, 64–65, *66*

INDEX

mix session. *See also* template
- DX editor role in, 163–64
- DX session merged with mix template in, 162–63
- final dub and creation of, 162–63
- preferred equipment, 162
- Pro Tools use in, 161, 162, 163, 164
- routing check during, 171

mix template. *See* template
mix window, *168*
mix workflow
- DX place in, 192
- final dub and Pro Tools use in, 160–61
- template, 192

monitoring system, 69
mono aux track, *170*, 171
mono optical sound playback, 14, 15–16
MP. *See* Dolby Motion Picture Matrix
MPEG (Motion Picture Experts Group), 41
multi-channel surround-sound playback, 16
multitrack hard-disk recorder. *See also* digital-multitrack field recorders and mixers
- digital types of, 67, *68*
- features and functions of, 68
- as location sound equipment, 67–68
- pre-buffer aspect of, 68
- production sound mixer employing, 46

multitrack recording, 15–16
Murch, Walter, 72
music, in television and film
- clicks in, 136
- composer studio and mixing, 131–32, *132*
- DAW in mixing, 129, *130*, 141
- decca tree technique in mixing, *139*, 139–40, *140*
- demo mixing in, 133
- film music mixing, 128–29, *130*
- final film music stem mix example in, 141
- libraries, 116
- locked picture in mixing, 134–35
- mix/deliverables in mixing, 140–41
- orchestra recording in, 128
- pre-records/pre lays in mixing, 135–36
- role of, 127
- score in, 5, 115, 117, 127
- songs in, 125–26
- soundtrack, 116
- source, 6, 115, 117, 118
- stem mixing in, 134
- temp music/score as part of, 116, 120
- theaters and mixing, 129

music-and-effects-only mix (M&E)
- ambience in, 199
- BGs in, 201
- DAWS format transfer for, 198
- DX in film/TV removal and replacement in, 198, 199, 204
- final format for, 198
- in foreign language replacement, 100
- future of, 206
- FX in, 199, 201–3, 204
- international distribution requiring, 197, 198
- scenarios, 199–200
- song replacement in, 200

music-and-effects-only mix (M&E), mixing
- approach breakdown, 204
- delivery format, 204–5
- final mix in, 202, 203
- FX and SFX added in, 202–3, 204
- original mix and mixers, 203
- PFX in, 203, 204
- preparation for, 203–4
- printmaster and stems in, 204
- producer/director involvement in, 205
- techniques, 201–6
- time frame impacting, 205

music editing
- categories and subcategories of, 115–16
- conforming in, 122–23
- cue label in, 117
- *The Dark Knight* as example of, 120–21
- DAWS, 124, *124*
- defined, 115
- process of, 117–19
- spotting in, 117, 118
- synchronization in, 125
- techniques for placing and, *124*, 124–26
- temp and source music in, 116, 120–21
- temp dubs in, 121

music editor
- composer relationship to, 120, 133
- conforming and, 122
- cue sheets prepared by, 123

Index **223**

editing and placement techniques of, *124*, 124–26
role of, 115, 117
in sound crew, 33
music (MX), 90
conforming, 122–23
EQ, 191, *191*
mixer, 33
plug-ins and processors for, 173
production, 116
supervisor, 33
template for units of, *190*, 190–91
trim, *190*, 191
MX. *See* music

N
narration, 98
noise reduction
Dolby A, 18
in sound evolution, 17
TOGAD for, 17
NTSC (National Television System Committee), 37, 40
Nuendo/Cubase, *10*

O
OMF (Open Media Framework) files, 76–77
1080i/1080p, 40
orchestra recording
clicks for tempo reference in, 136
conductor balancing, 138
decca tree technique in, *139*, 139–40, *140*
demystified, 137–38
live mixing and, 137–38
microphones in, 137–38
in music mixing for film, 128
organization, *29, 30*

P
PA. *See* production assistant
pan pot, 17
PFX. *See* production sound effects
picture editor, 31
playback rate, 35
The Player (Altman), 23
players, filmmaking, 28–29
plug-ins and processors
for DX mixing, reassigns, SFX, FO, and MX, 173–91

futz track, 181, *181, 182*
print master and meter, 193, *194*
for templates, 173–91
for TV dialogue editing, 93
POC. *See* production coordinator
positional reference, 35
post production. *See also* audio post production
archiving in, 28
delivery impact on, 207
DX editing process in, 98
in filmmaking process, 26–27
final dub in, 27, 155
mixing template, 165
reality TV and editing in, 94
rough cut during, 26, 143
supervisor, 3–4
temp dubs in, 26–27
track counts, 27
as union job, 51
post production media
digital audio file formats in, 38–39
digital formats in, 41
film/video formats in, 39–41
synchronization in, 35–38
Telecine machines and process in, 42–43
pre-dub
budgeting for, 147–48
effects impacted by, 146
final dub impact from, 154
final mix impacted by, 146
process, 143, 148, 152, 153
sound stage requirements for, 147
temp dubs, 27, 121, 143–44
time factor for, 144, 145, 147
TV and uses of, 144–45
pre-dub, session
conforming in, 152
definition and nature of, 148–49
fades and crossfades in, 150, *151*
handles in, 149, *150*
trimming in, 149
pre-dub/temp mix
DAWS use in, 149, 150, 153, 154
in film, 143–44
re-recording mixer role in, 146
sound supervisor for, 145, 146–47
track count in TV, 147
of trailers for radio and TV, 152–54
in TV, 144–48

pre-production
    deliverables' specifications in, 208
    in filmmaking process, 24–25
    story-boarding during, 25
pre-records/pre lays
    in music mixing for TV and film, 135–36
    score and, 135
    source music, 115
    stem mixing and, 135–36
print master. *See also* final mix
    in I/O routing, 167
    M&E mixing and original, 204
    meter plug-in on, 193, *194*
producer, 30, 205
production
    audio, 2
    dailies assembled during, 25–26
    in filmmaking process, 25–26
    music, 116
production assistant (PA), 23, 31
production coordinator (POC), 31
production dialogue
    ADR replacing, 83
    definition and nature of, 83, 84
    DX editor role in, 87
    editing, 2, 84
    for reality TV and TV dialogue editing, 94–95
    terms glossary for, 84–86
production sound effects (PFX), 93, 203, 204
production sound mixer
    as department head, 46
    equipment for, 46
    in location sound crew, 45–46, *47*
    Macpherson as, *47*, 55
    multitrack hard-disk recorder employed by, 46
    nature and function of, 45–46
production sound report, *52*
Pro Tools
    DAWS session setup page, 7
    final dub and mixing workflow on, 160–61
    mix session use, 161, 162, 163, 164
    sound design impact of, 82
    as TV dialogue editing delivery platform, 94
    workflow mix goals in, 161
    workflow mix session setup using, 161

Q
QuickTime, 41, 135, 153

R
reality television
    ADR for, 95
    cavity microphone in, 95
    "Frankenbits" dialogue editing for, 94
    post production editing in, 94
    TV dialogue editing and production dialogue for, 94–95
reassigns, 177–80, *178*
recording, 104, 107. *See also* orchestra recording
recordist, 159–60. *See also* sound recordist
reel mixing, 163
repurposing, 122
re-recording mixer, 3
    final dub role of, 158–60
    FX role of, 113
    pre-dub/temp mix TV work for, 146
    recordist as assistant to, 159–60
    in sound crew, 33
    spotting involvement of, 158–59
    supervising sound editor conjoining with, 158
resolution, 40
resolved system, 6
reverb
    DX unit, 182–83, *183*
    FO, 189, *189*
    in I/O routing, 166–67
    SFX, 186, *186*
    template settings, 169, *169*
room tones/filler, 90, 91
rough cut, 26, 143
routing. *See also* I/O routing
    deliverables and, 208
    in location sound equipment, 67
    mix session and checking, 171
    synchronization, 67

S
Schelly, Vincent, *49*
score
    conforming in sessions for, 122–23
    locked picture relationship to, 134–35
    in music for TV and film, 5, 115, 117, 127
    pre-records/pre lays and, 135
    scoring mixer and, 5, 129
    temp, 116, 120

Index

scoring mixer, 138
   composer relationship to, 128, 133
   nature and function of, 128, 129
   score and, 5, 129
screenplay, 24
SD. *See* Standard Definition
SDDS. *See* Sony Dynamic Digital Sound
SFX. *See* sound effects
Shepard tone, 74
shotgun microphone, 57–59, *58*, *59*
SMPTE (Society of Motion Picture and Television Engineers) time code
   drop-frame rate, 37
   in film-to-video transfers, 54
   in sound log, 52
   synchronization through, 36, *36*
songs, 125–26, 200
Sony Dynamic Digital Sound (SDDS), 21
sound assistant, 50–51
sound check, 56
sound crew, 32–33. *See also* location sound crew; *specific topics*
sound design
   for *The Dark Knight*, 74–75
   defined, 72
   digital and analogue technology in, 72
   for film, 1
   SFX containing, 72–73
   sound selection in, 73
   technology and Pro Tools impact on, 82
   Van Slyke on future of, 82
sound designer
   constant readiness for, 81
   in SFX, 4
   Van Slyke as veteran, 81–82
sound effects editor
   BGs and backgrounds pass used by, 77
   conforming employed by, 79
   DAWS employed by, 76, 77
   dub stage role of, 80
   example workspace and, 78, *78*
   hard effects pass by, 77
   OMF files used by, 76–77
   primary function of, 76
   in SFX, 4, 32, 76–78, *78*
   supervising, 73–75
sound effects (SFX). *See also* production sound effects
   audio post production role of, 71
   BGs and room tones in, 75–76
   compressor/limiter, 185, *186*
   conforming in, 79
   current use of, 72
   in DAWS, 4
   dub stage delivery, 80
   editors, 4, 32, 76–78, *78*
   for episodic TV, 81–82
   film and TV categories of, 72
   in M&E mixing, 202–3, 204
   mixer, 32
   nature and process of, 4
   past use of, 71
   plug-ins and processors for, 173, 184–86
   reverb, 186, *186*
   sound design within, 72–73
   summary of working in, 82
   supervising sound editor in, 73–75
   template and units of, *184*, 184–86
sound evolution, for film and television
   digital theater sound in, 21
   Disney techniques for, 16, 17
   Dolby Stereo development in, 18
   first "talkie" films in, 14
   multi-channel surround-sound playback in, 16
   noise reduction in, 17
   pan pot for sound motion in, 17
   sound synchronization in, 13–14
   in theaters, 14–15
   THX system in, 19–20
   timeline for, 13–15
sound kit/sound cart, 50, 51
sound logs
   digital-multitrack field recorders and data entry of, 52–53
   in film-to-video transfers, 53
   for location sound crew, 52–53
   roll, scene, and take in, 52
   SMPTE time code and comments in, 52
sound recordist, 73–74
sound reels, 88
sound selection, 73
sound stage, 147, 156. *See also* dub stage
sound supervisor, 90, 145, 146–47
soundtrack, 79, 116
source music
   in film or TV, 115, 117, 118
   nature and process of, 6
   song or pre-record, 115

INDEX

spotting
    DAWS use in, 5, 106, *107*, 112
    FX, 104–6, 112
    in music editing, 117, 118
    notes, 118–19, *119*, 125
    re-recording mixer involvement in, 158–59
    supervising sound editor in, 104, 106, 113
Standard Definition (SD), 40
Star Wars, 2
Steamboat Willie, 14
stem mixing
    final dub required final mix and, 165
    in M&E mixing, 204
    mix/deliverables and, 140–41
    in music mixing for TV and film, 134
    pre-records/pre lays and, 135–36
stem record tracks, 167
Stereo Variable Area (SVA), 18
Stokowski, Leopold, 17
story-boarding, 25
studio, 209, 210–11
studio space, 96–97
supervising sound editor
    comprehensive SFX list created by, 73
    FX role and spotting by, 104, 106, 113
    nature and function of, 73
    re-recording mixer conjoining with, 158
    in SFX, 73–75
    in sound crew, 32
    sound recordist selection by, 73–74
    surround environment monitoring, 155–56
SVA. *See* Stereo Variable Area
sync effect acting, 4, 99
synchronization
    of DAWS and video through time code, 11–12
    defined, 35
    drop-frame/non-drop-frame rates in, 37–38
    film-to-video transfers' need for, 53
    kinetescope/kinetephone connected for sound, 13
    in music editing, 125
    positional reference and playback rate in, 35
    in post production media, 35–38
    routing, 67
    SMPTE time code for, 36, *36*
    sound evolution in sound, 13–14
    Tri-Ergon Process of sound, 14
synopsis, 24

T

"talkie" films, 14
team effort, xi, 1
technology
    audio post production and 7.1 digital, 20, 21
    digital, xi
    sound design employing digital and analogue, 72
    sound design impact of improved, 82
Telecine machines and process
    frame rates in, 42–43
    mechanics of, 42
    in post production media, 42–43
    purpose of, 42
    2-3 pulldown process, 42–43
television (TV). *See also* dialogue editing, television; music, in television and film; pre-dub/temp mix; reality television; sound evolution, for film and television; video quality standards
    analog, 41
    drop-frame/non-drop-frame rates and compatibility for color/black-and-white, 37
    dub stage differences between film and, 80, 155, *156*, 156–57, *157*, *158*
    DX sources in, 199
    HD, 40, 41
    M&E DX removal and replacement in, 198, 199, 204
    organization in production of, *30*
    pre-dub/temp mix in, 144–48
    pre-dub uses in, 144–45
    SFX categories in, 72
    SFX for episodic, 81–82
    time frame in episodic, 81
    voice casting for foreign adaptation, 198
temp and source music
    in music editing, 116, 120–21
    music in film and TV using, 116, 120
    score, 116, 120
temp dubs
    in music editing, 121
    in post production stage, 26–27
    pre-dub, 27, 121, 143–44
    as rough cut audio mix, 143
template
    DAWS and creating, 165, 166, *166*, 173
    DX unit and equipment used in, 173–79, *179*, *180*
    final dub instruction example for stereo, 166–73

Index   **227**

FO, *187*, 187–89
futz track creation, 181, *181, 182*
I/O routing in final dub, 165–73, *166*
levels, 193–95
limiter settings for, *170*
mix session through merging DX session with mix, 162–63
mix workflow, 192
mono aux track for, *170*, 171
plug-ins and processors used for, 173–91
post production mixing, 165
reverb in settings for, 169, *169*
session setup, *172*
SFX unit, *184*, 184–86
signal test, *171*
temp mix, 143. *See also* pre-dub/temp mix
theaters
   digital sound in, 21
   Fantasia impact on sound in, 15
   music mixing and, 129
   sound evolution in, 14–15
   THX system addressing playback systems and acoustics in, 20
   THX system and dubbing, 19
THX (Tomlinson Holman EXperiment), 156
   Baffle Wall, 20
   dubbing theater in, 19
   playback system, 20
   sound evolution through development of, 19–20
   sound system standards of, 19, 20
   theater playback systems and acoustics addressed by, 20
time code
   for DAWS and video synchronization, 11–12
   drop-frame/non-drop-frame rate and DFTC, 38
   synchronization through SMPTE, 36, *36*
   video and burned, 11
time frame
   episodic TV, 81
   M&E mixing impacted by, 205
   pre-dubs factoring, 144, 145, 147
tone-operated gain-adjusting device (TOGAD), 17
track abbreviations, 90
track counts, 27, 147
trailers, for radio and TV, 152–54
treatment, 24

Tri-Ergon Process, 14
trimming, 149
TV. *See* television

U
union, 51

V
Van Slyke, David, 81–82
video and videotape. *See also* film-to-video transfers
   B&W format originally used in, 40
   DAWS importation of, 11
   film/video format and use of, 40
   quality standards, 40–41
   time code burned into, 11
   time code for DAWS synchronization with, 11–12
video quality standards
   HD, 40
   1080i/1080p, 40
   resolution and aspect ratio in, 40
   SD, 40
visual presentation, xi
VO. *See* voice-over
Vogt, Hans, 14
voice casting, 198
voice-over (VO), 98
Volkmann, John, 15–16

W
Walla sound effect, 85
WAV files, 210
windsocks. See zeppelins and windsocks
wireless microphone system
   diversity *versus* single antenna systems for, 61
   lavaliere, 61
   renting *versus* buying, 62

X
X track, 91

Z
zeppelins and windsocks, *62*, 62–63, *63*
Zimmer, Hans, 27, 120, 121

More Great Books & DVDs from

berklee press

A MODERN METHOD FOR GUITAR – VOLUME 1
by William Leavitt •
featuring Larry Baione
50448065 Book/DVD-ROM Pack.............$34.99

THE FUTURE OF MUSIC
Manifesto for the Digital Music Revolution
by Dave Kusek & Gerd Leonhard
50448055 ....$16.95

THE CONTEMPORARY SINGER – 2ND EDITION
Elements of Vocal Technique
by Anne Peckham
50449595 Book/CD Pack $24.99

BERKLEE MUSIC THEORY – BOOK 1 – 2ND EDITION
by Paul Schmeling
50449615 Book/CD Pack.......$24.95

FOR MORE INFORMATION, SEE YOUR LOCAL MUSIC DEALER,
OR WRITE TO:

HAL•LEONARD® CORPORATION
7777 W. BLUEMOUND RD. P.O. BOX 13819 MILWAUKEE, WI 53213

Prices, contents, and availability subject to change without notice.

0413

evolve.

DON'T BE PART OF MUSIC HISTORY.

Learn to adapt with forward-thinking online music courses and programs from Berkleemusic, the Continuing Education Division of Berklee College of Music.

- Music Publishing 101
- Mixing and Mastering with Pro Tools
- Music Theory 101
- Guitar Scales 101
- Master Certificate in Production
  (8-Course Program)

Berklee music
learn music online

Call Our Advisors Today
1.866.BERKLEE
www.berkleemusic.com